THE GOD OF ISRAEL AND CHRISTIAN THEOLOGY

THE GOD OF ISRAEL
AND
CHRISTIAN THEOLOGY

R. Kendall Soulen

Fortress Press
Minneapolis

THE GOD OF ISRAEL AND CHRISTIAN THEOLOGY

Cover and text design by Joseph Bonyata

Library of Congress Cataloging-in-Publication Data

Soulen, R. Kendall
    The God of Israel and Christian theology / R. Kendall Soulen.
        p.   cm.
    Includes bibliographical references and index.
    ISBN 0-8006-2883-7
    1. Judaism (Christian theology)—History of doctrines.
2. Christianity and other religions—Judaism. 3. Judaism—
Relations—Christianity. 4. Christianity and antisemitism.
I. Title
BT 93-S35   1996   95-46692
231.7'6—dc20   CIP

Manufactured in the U. S. A.   AF 1-2883
00   99   98   97   96   1   2   3   4   5   6   7   8   9   10

CONTENTS

PART TWO
THE UNITY OF THE CANON AFTER CHRISTENDOM

To Richard Nevins Soulen
and Margaret Ann Soulen,
my first and best teachers

PREFACE

THE GOD OF ISRAEL IS THE FIRM FOUNDATION and inescapable predicament of Christian theology. Pursued without reference to the God of Israel, Christian theology is hopelessly exposed to the charge of being mere vanity, for the gospel about Jesus is credible only if predicated on a living God who "gives life to the dead and calls into existence the things that do not exist" (Rom 4:17). But pursued with reference to the God of Israel, Christian theology is immediately engaged in a fight for its life, pressed on every side by perplexities and difficulties with which it must wrestle but which it cannot master. Not least among these perplexities is that Christian theology serves an overwhelmingly gentile church that exists alongside another community, the Jewish people, which also glorifies the God of Israel but which cannot hear the gospel tidings of the living God.

There is, of course, a third option, that of lukewarm Laodicea. The theology of Laodicea is neither hot nor cold because it is afraid to abandon the God of Israel altogether but unwilling to embrace perplexities it cannot master. There are, perhaps, just two main epochs when Christian theology has been almost wholly deprived of the seductive comforts of Laodicea and has had to wrestle with Jacob's angel in full recognition that its life was at stake.

The first period coincided with the great trauma of the early church's initial separation from the Jewish people. The possibilities of this initial period, grappled with above all by Paul in Rom 9–11, were soon foreclosed. An increasingly gentile church sought relief from its quandary by declaring itself the "new spiritual Israel" that had superseded the old carnal Israel in God's election and design. For the next two millennia, during which the gentile church became ever more at home in the cultures it dominated, this teaching of supersessionism was seldom challenged. "For you say, 'I am rich, I have prospered, and I need nothing.' You do not realize that you are wretched, pitiable, poor, blind, and naked" (Rev 3:17).

The second era, which began in our time and continues still, was inaugurated by events that shattered the equanimity of Laodicean theology and made its poverty impossible to hide: the Holocaust, in which Christians have had to confess their own complicity, and the return of the Jewish people to the land God promised to Abraham. Under the new conditions created by these events, Christian churches have begun to consider anew their relation to the God of Israel and the Israel of God in the light of the Scriptures and the gospel about Jesus. Revisiting the teaching of supersessionism after nearly two thousand years, many churches have now publicly confessed that fidelity to the gospel requires the rejection of supersessionism and the affirmation of God's own unbroken fidelity to the Jewish people. Yet far from bringing the church's relation to the God of Israel to equilibrium, this confession has thrust the church into new and far-reaching perplexities. For the rejection of supersessionism is fraught with profound implications for the whole range of Christian theological reflection, and the full extent of these implications is still far from fully clear. But perplexities such as these come with the promise of blessing, for they arise out of wrestling with the living God.

At one level, this book is an effort to think through the systematic implications of the church's new posture toward the God of Israel and the Jewish people. Taking the contemporary churches' rejection of supersessionism as its starting point, the book asks two questions: how deeply is supersessionism implicated in the traditional fabric of Christian theology? And how can Christians read the Bible and articulate their most basic convictions in ways that are not supersessionist? In short, how can Christians be really Christian without being triumphalist toward Jews?

At another level, however, the present book seeks to advance a larger systematic argument about the God of Israel and Christian theology in the present time, a time that has sometimes been characterized as "after Christendom." The book argues that the integrity of Christian theology after Christendom requires a renewed conversion of basic Christian forms of thought toward the God of Israel. Such a conversion is necessary, I argue, because Christian theology in its dominant classical and modern forms embodies what is in effect an incomplete conversion toward the living God, the God of Abraham, Isaac, and Jacob. The crucial marks of that incomplete conversion are a triumphalist posture toward the Jewish people and a latently gnostic assessment of God's engagement in the realm of public history.

Indeed, these twin limitations offer a reasonable characterization of what is to be understood by Christendom as a theological and social construct. "Christendom" names the church's theological and social posture when it is triumphalist toward Jews and gnostic toward God's engagement in history. The God of Israel, in contrast, names the God who is identified by fidelity to the Jewish people through time and therefore by engagement with human history in its public and corporate dimensions. If it is true that the gospel about Jesus is credible only as predicated of the God of Israel, then the integrity of Christian theology after Christendom depends upon bringing traditional forms of Christian thought into a further degree of congruence with the God of Israel. That is the larger task to which the present book seeks to contribute.

Finally, a word about the limits of my argument. Some readers may be tempted to judge the constructive part of this book according to whether it seeks to vindicate classical ecumenical affirmations in the areas of Trinity and christology. They will discover that I do not attempt to address that question in these pages. Instead, I limit myself to the exposition of what I take to be the theologically more basic claim, namely, the God of Israel has acted in Jesus Christ for all. The proposal sketched here does provide, I think, a framework that can accommodate the truth of classical trinitarian and christological affirmations, but that is a claim I hope to develop elsewhere.

Adequately thanking those who have helped me in writing this book is a task as pleasurable to attempt as it is impossible to fulfill. The earliest seeds of this endeavor were planted under the benevolent and much-forgiving direction of Hans Frei in a study I undertook with him on the interpretation of Romans by Martin Luther and Karl Barth. While Hans Frei died before the present book reached more than inchoate form, his generous spirit provided the initial place where its fledgling ideas took root.

I received early stimulation and direction for this work from wonderful conversations with my friends and colleagues Joe Mangina, Matthew Hawk, Gene Rogers, Nick Healy, and Kathy Grieb. George Lindbeck devoted generous time and critical attention to the earliest (and most impenetrable) drafts of this work and has been a ready source of encouragement and useful criticism ever since. He also introduced me to the work of Michael Wyschogrod, whose work provided a decisive stimulus for this book, and who has graciously read and commented on this work at several stages.

David Kelsey and Kathryn Tanner kept me on track during periods of discouragement and provided insightful theological counsel at crucial stages. I am also grateful to Cyril O'Regan, M. Douglas Meeks, Stanley Hauerwas, Walter Lowe, Bruce Marshall, and Patrick Miller, all of whom read drafts of this manuscript and offered encouragement and valuable advice. I owe a special word of gratitude to Rusty Reno, who has taken a generous interest in this project from the start and who has read the work through more than once with an open heart and a sharp pencil.

This book would not have been written without the support of my wife, Allison Rutland Soulen, to whom I am more grateful than I can say. I also profited enormously from the encouragement and editorial acuity of my parents, Dr. Richard Nevins Soulen and Mrs. Margaret Ann Soulen, and my parents-in-law, Dr. Walter Blake Rutland and Mrs. Ann Carolyn Rutland. Leila Rebecca Rutland Soulen, my infant daughter, made the final stages of work on this project inexpressibly more joyful than they could otherwise have been.

Gregory Nolff assisted me greatly in preparing the manuscript for publication. I am grateful for his able work, and for that of Ken Harrington, who proofread several chapters.

1

THE GOD OF ISRAEL
AFTER CHRISTENDOM

E VER SINCE CHRISTIANS FIRST APPEARED ON THE SCENE, they
have confessed that the God of the Hebrew Scriptures acted in
Jesus of Nazareth for all the world. That is the center of Christian
faith. All the rest turns on this.

A curious consequence of this confession is that simply because
Christians are Christians they inevitably adopt some specific posture toward the Jewish people, a posture that is always theological
and practical at once. The reasons for this are not hard to discern.
Because Christian faith concerns the God of the Hebrew Scriptures,
it concerns One who has chosen to be identified as the God of Abraham and his children after the flesh, the Jews. Because Christian
faith concerns Jesus of Nazareth, it concerns one who was himself a
Jew and a member of the household of Israel. Finally, because
Christian faith concerns something that has happened for all, it
concerns something that has happened also for the sake of the Jewish people. The question, then, has never been whether Christians
should speak and act with reference to the Jewish people. Rather,
the question has been *how* they should do so, and how what they
would say and do would affect the existence of the Jewish people.

For most of the past two millennia, the church's posture toward
the Jewish people has come to expression in the teaching known as
supersessionism, also known as the theology of displacement.
According to this teaching, God chose the Jewish people after the
fall of Adam in order to prepare the world for the coming of Jesus
Christ, the Savior. After Christ came, however, the special role of
the Jewish people came to an end and its place was taken by the

1

church, the new Israel. The church, unlike the Jewish people, is a spiritual community in which the carnal distinction between Jew and Gentile is overcome. Accordingly, the church holds that the preservation of Jewish identity within the new Israel is a matter of theological indifference at best, and a mortal sin at worst. Yet the Jews themselves failed to recognize Jesus as the promised Messiah and refused to enter the new spiritual Israel. God therefore rejected the Jews and scattered them over the earth, where God will preserve them until the end of time.

In the early nineteenth century, some progressive Christian theologians carried the idea of supersessionism to a new level. According to them, the God of Jesus Christ was not revealed by the Hebrew Bible at all, and therefore had never entered into a special relationship with the Jewish people in the first place. Accordingly, these theologians held that the continued existence of the Jewish people was a matter of theological indifference not only within the church but also outside it. The Jews were simply a vestige of an earlier age of religious consciousness, and their eventual extinction could be expected with the gradual advance of Christian civilization.

Finally, in the 1930s some German Christians began to expel Christians of Jewish descent from their pulpits and parishes. Soon afterward, other Germans, many of them baptized, began to take Jews from their homes and put them in concentration camps. Many Christians around the world were aware of this, but most did not regard it as a matter calling for a specifically theological or practical response. On the whole, they continued to speak and act toward the Jewish people as they had always done. When the camps were opened in 1945, it became clear that the Nazis had exterminated millions of Jews by gassing them and burning their bodies in ovens.

In the decades since the Second World War, the church's posture toward the Jewish people has slowly begun to change. One of the most important features of this change has been a critical reevaluation of the teaching of supersessionism. After examining again the sources of their faith, some churches have concluded that the teaching that the church displaced the Jewish people in God's plan is wrong or at least seriously misleading. In its place they have affirmed that the church has not superseded the Jewish people in God's plan and that God remains faithful to God's election of the Jewish people. To cite one example, the Presbyterian Church (USA) has declared:

Supersessionism maintains that because the Jews refused to receive Jesus as Messiah, they were cursed by God, are no longer in covenant with God, and that the church alone is the "true Israel" or the "spiritual Israel." When Jews continue to assert, as they do, that they are the covenant people of God, they are looked upon by many Christians as impertinent intruders, claiming a right which is no longer theirs. The long and dolorous history of Christian imperialism, in which the church often justified anti-Jewish acts in the name of Jesus, finds its theological basis in this teaching. We believe and testify that this theory of supersessionism or replacement is harmful and in need of reconsideration as the church seeks to proclaim God's saving activity with humankind.[1]

The declaration goes on to state:

God's covenants are not broken. "God has not rejected his people whom he foreknew" (Rom 11:2). The church has not "replaced" the Jewish people . . . . Hence, when speaking with Jews about matters of faith, we must always acknowledge that Jews are already in a covenantal relationship with God.[2]

The declaration is indicative of the sea-change that is taking place in significant parts of the Christian church. While the change has been gradual and uneven, it undoubtedly represents a development of historic significance for Christian theology. For the first time in nearly two millennia, the church is seeking to put its relationship to the Jewish people on a new foundation.

This volume takes as its point of departure the fact that significant parts of the Christian church today reject supersessionism and affirm God's fidelity to the Jewish people. From there we ask: *what are the implications of this new development for the rest of Christian theology?* Part One argues that supersessionism has shaped the narrative and doctrinal structure of classical Christian theology in fundamental and systematic ways. Hence the rejection of supersessionism entails the reevaluation of the whole body of classical Christian divinity. Part Two suggests one way in which Christians might reconceive the coherence of Christian theology in a manner that is free of supersessionism yet consonant with the evangelical center of Christian faith—the God of Hebrew Scriptures has acted in Jesus of Nazareth for all the world.[3]

My treatment of the problem of supersessionism and Christian theology is shaped by four central convictions. First, supersession-ism raises specifically theological problems about the truth and coherence of Christian faith and must therefore be addressed at the level of systematic theological reflection. Second, the effort to tran-scend supersessionism requires serious encounter with the theolog-ical claims of Jewish faith. Third, the systematic implications of supersessionism for Christian theology are best understood when attention is focused on the way in which Christians interpret the narrative unity of the Christian Bible. Fourth, when viewed in the context of the church's traditional understanding of the canon's narrative unity, supersessionism is seen to distort not only the church's posture toward the people Israel but other aspects of the church's faith and life as well.

SUPERSESSIONISM AS A PROBLEM
FOR SYSTEMATIC THEOLOGY

The present work holds that supersessionism raises problems of a specifically theological nature that must be addressed at the level of systematic theological reflection. Simply put, supersessionism is a specifically theological problem because it threatens to render the existence of the Jewish people a matter of indifference to the God of Israel. Just in this way, supersessionism introduces a profound note of incoherence into the heart of Christian reflection about God. While it may be possible to imagine a god who is indifferent to the existence of the Jewish people, it is impossible so to imagine the God of the Hebrew Scriptures, the God of Israel. If Christians nev-ertheless claim to worship the God of Israel while teaching God's indifference toward the people Israel, they are engaging in a massive theological contradiction. Moreover, they throw the credibility of the Christian confession itself into doubt. If the God of Israel is ulti-mately indifferent even to the existence of the Jewish people, how seriously can one take God's engagement with the rest of creation? If the God of Israel is indifferent to the bodies of the Jewish people, how seriously can one take the resurrection of Jesus of Nazareth from the dead? If the God of Israel ordains a salvation in the midst of history that renders the existence of the Jewish people irrelevant, what can be the power of this salvation to mend the wounds of human history as a whole?

Certainly, one can criticize supersessionism on grounds that are not specifically theological. For instance, one might argue on psychological grounds that supersessionism is problematic because it instills feelings of hatred and contempt toward Jews. Yet even if such claims could be proven false, supersessionism would remain problematic on theological grounds. If Christians today are rethinking their traditional theological posture toward the Jewish people, it must be because of the reasoned conviction that in doing so they are being more truthful and more faithful to the God whom they worship and confess. To do so merely out of a desire to avoid offense or in a spirit of "theological reparations" would contribute nothing to the genuine reform of Christian living, and would in the long run contribute only to cynicism and disappointment. Only when recognition of supersessionism's theological inadequacy stands at the center of the church's new posture toward the Jewish people are there real grounds to hope for a renewal of Christian theology and Christian living.

SUPERSESSIONISM AND DIALOGUE

The church's theology of displacement took shape at a time when theological contact between the church and the Jewish people was virtually non-existent. A second conviction informing this essay is that the path beyond supersessionism must go by way of renewed encounter with the theological claims of Jewish existence. In recent years, no one has contributed more to the hard work of theological dialogue between Christians and Jews than the Jewish theologian Michael Wyschogrod. Wyschogrod offers the Christian reader a statement of Jewish theology that is deeply rooted in Jewish tradition yet conversant with Christian theology and its questions. He therefore offers a natural point of orientation for a Christian theology that seeks to overcome the legacy of supersessionism.

At the heart of Wyschogrod's theology is his affirmation of God's free, irrevocable election of Israel as the people of God.[4] The mystery of this election is that it concerns a natural human family. God could have chosen according to some spiritual criterion: election according to faith or according to moral excellence. Instead, God chose the seed of Abraham, Isaac, and Jacob, a human family neither better nor worse than others. As a result, Israel's election is a corporeal election, and the foundation of Judaism is nothing other than the family identity of the Jewish people. Even in the exceptional case of the person who converts to Judaism, Jewish identity consists centrally in membership in the family descended from Abraham, Isaac, and Jacob.[5]

In addition to its family identity as the seed of Abraham, Judaism also involves a whole complex of obligations, traditions, and beliefs. Of these, none is more important or central to Jewish life than the obligation to observe the commandments of the Torah. An Orthodox Jew, Wyschogrod holds that the Torah constitutes God's special claim upon the obedience of the Jewish people in general and upon each Jew in particular. Jewish neglect of the Torah constitutes serious disobedience against God. Yet crucial though the Torah is to Jewish life, even it is superstructure rather than foundation:

> The foundation of Judaism is the family identity of the Jewish
> people as the descendants of Abraham, Isaac, and Jacob. Whatev-
> er else is added to this must be seen as growing out of and related
> to the basic identity of the Jewish people as the seed of Abraham
> elected by God through descent from Abraham. This is the crux
> of the mystery of Israel's election.[6]

The fundamental reality of Judaism is the corporeal election of Abraham's children. Everything else, even the Torah, rests upon this.[7]

Wyschogrod acknowledges that joining the divine election to the corporeal reality of a particular people invites serious objections.[8] As Judaism itself teaches, God's nature is spiritual. Therefore it would seem only natural for God's election to be based on religious sensibility or moral accomplishment rather than carnal descent. The elect would then consist of all those who are spiritually and morally akin to God, from whatever people or nation they descend. Wyschogrod admits that God could have chosen to engage the world in this way. Yet had God done so, Wyschogrod argues, the cost would have been great. The human creature is not only spiritual but material. If God had chosen to engage the human creature only in the spiritual aspect of its being, then the greater portion of what constitutes humanity would have been left out of the relation with God. By electing Israel, God chose to embrace a people in the fullness of its humanity. In this way, God confirms the human creature as it was created to live in the material cosmos.[9]

Wyschogrod points out another consequence of God's election of a human family rather than a spiritual or ethical elite. By making election a matter of descent, God has made it very difficult for members of the elect community to escape their identity as God's chosen.[10] In contrast, an election based on faith or ethics would be terminated by a change in belief or conduct. A Jew, however, cannot resign his or her election. By electing to be the God of Israel, God has bound God's name to the world in a way that cannot easily be dissolved. In Wyschogrod's memorable phrase, Israel "is the carnal anchor that God has sunk into the soil of creation."[11]

But why should God be a God of election at all? Does not God love all persons equally? Why should God choose one people and not another? Wyschogrod's insistence upon God's freedom prohibits him from saying that God had to elect one family over the rest. Yet given the fact that God has done so, it is possible to seek reasons for what God has done in order to display grounds for human gratitude.[12]

Wyschogrod notes that love is sometimes distinguished into two kinds, agape and eros.[13] Agape is charity in the purest sense while eros is sensual love. Agape is without superiority or condescension, while eros is vulnerable to passion, desire, and jealousy. Agape is disinterested and impartial, while eros is concerned with this person rather than that one. For Wyschogrod, this account of love is suspect because it bifurcates the human condition in an unreal way. In this respect it resembles the distinction between body and soul. Body and soul are aspects of the one being that God created in God's image. To regard a person primarily as soul rather than as a concrete unity is to risk missing the human being who is really there. Similarly, true love is impossible without an element of eros that orients agape on the reality of the particular one who is loved. This introduces an element of exclusivity into true love. Without this directedness and exclusivity, agape becomes fictitious:

> Undifferentiated love, love that is dispensed equally to all must be love that does not meet the individual in his individuality but sees him as a member of a species, whether that species be the working class, the poor, those created in the image of God, or what not. . . . In the names of these abstractions men have committed the most heinous crime against real, concrete, existing human beings. . . .[14]

Real encounter is possible only when humans are regarded as more than instances of a class. Genuine human love is directed to the concrete individuality of the other; therefore, genuine human love requires exclusivity.[15]

Wyschogrod observes that God's love is usually said to resemble agape rather than eros. As agape, God's love cannot exclude. According to Wyschogrod, however, it belongs to the glory of the biblical God that God chose to love humanity in a human way. Precisely because God is deeply concerned with human creation, God loves it with a differentiated love. By electing Abraham and his seed, God has chosen in favor of genuine encounter with the human creature in his or her concreteness. The unsubstitutability of God's love for Israel is the guarantee of God's love toward all persons, elect and non-elect. The distinction between Jew and Gentile—far from indicating a limit or imperfection of God's love—testifies to God's willingness to engage all creation on the basis of divine passion.[16]

The universal significance of God's love for Israel is revealed in God's promise to Abraham that all the world should be blessed in him:

> Because He said: "I will bless those who bless you, and curse him that curses you; in you shall all the families of the earth be blessed" (Gen 12:3), He has tied His saving and redemptive concern for the welfare of all men to His love for the people of Israel.[17]

God's promise to Abraham links God's blessing not to some generic feature of human identity that all people share but to encounter between those who are and who remain genuinely different. As a result, there are no "general" or "universal" paths that lead to the God of Israel. Apart from a relationship to the people Israel, no relationship to the God of Israel is possible.[18] God is the Creator and Ruler of the universe, but God does not draw near as the conclusion of cosmological or ontological proofs for the existence of God. God draws near as the God of Abraham who took the people Israel out of the land of Egypt and who remains this nation's God to the end of time.[19]

Having viewed at least some basic features of Wyschogrod's theology, we can turn our attention to his understanding of Christianity. From Wyschogrod's perspective, what is Judaism to make of Christian faith? Wyschogrod discusses Christianity with special reference to christology and ecclesiology, so we will consider these two areas separately.

Christians claim that Jesus of Nazareth is the Messiah of Israel and the Son of God. For Jewish faith, these claims are extremely problematic. In itself, the claim that any given person was or was not the Messiah is not a matter of ultimate importance for Jews; that is, it is a point on which Jews can be mistaken while remaining good Jews. Nevertheless, the claim that Jesus was the Messiah is difficult for Jews to accept because Jesus did not perform a key messianic function: he did not usher in the messianic reign. More difficult by far, however, is the Christian claim that God was incarnate in Jesus. For a Jew to be mistaken in this belief would mean a grave violation of the prohibition against idolatry.[20]

Are Jews therefore free to reject out of hand the church's claims about God's incarnation in Jesus? Wyschogrod does not think so, for that would be to impose external constraints on God's freedom, something hardly compatible with authentic Jewish thought. Israel would be entitled to reject the church's claims about Jesus out of hand only if these claims implied that God had repudiated God's promises to Israel. That is something that Israel can be sure that God will never do, not because God is unable but simply because God honors God's promises. The question, then, is whether christology involves the abrogation of God's promises to Israel. Wyschogrod does not believe that this is necessarily the case. He suggests that the doctrine of God's incarnation in Jesus could be understood as a kind of intensification of God's covenant with Israel. Although the incarnation is not foreseen in the Hebrew Bible, once the fact of the incarnation is assumed (as it is by Christians), it can be regarded as an extension of the Bible's basic thrust:

> [The covenant between God and Israel] depicts a drawing togeth-er of God and Israel. In some sense . . . it can also be said to involve a certain indwelling of God in the people of Israel whose status as a holy people may be said to derive from this indwelling. Understood in this sense, the divinity of Jesus is not radically dif-ferent—though perhaps more concentrated—than the holiness of the Jewish people.[21]

The Christian doctrine of the incarnation can be viewed as a development of the Bible's account of God's movement toward human creation in the people Israel. In this respect at least, Wyschogrod suggests, the difference between Judaism and Christianity may be regarded as one of degree rather than kind.[22]

None of this means that Wyschogrod regards the christological impasse between Judaism and Christianity as overcome, an impasse that Wyschogrod has described as "the encounter of the irresistible force with the immovable object."[23] But it does imply the following:

> The disagreement between Judaism and Christianity [with respect to the incarnation], when understood in this light, while not reconcilable, can be brought into the context within which it is a difference of faith regarding the free and sovereign act of the God of Israel.[24]

If Judaism does not accept Christianity's faith in Jesus of Nazareth, it is not because this faith as such runs counter to the basis of Jewish existence but because "Judaism does not hear this story, because the Word of God as it hears it does not tell it and because Jewish faith does not testify to it."[25]

In contrast to Wyschogrod's cautiously conciliatory tone with respect to the issue of christology, it is with considerable ambivalence that Wyschogrod turns to the church. Here is a community assembled from all the nations who are united not by common descent or language but by a common desire to worship the God of Israel. What should a Jew make of this astonishing phenomenon?

In Wyschogrod's judgment, Jews should approach the phenomenon of the church with hopeful respect. Wyschogrod holds that Israel's own trust in God leads it to expect a day when the nations will join Israel in the praise of God's name. To this extent, at least, the church appears congruent with Israel's own pattern of expectations, since the church has helped to spread the knowledge of God to the ends of the earth:

> The wonder is that nations . . . have come within the orbit of the faith of Israel, experiencing man and history with Jewish categories deeply rooted in Jewish experience and sensibility. How can a Jewish theologian not perceive that something wonderful is at work here, something that must in some way be connected with the love of the God of Israel for all his children, Isaac as well as Ishmael, Jacob as well as Esau.[26]

By means of the church, the categories that inform Jewish life—categories such as sin and redemption, the Messiah, sacrifice, the Passover, Jerusalem—have entered into the consciousness of the nations.

Ultimately, however, the question of whether Israel can see in the church a sign that is congruent with Jewish faith depends upon the church's attitude toward the Jewish people. Are the nations prepared to receive God's blessing in the context of God's covenant with Israel? Or do they seek to do away with God's beloved child in order to usurp its place in God's affection? Unfortunately, the phenomenon of the church is deeply ambiguous on this point. Traditionally, the church has failed to understand itself in light of God's fidelity to the people Israel. Instead it has proclaimed itself to be the true spiritual Israel, comprising the faithful of all nations, in relation to which the old carnal Israel existed merely as a temporary foreshadowing.

For Wyschogrod, the acid test of the church's theological posture toward Israel's election is the church's conduct toward Jews in its own midst, that is, toward Jews who have been baptized. For it is here that the church demonstrates in an ultimate way whether it understands itself in light of God's eternal covenant with the seed of Abraham. If the church acknowledges the abiding reality of Israel's corporeal election, it will naturally expect baptized Jews to maintain faithfully their Jewish identity. But if the church truly believes that it has superseded God's covenant with Israel, it will prohibit or discourage Jews from preserving their identity as Jews and members of the Jewish people. In short, the problem of supersessionism turns on the church's capacity to acknowledge the abiding religious significance of Israel's corporeal election and hence the abiding religious significance of the distinction between Gentile and Jew.[27]

Wyschogrod argues that the church's early position on this crucial issue differs from what later became its standard view.[28] At an early date, followers of Jesus envisioned the church as a single fellowship with two branches, the Jewish and the Gentile. Jewish and gentile Christians shared a common faith in Jesus, but they differed in that Jews remained obedient to the Torah while Gentiles were bound only by the Noachide laws (see Acts 15). This understanding of the church continued to presuppose God's election of the stock of Abraham. To this belief it added the conviction that Gentiles can be followers of Jesus *as Gentiles*, that is, apart from circumcision and observance of the Torah.

Gradually, however, this view of the church was replaced by a different one according to which Christ's coming meant the complete erasure of the distinction between Jew and Gentile. This view makes the continuation of Torah obedience among baptized Jews anomalous, and as a consequence it discourages the preservation of Jewish identity over time. This shift in practice, together with the negative judgment that it embodies regarding the significance of Israel's corporeal election, is the heart and soul of supersessionism. Since the church did not insist that Jews retain their identity even in the church, "it can be inferred that . . . the church seriously holds that its election supersedes that of the old Israel."[29] Now the church views itself as the true spiritual community that was the goal of God's plan all along.

Clearly, the second view represents the church's classical understanding of itself. The basis of this self-understanding is the spiritualization of God's covenant with Israel. The church declares that the only thing that matters before God is one's inward spiritual identity as one who believes, not one's corporeal identity as either Jew or Gentile. In this way, the church frees membership in the covenant from all consideration of membership in a natural human family. But it does so at the cost of casting off the carnal anchor that joins the God of Israel to creation in the people Israel. At this point, Israel can no longer meet the church with respectful disagreement, as it could with regard to its christological claims. By claiming to be God's new people, the church directly assaults the trustworthiness of God's promise to Israel. Israel can regard this only as another example of the nations' protest against the election of the stock of Abraham, a protest that Israel must repudiate as a rebellion against God's word.[30]

For Wyschogrod, Christian supersessionism reflects a basic rebellion against the categories of Jewish and Gentile identity and the mysterious difference that they entail. According to Wyschogrod, the church cannot "go behind" God's election of Israel to a more general, spiritual plane of God's relationship to humanity without paying a heavy price. That price is an inevitable estrangement from the God of the Scriptures, the God of Abraham, Isaac, and Jacob.

SUPERSESSIONISM AND THE CHURCH'S STANDARD CANONICAL NARRATIVE

Overcoming the theology of displacement is one of the main theological tasks facing the Christian church today. Many churches have already taken a first step in this direction by repudiating supersessionism and affirming God's fidelity to God's covenant with Israel. But more than this is required. The church must also engage in fresh theological thinking on basic issues of Christian faith. This includes, to be sure, renewed investigation into the meaning of such central Christian doctrines as God, Jesus Christ, the church, eschatology, and so forth. Yet it would be mistaken to think that Christians can overcome the theology of displacement simply by addressing Christian doctrines seriatim. Much recent theology has argued convincingly that doctrines are not the most basic elements of a community's thought and life, at least not in the case of Christianity and Judaism.[31] Christian doctrines presuppose a more basic storied account of God's relations with humankind, and it is this storied account that forms the bedrock of the church's convictions, practices, and character. Ultimately, therefore, what is required in order to overcome the legacy of supersessionism is a fresh way of telling the Christian story, a way that is faithful and evangelical and just so free of the incoherence of supersessionism. This brings us to a third conviction informing this work, namely, the centrality of a canonical narrative in the work of Christian theology.

A key claim of this volume is that in order to understand and ultimately to overcome the legacy of supersessionism in Christian theology, we must focus attention on how Christians have understood the theological and narrative unity of the Christian Bible as a whole. This task is facilitated by the concept of a canonical narrative. *A canonical narrative is an interpretive instrument that provides a framework for reading the Christian Bible as a theological and narrative unity.* As used in this essay, a canonical narrative is to be clearly distinguished from the biblical canon itself. The biblical canon is the collection of texts that constitute the sacred writings of the church. In contrast, a canonical narrative is a framework for *interpreting* the biblical canon. Arising from the biblical canon, but not simply identical with it, a canonical narrative reflects a fundamental decision about how the Bible "hangs together" as a whole. The need for a canonical narrative arises because the Bible is an extraordinarily complex text whose unity and coherence are subject to question and debate. This is especially true in light of the Christian Bible's peculiar double structure, consisting in the Scriptures and the Apostolic Witness (commonly known as the Old and New Testaments).[32] A canonical narrative shows how this twofold canon coheres as a single witness to the core confession of Christian faith: the God of Israel has acted in Jesus Christ for all the world. By accomplishing this, a canonical narrative establishes the hermeneutical foundation of Christian theology and doctrine.

The idea of a canonical narrative as used in this volume closely resembles Charles Wood's concept of a canonical construal.[33] A canonical construal, according to Wood, embodies a basic decision regarding how the Bible should be interpreted as a whole. It involves "a working understanding of the inner configurations, interrelationships, and relative functions of the various components of the canon."[34] Wood points out that when the Bible is interpreted in light of a canonical construal, it is much more than the mere sum of its parts. Just as salt is not simply the product of certain quantities of sodium and chlorine, but the product of their interaction, so the Bible interpreted by means of a canonical construal is not merely an anthology of writings. "It is the new instrument produced by the working together of these parts when they are taken in a certain way, that is, according to the canonical construal which has been adopted."[35]

I prefer to speak of a canonical narrative rather than construal because the term *narrative* identifies the particular kind of construal upon which Christians have in fact traditionally relied. The interpretive framework that Christians commonly use to read the Bible has the basic character of a story. This is hardly surprising in view of the prominent role that narrative plays in the biblical text itself. As Wood has remarked:

> When one regards the biblical canon as a whole, the centrality to it of a narrative element is difficult to overlook: not only the chronological sweep of the whole, from creation to new creation, including the various events and developments of what has sometimes been called "salvation history," but also the way the large narrative portions interweave and provide a context for the remaining materials so that they, too, have a place in the ongoing story, while these other materials—parables, hymns, prayers, summaries, theological expositions—serve in different ways to enable readers to get hold of the story and to live their way into it.[36]

Granting the central role that narrative plays in the Bible, it is nonetheless important to bear in mind that a canonical narrative— even one hallowed by tradition and familiarity—is not simply identical with the biblical narratives themselves, nor indeed with any part of the biblical text. A canonical narrative provides an interpretive construal of the Bible that is logically distinct from the biblical text itself. In effect, a canonical narrative is a story that permits Christians to read the multiplicity of biblical stories (and legal codes, genealogies, letters, etc.) in reasonably coherent and consistent terms.

Christianity's traditional canonical narrative was forged in the latter half of the second century, at about the same time that the Christian Bible took its characteristic and lasting shape as a single canon consisting of two parts, the Scriptures and the Apostolic Witness. From the beginning, the traditional canonical narrative has provided an interpretive framework that shows how the church's canon forms a single coherent witness to the God of Israel's action in Jesus Christ. The framework organizes the entire biblical text in light of two chief ways in which God, the Creator of the world, engages human creation: as Consummator and as Redeemer. The story coordinates God's work as the Consummator of creation with Adam and Eve, and tells how God having created the first parents initially proposed to consummate or perfect and fulfill them by bringing them to eternal life. The story then relates how God's consummating work suffered a calamitous setback in the event known as the fall, whereby the first parents through their disobedience unleashed the destructive powers of sin, death, and evil upon themselves and the good creation. God then graciously resolved to engage humankind specifically as Redeemer in Christ, in order to rescue humankind from the consequences of the fall and in order to vindicate God's original intention to consummate human creation. Fitting the work of redemption to the times, God ordered the economy of salvation in Christ in a twofold form: prophetic and definitive. The prophetic form, commonly called the Old Covenant or Old Testament, coincides chiefly with God's history with Israel from Abraham to the incarnation. The definitive form, commonly called the New Covenant or the New Testament, coincides with God's history with Jesus Christ and the church from the incarnation to the day of judgment.

This account of the Bible's narrative unity has exercised unparalleled influence on the church's theological imagination from the second century to the present day. In particular, it has shaped the way Christians have conceived two relations that are fundamental to the whole fabric of Christian theology: the relation of God's work as Consummator and God's work as Redeemer, and the relation of the Scriptures and the Apostolic Witness. The standard canonical narrative (or standard model) defines the first relationship by means of the story of creation-for-consummation, fall, redemption in Christ, and final consummation, and it defines the second relationship by means of the conception of the unity-in-difference of the Old and New Covenants or Testaments. While mainstream Christian traditions have been replete with contentious and ongoing debates about virtually every aspect of Christian theology, these debates have taken place largely within the hermeneutical parameters established by the standard model.

Charles Wood observes that any canonical construal can be expected to give rise to its own set of questions and problems, some fairly obvious, others latent, and that it may be only after some considerable time that one is in a position to assess the limitations of a construal and to suggest revisions or alternatives.[37] Part One of this work argues that supersessionism is one such latent problem connected with the church's standard canonical narrative. I explore the connection between the standard canonical narrative and the theology of displacement by looking at three pairs of pivotal Christian thinkers: Justin Martyr and Irenaeus of Lyon, Immanuel Kant and Friedrich Schleiermacher, and Karl Barth and Karl Rahner. As our study of these figures unfolds, it will become clear that the theology of displacement is not a superficial feature of the standard model. On the contrary, supersessionism is directly implicated in the model's "deep grammar," including how it constructs the relationship of God's works as Consummator and as Redeemer, and the relationship of the Scriptures and the Apostolic Witness.

At the deepest level, the problem with the standard canonical narrative is that it makes God's identity as the God of Israel largely indecisive for shaping theological conclusions about God's enduring purposes for creation. The model renders the center of the Hebrew Scriptures—the eternal covenant between the God of Israel and the Israel of God—ultimately indecisive for understanding how God's works as Consummator and as Redeemer engage creation in lasting and universal ways. In a real sense, the standard model embodies a kind of toned down Christian gnosticism. As conceived by the standard model, God's action in Jesus Christ entails deliverance—not indeed from the work and realm of creation—but nevertheless from a history in which God's relationship with the Jewish people plays a central and enduring role. This is a gnosticism not of being but of history, a point that brings us to a fourth and final major conviction informing this volume.

SUPERSESSIONISM AND THE FLIGHT FROM HISTORY

One cost of the church's standard canonical narrative is that it fosters and supports a triumphalist posture toward the Jewish people. However, the standard canonical narrative has exacted other costs as well. For the same reason that the standard model is supersessionist, it has also tended to contribute to a double impoverishment of the Christian theological imagination. On the one hand, the standard model has led to a loss of biblical orientation for Christian theology, especially with regard to the Scriptures of Israel. On the other, it has led to a loss of creative theological engagement with the hard edges of human history. As a result, the standard model has fostered and supported a damaging dislocation of the gospel about Jesus Christ. Estranged from its proper context in the Scriptures of Israel and in public history, the gospel has been resettled in very different contexts. Alienated from the Hebrew Scriptures, the gospel has been interpreted in the context of accounts of human religiosity more or less foreign to the theological idiom of the Bible. Disconnected from the sweep of public history, the gospel has been contextualized one-sidedly in the realm of the personal and private.

Strikingly, one of the first modern theologians to identify and protest against this double dislocation of the gospel was a man who wrote from within the death camps of Nazi Germany, in part at least on account of his own theological and practical posture toward the Jewish people. In his elliptical call for a "religionless Christianity," Dietrich Bonhoeffer (1906–45) summoned Christian theology to emancipate itself from an unbiblical subservience to metaphysical and individualistic interpretations of the gospel. "What does it mean to 'interpret in a religious sense?'" he asked. "I think it means to speak on the one hand metaphysically, and on the other hand individualistically. Neither of these is relevant to the biblical message or to the man of today."[38]

Bonhoeffer's remarks are probably best remembered today as a protest against privatized understandings of the gospel and as a call for Christians to rediscover the meaning of their faith in the midst of public history. In this respect, Bonhoeffer is rightly honored as an early witness to a concern that has since come to characterize much of the theological literature of recent decades. Less well remembered, perhaps, is the fact that Bonhoeffer's own search for a worldly Christianity went hand in hand with his discovery of the Hebrew Scriptures as the indispensable context of the gospel:

> The transcendence of epistemological theory has nothing to do with the transcendence of God. God is beyond in the midst of our life. The church stands, not at the boundaries where human powers give out, but in the middle of the village. *That is how it is in the Old Testament, and in this sense we still read the New Testament far too little in the light of the Old.* How this religionless Christianity looks, what form it takes, is something that I'm thinking about a great deal, and I shall be writing to you again about it soon.[39]

Bonhoeffer did not live to give his musings final shape. But it is evident that his call for a "religionless Christianity" cannot be properly understood apart from his renewed interest in the Hebrew Bible. Bonhoeffer's concern was not to "modernize" Christian faith after the liberal fashion of the day but rather to make it more faithful by situating the gospel in the context of public history and the Scriptures of the Jewish people.

I argue that there is a systematic connection between the doctrine of supersessionism and the weaknesses that Bonhoeffer identified in traditional patterns of Christian thought and that have since claimed the attention of many others.[40] Just as a flaw in the heart of a crystal distorts all of the light that passes through it, the logic of supersessionism has tended to distort the doctrinal patterns of Christian thought in ways that have hindered areas of Christian discipleship far beyond the church's posture toward Israel. If this is the case, then the task of overcoming supersessionism is vital not only for the renewal of the church's relation to the Jewish people but for the renewal of its relation to the Bible and to the world.

A ROAD MAP

Part One addresses the logic and limitations of the church's standard construal of the Bible's narrative unity. The standard canonical narrative provides an interpretive framework that shows how the church's twofold canon of Scriptures hangs together as a coherent witness to the church's central confession: the God of Israel has acted in Jesus Christ for all the world. The standard model knits the Christian Bible into a coherent whole by advancing a particular storied account of two vital relationships that underlie the whole fabric of Christian theology: the relationship of God's work as Consummator and God's work as Redeemer, and the relationship of the Scriptures and the Apostolic Witness.

Chapter 2 examines the origins of the standard model in the work of Justin Martyr (c.100–c.165) and especially Irenaeus of Lyon (c.130–c.200). These two theologians forged the standard model at a time when the second-century church was seeking to defend its basic confession against three chief adversaries: pagans, Jews, and gnostic Christians. The great accomplishment of Justin and especially of Irenaeus was to propose an interpretive framework for reading the Bible in light of which the church could defend its basic confession against each of these adversaries. I argue, however, that the cost of their particular solution was great. In their vision of the Bible's coherence, the great bulk of the Hebrew Scriptures, and above all God's history with Israel and the nations, is rendered ultimately indecisive for shaping conclusions about how God's works as Consummator and as Redeemer engage creation in enduring and universal ways. One consequence was the logic of supersessionism, according to which the "spiritual" church is destined from all eternity to replace carnal Israel in God's plans. A second consequence was a certain tendency to contextualize the gospel of Jesus Christ within metaphysically abstracted understandings of God's purposes for creation. This in turn fostered a loss of creative theological contact with the Hebrew Scriptures and public history in the formulation of Christian doctrine.

Chapter 3 carries the discussion of the standard model into the early modern era. Kant (1724–1804) and Schleiermacher (1768–1834) bring to a logical conclusion the decisive feature of the standard model, namely, its tendency to render God's identity as the God of Israel irrelevant for shaping conclusions about God's enduring purposes for creation. Indeed, Kant and Schleiermacher explicitly refuse to identify the God of Christian faith with the God of Israel. As a result, the supersessionism that already characterized the standard model in its classical form undergoes a dramatic exacerbation in the modern period. Classical Christian theologians had merely subordinated God's history with the Jewish people to the standard model's dominant story of creation-for-consummation, fall, redemption in Christ, and final consummation. By contrast, Kant and Schleiermacher exploit the logic of the standard model in order to expel altogether God's history with the Jewish people from the body of Christian faith. As a consequence, the existence of the Jewish people becomes a matter of theological indifference for Christians not only within the sphere of the church but within human history in general.

At the same time, the example of early modern theology suggests that sharpened supersessionism exacerbates the dual impoverishment of the Christian imagination identified by Bonhoeffer. The constructive theologies of Kant and Schleiermacher evince a further erosion of Christian theology's capacity to engage constructively with the biblical story and public history. The loss of engagement with the biblical story now extends beyond the Scriptures of Israel and begins to blunt contact with the Apostolic Witness itself. Simultaneously, God's enduring purposes for creation drift ever more completely into a sphere of individual consciousness and inwardness.

Chapter 4 concludes the analysis of the standard model by examining two of its greatest postmodern exponents, Karl Barth (1886–1968) and Karl Rahner (1904–1984). Barth and Rahner are both keenly sensitive to the dual impoverishment of the standard model that is the legacy of early modern theology. Barth is especially concerned with theology's loss of biblical substance and orientation. Rahner is especially concerned with theology's loss of engagement with the contingent and historical features of human identity. Furthermore, both theologians are aware that what is ultimately at risk in both instances is theology's orientation on the living God of the Bible.

Strikingly, both theologians address the crisis of the standard model by redescribing God's work as Consummator in profoundly original ways. Barth identifies God's consummating work with reference to God's covenant with the Jewish people. Rahner identifies God's consummating work with reference to a historical and contingent feature of human identity. In these two complementary ways, Barth and Rahner significantly modify the traditional logic of the standard model and provide important resources for imagining an alternative account of the Bible's narrative coherence.

Nevertheless, the great weakness of Barth and Rahner is that they fail to recognize and confront the root problem of the standard model, namely, supersessionism. As a result, both men transmit the logic of supersessionism into the post-Holocaust era. Furthermore, both men ultimately fail to address convincingly the dual crisis of the standard model. Despite Barth's exegetically brilliant association of God's consummating work with God's election of Israel, his vision of consummation ultimately collapses into the single person of Jesus Christ, who threatens to absorb all biblical substance into himself. And despite Rahner's linkage of God's consummating work with the historical dimension of human existence, his vision of consummation ultimately collapses into the inward dynamism of human consciousness. In both cases, what is lost is a clear account of how the texture of the biblical witness intersects with the public reality of human history.

Part Two takes up the volume's second constructive task. At stake in this part is learning to grasp the theological unity of the Bible in a manner that does not "nullify the faithfulness of God" (Rom 3:3). Drawing on what we have learned about the logic of supersessionism, I suggest an alternative account of the canon's narrative and theological unity. The account aims to show that Christians can interpret the canon as a coherent witness to the church's basic confession in a manner that overcomes the logic of supersessionism and that coheres fully with the contemporary church's affirmation of God's irrevocable election of the people Israel. In addition, I suggest that by conceiving the unity of the canon in nonsupersessionist ways, Christians can take an important step toward remedying the false contextualization of the Bible identified by Bonhoeffer in his call for a worldly Christianity.[41]

PART ONE

THE LOGIC AND LIMITATIONS
OF THE
STANDARD CANONICAL NARRATIVE

2

A FLAW IN THE HEART
OF THE CRYSTAL
JUSTIN AND IRENAEUS

THE STANDARD CANONICAL NARRATIVE

During the latter half of the second century, the church's original canon of Jewish Scriptures was expanded to include a second collection of Jewish writings that later became known as the New Testament.[1] With the expanded canon came the need for an interpretive framework or canonical narrative that would enable Christians to read their twofold canon as a theological unity. By the beginning of the third century at the latest, such a canonical narrative was securely in place. In its basic lineaments, it was the common possession of Christian theologians throughout the patristic era, and from their hands it was bequeathed to later epochs of the church.

The canonical narrative that prevailed is a story that, at least until quite recently, was familiar to virtually every Christian. The story recounts God's history with human creation in four crucial episodes: God's intention to consummate the human pair whom God has created, the first parents' disobedience and fall, the redemption of lost humanity in Christ, and final consummation. The story is found in abbreviated form in the church's creeds and provides the basic outline for most works of Christian theology.

The story's plot turns on two different ways in which the Creator engages human creation: as Consummator and as Redeemer. As the Consummator of creation, God appoints a supreme goal for humankind and draws it toward that goal through God's own constant consummating activity. God's work as Consummator establishes an initial axis of narrative tension that determines the

25

canonical narrative's overarching sweep. The story line of consummation is not dependent on the calamity of sin or indeed on any other narrative complication. The tension arises solely through the final end that God appoints for human creation and is resolved when God brings humanity to the goal for which it was created.

In addition to God's work as Consummator, God also engages human creation as Redeemer. By its nature, God's work as Redeemer presupposes a further narrative complication in addition to the initial story line established by God's work as Consummator. The additional complication is the brute fact of sin and evil. Sin radically threatens God's initial work as Consummator and unleashes destructive powers that corrupt the good inherent in creation itself. As Redeemer, God delivers the human creature from the destructive powers of sin, evil, oppression, and death. Furthermore, God restores the redeemed creature to the hope of final consummation.

Now, what gives the standard canonical narrative its characteristic logic is the way these two modes of God's engagement with creation are employed to organize the church's twofold canon into a narrative unity. The standard model coordinates God's work as Consummator with the opening chapters of Genesis and the story of Adam and Eve (Gen 1–2). God appoints for the first parents the supreme goal of eternal life with God, a goal that they can eventually attain through reliance upon God's consummating grace and obedience to God's command. Frequently, God's work as Consummator is coordinated even more specifically with Gen 1:26–27, according to which God created humankind in God's "image" and "likeness." While interpretations of the image of God vary, it is commonly understood as a capacity for eternal communion with God that belongs to humankind by virtue of its specific nature as a spiritual or rational creature. On this view, the goal that God appoints as Consummator is the fulfillment of humanity's specific nature through eternal fellowship with God.

God's work as the Consummator of Adam and Eve gives the standard canonical narrative an initial axis of narrative tension that is antecedent to sin and to the fall. The tension arises through God's appointment of eternal life as the goal of human nature and is resolved when humankind attains the end for which God created it. The initial story line of consummation, however, swiftly undergoes a catastrophic complication in the event commonly known as the fall. The standard model coordinates the idea of the fall with the events recounted in Genesis 3. By disobeying God's command, the first parents rupture God's work as Consummator in a way that is beyond human power to mend. They despoil the image of God in which they were created and forfeit the ultimate goal of eternal life. What is more, they bring themselves and their progeny under the threat of divine judgment and the powers of sin, corruption, and death.

God's frustrated intention to consummate the first parents establishes the soteriological context of God's work as Redeemer in Jesus Christ. The standard model conceives of God's redemptive work in Christ as the center and turning point of God's single over-arching plan to save humanity, a plan that spans the ages from the fall to the day of judgment. God's overarching redemptive work is also known as the economy (*oikonomia*) of redemption, a term that refers to God's saving management (*nomos*) of the household (*oikos*) of creation.[2] God adapts the economy of redemption to the needs of fallen humanity by ordering it in two chief dispensations. The first dispensation, called the Old Covenant or Old Testament, prepares humanity for redemption by pointing forward to Christ in a carnal and prophetic way. The second chief dispensation, called the New Covenant or the New Testament, testifies to redemption in Christ in a definitive and spiritual way. According to the standard model, therefore, Jesus Christ is the center and substance of both the Old and the New Covenants. The Old Covenant points forward to Christ, the New Covenant points back. Accordingly, the standard model also regards Jesus Christ as the hermeneutical focal point or *scopus* of the Christian canon as a literary entity. The Scriptures testify to Christ prophetically, while the Apostolic Witness does so historically. Eventually, these two parts of the canon come to be called the Old and New Testaments.

Under the dispensation of the Old Testament, Jesus Christ is made known by the law and the prophets in the context of God's covenant with Israel, from whom Jesus Christ himself is descended according to the flesh. The Old Testament dispensation has *redemptive power solely by virtue of its reference to the future coming of Christ*. Circumcision, promises, law, temple, Israel's history, and so forth all point in various ways toward Christ and the church, and thereby make faith possible in the time before Christ. Those Israelites who grasped the Mosaic dispensation according to its inward, christological substance were saved, while those who took the Old Covenant according to its outer, carnal form alone remained under Adam's curse.

Under the dispensation of the New Testament, God's work as Redeemer is actually enacted in Jesus Christ and the outpouring of the Holy Spirit, and made available to the world through the preaching and sacraments of the church. Now for the first time God administers the economy of redemption in an outer form that corresponds directly to its inward, christological substance. The prophecies, types, and figures of the Old Testament are fulfilled and superseded by their New Testament equivalents. So baptism replaces circumcision, the Eucharist replaces Passover, and so forth.

Christ's advent therefore marks the point at which God's one overarching economy of redemption changes from its prefigurative to its definitive form. As a result, the visible community of salvation also undergoes a transformation from its prefigurative to its definitive form. Before Christ's coming, the visible community of salvation was defined by carnal descent from Abraham, Isaac, and Jacob. After Christ's coming, the visible community is defined by baptism and confession of faith in Jesus Christ, which is open to all without distinction. Accordingly, the carnal distinction between Jew and Gentile loses whatever theological significance it previously possessed. While some Jews receive the gospel and join the church, most do not. As a result, God punishes the unbelieving Jews and scatters them over the earth, where they will remain until the day of judgment.

The standard canonical narrative concludes by pointing forward to Christ's second advent at the end of time. Christ's second coming inaugurates a series of end-time events, especially the general resurrection of the dead, the last judgment, and the separation of the saved and the damned. These events resolve both axes of tension in the plot of the canonical narrative by completing God's redemptive work in Christ and by fulfilling God's original consummating intention to bring humanity to eternal life.

PROBLEMATIC ASPECTS

The canonical narrative just outlined has provided an enormously influential solution to the problem of how the Bible hangs together as a unified witness to the central confession that "the God of Israel has acted in Jesus Christ for the sake of all." The model gives classic definition to two relationships that, as we have noted, are of the utmost importance to Christian theology: the relation of God's work as Consummator and as Redeemer, and the relation of the Scriptures and the Apostolic Witness. The model defines the first relationship by means of the story of creation-for-consummation in Adam, Adam's fall, redemption in Christ, and final consummation. And it defines the second relationship in terms of the unity-in-difference of the Old and New Testaments as complementary parts of God's one economy of redemption in Christ. Yet its familiarity notwithstanding, the standard canonical narrative has been rendered problematic by the church's contemporary rejection of supersessionism. For, as I argue in the rest of this chapter, the standard model is deeply implicated in the problem of supersessionism. This is so for obvious narrative reasons and for less apparent structural reasons as well.

To begin with the obvious narrative problem, the standard model is supersessionist simply by virtue of the story that it tells. According to the standard model, Israel and the church both depend exclusively upon Christ for their soteriological significance. But Israel corresponds to Christ in a merely prefigurative and carnal way, whereas the church corresponds to Jesus Christ in a definitive and spiritual way. Hence Christ's advent brings about the obsolescence of carnal Israel and inaugurates the age of the spiritual church. Everything that characterized the economy of salvation in its Israelite form becomes obsolete and is replaced by its ecclesial equivalent. The written law of Moses is replaced by the spiritual law of Christ, circumcision by baptism, natural descent by faith as criterion of membership in the people of God, and so forth. As a result, *carnal Israel becomes obsolete.* This understanding of supersessionism can be called *economic* because the ultimate obsolescence of carnal Israel is an essential feature of God's one overarching economy of redemption for the world. Economic supersessionism is epitomized in the following passage by the second-century writer Melito of Sardis:

> The people [Israel] was precious before the church arose,
>   and the law was marvelous before the gospel was elucidated.
> But when the church arose
>   and the gospel took precedence
> the model was made void, conceding its power to the reality. . . .
>   the people was made void when the church arose.[3]

According to economic supersessionism, Israel is transient not because it happens to be sinful but because Israel's essential role in the economy of redemption is to prepare for salvation in its spiritual and universal form.

Economic supersessionism is often accompanied by a complementary narrative viewpoint that can be called *punitive* supersessionism. According to punitive supersessionism, God abrogates God's covenant with Israel (which is already in principle outmoded) on account of Israel's rejection of Christ and the gospel. Once again, the viewpoint is summed up by Melito:

> Therefore, O Israel,
> you did not quake in the presence of the Lord,
>   so you quaked at the assault of foes. . .
> you did not lament over the Lord,
>   so you lamented over your firstborn;
> you did not tear your clothes when the Lord was hung,
>   so you tore them over those who were slain. . .
> you did not accept the Lord,
>   you were not pitied by him. . .[4]

Because the Jews obstinately reject God's action in Christ, God in turn angrily rejects and punishes the Jews.

Punitive supersessionism may initially appear more problematic than economic supersessionism because it is more palpably polemical toward Israel. In fact, however, economic supersessionism poses a far more difficult problem for Christian theology today. While economic supersessionism need not be overtly hostile toward the Jewish people, it logically entails the ontological, historical, and moral obsolescence of Israel's existence after Christ. The absence of an obviously antagonistic posture toward the Jews should hardly make this perspective more congenial to churches that have found it necessary to reject theological triumphalism toward Jews. Furthermore, economic supersessionism shapes the way Christians read great expanses of the biblical story (from Abraham to Christ and Pentecost), and is therefore deeply interwoven with the narrative and conceptual fabric of the standard model as a whole. In contrast, punitive supersessionism forms little more than an appendix to the standard model's main story line, since it concerns God's rejection and punishment of unbelieving Israel after Christ. All of this suggests that while Christian theology today can reject punitive supersessionism with relative ease, doing so does not guarantee that the theology of displacement has been overcome. The logic of economic supersessionism may remain. This is the case, for example, whenever Christians hold that Israel's existence has been rendered obsolete in principle but that God nevertheless remains faithful to Israel in fact despite its unbelief.[5]

Yet the problem of supersessionism in the standard model extends deeper than either economic or punitive supersessionism. In addition to these two explicit doctrinal perspectives, the standard model is also supersessionist in a *structural* sense, that is, by virtue of the manner in which it construes the narrative unity of the Christian Bible as a whole. The standard model is structurally supersessionist *because it unifies the Christian canon in a manner that renders the Hebrew Scriptures largely indecisive for shaping conclusions about how God's purposes engage creation in universal and enduring ways.* Whereas economic and punitive supersessionism designate discrete problems *within* the standard model, structural supersessionism designates a problem that pervades the standard model as a whole.[6]

To grasp supersessionism as a structural problem, consider the following. The standard canonical narrative turns on four key episodes: God's intention to consummate the first parents whom God has created, the fall, Christ's incarnation and the inauguration of the church, and final consummation. These four episodes play a uniquely important role in the standard model because together they constitute the model's basic plot or story line. They relate how God's works as Consummator and as Redeemer engage human creation in ways that have universal and lasting significance. In this way, the four episodes determine the basic narrative and conceptual structure of the standard model as a whole. For convenience's sake, I will call this fourfold plot structure the standard model's *foreground.* The four episodes constitute a foreground of sorts because they stand in direct dramatic relation to one another and thereby determine the dramatic context of the rest of the canonical text. Like the synopsis of a play or opera, they establish the storied context in which every other character, incident, or plot development is conceived.

Now, if one considers the narrative content of the standard model's foreground, two facts stand out. First, the foreground portrays God's engagement with human creation in cosmic and universal terms. Christ figures in the story as the incarnation of the eternal Logos, humankind appears as descendants of the first parents and as possessors of a common human nature, and so on. Second, the foreground completely neglects the Hebrew Scriptures, with the exception of Genesis 1–3! The story tells how God engaged Adam and Eve as Consummator and how God's initial consummating plan was almost immediately disrupted by the fall. The foreground story then leaps immediately to the Apostolic Witness interpreted as God's deliverance of humankind from the fall through Jesus Christ. So conceived, God's purposes as Consummator and Redeemer engage human creation in a manner that simply outflank the greater part of the Hebrew Scriptures and, above all, their witness to God's history with the people Israel.

What then becomes of the center of the Hebrew Scriptures, namely, the God of Israel's history with the Israel of God? Not surprisingly, it recedes into what I will call the background of the standard canonical narrative. The term *background* is not intended to suggest that God's way with Israel necessarily receives a *quantitatively* small amount of exegetical and theological attention in comparison with the foreground. That is sometimes but by no means always the case. The point is rather a *qualitative* one. The term *background* points to the fact that God's history with Israel plays a role that is ultimately indecisive for shaping the canonical narrative's overarching plot. God's history with Israel does not form an indispensable narrative element of either God's initial work as Consummator or God's work as Redeemer in its definitive form. Bracketed between these two decisive modes of God's engagement with creation, Israel's history is portrayed as nothing more than *the economy of redemption in prefigurative form*. So construed, Israel's story contributes little or nothing to understanding how God's consummating and redemptive purposes engage human creation in universal and enduring ways. Indeed, the background can be completely omitted from an account of Christian faith without thereby disturbing the overarching logic of salvation history. This omission is reflected in virtually every historic confession of Christian faith from the Creeds of Nicaea and Constantinople to the Augsburg Confession and beyond.[7]

As the example of the creeds suggests, the structural supersessionism of the standard model has profound significance for the doctrinal and theological conclusions that Christians draw about every aspect of their faith. The standard model incorporates God's history with Israel into the Christian story only as it simultaneously renders it largely indecisive for grasping the story's overarching plot. Insofar as theology formulates its dogmatic or systematic conclusions with reference to the Bible's overarching plot, the standard model effectively renders God's history with Israel mute for the purposes of theological reflection.

To sum up, the standard canonical narrative unifies the Christian canon into a single coherent witness only as it simultaneously refracts that witness asymmetrically into a dominant creaturely-universal foreground and a subordinate Israelite background. The creaturely-universal foreground relates how God's works as Consummator and as Redeemer engage creation in universal and enduring ways yet in a manner that simply outflanks the bulk of the Hebrew Scriptures and the story of Israel. The Israelite background takes account of the center of the Hebrew Bible and its testimony to the story of Israel yet in a way that renders these largely irrelevant for shaping conclusions about God's overarching purposes for creation. *As a result, God's identity as the God of Israel and God's history with the Jewish people become largely indecisive for the Christian conception of God.* The conclusion that these considerations point to is simply this: the problem of supersessionism in Christian theology goes beyond the explicit teaching that the church has displaced Israel as God's people in the economy of salvation. At a deeper level, the problem of supersessionism coincides with the way in which Christians have traditionally understood the theological and narrative unity of the Christian canon as a whole.

THE ORIGINS OF THE
STANDARD CANONICAL NARRATIVE

The canonical narrative sketched above originated in part as a response to the apologetic situation of the second-century church. The church was then an overwhelmingly gentile community engaged in a protracted struggle to define its theological identity against three sets of opponents: Jews, pagans, and Gnostics. In each case, the church found it necessary to defend its central confession at a different point. *Against the Jews,* the church had to defend the claim that the God of Hebrew Scriptures had acted for all the world *in Jesus Christ. Against the pagans,* the church had to defend the claim that God had acted in Jesus Christ *for all the world,* that is, *with saving significance for everyone.* And finally, *against the gnostics,* the church had to defend the claim that One who acted for all the world in Jesus Christ was *the God of Hebrew scriptures.* The genius of the standard canonical narrative was to provide a synoptic construal of the Bible that allowed the church to expound its basic confession in a consistent and comprehensive fashion along each of these three hostile fronts.[8]

The creation of a framework for reading the Christian Bible was to a considerable degree the accomplishment of Justin Martyr and especially Irenaeus of Lyon.[9] Justin wrote when the Hebrew Scriptures still constituted the sole Bible of the Christian church, and on that basis he championed Christian faith against pagans and Jews. Irenaeus wrote one generation later when the Apostolic Witness was an accepted part of the Christian Bible, and on that basis he defended Christian faith against the threat of gnosticism. While Justin is generally reckoned to be the first Christian theologian to provide a comprehensive "salvation-historical" framework for interpreting the Hebrew Scriptures, Irenaeus deserves credit for being the first to propose a comprehensive framework for reading the church's twofold canon. Irenaeus' achievement provided the basic design for what would become the church's standard canonical narrative.

To be sure, both Justin and Irenaeus drew on previous traditions of Christian exegesis, including traditions found in the Apostolic Witness itself. Nevertheless, Justin and Irenaeus created a framework for reading the Bible that was much more than a mechanical reproduction of previous tradition. It was an original and imaginative statement about how the Christian canon hangs together as a whole and in its parts. Unfortunately, it was also a statement that made supersessionism central to the logic of Christian theology for centuries to come.

JUSTIN MARTYR:
A FRAMEWORK FOR THE SCRIPTURES OF ISRAEL

Justin Martyr was a transitional figure in the early church. He was one of the last Christian theologians to regard the church's Bible as identical with the Hebrew Scriptures but one of the first to take up the task of giving a reasoned defense and recommendation of Christian faith to outsiders. Justin's surviving works are the *First* and *Second Apologies*, which expound and defend Christian doctrine for pagan audiences, and *Dialogue with Trypho*, which purports to record Justin's lengthy conversation with Trypho, an educated Jew, about the merits of Christian faith. In these works, Justin developed a comprehensive narrative framework for reading the Hebrew Scriptures that anticipates the shape of the standard model in important ways.[10]

Justin's framework anticipates the standard model in two main respects. First, he organizes the Scriptures in light of a vision of salvation history that possesses both foreground and background dimensions.[11] The foreground consists in the cosmic drama between the Creator and human creation that culminates in the incarnation of the Logos, in the spiritual community he founds, and in his return at the end of the age. The background consists in the Creator's troubled history with Abraham's children after the flesh, the Jews. Justin regards both dimensions of salvation history as indispensable for Christian faith, but for different reasons. The cosmic foreground is significant because it relates how God directly engages each person's nature and destiny as a rational creature. The background, in contrast, is significant because it proves the truth of the foreground by prophecy, signs, and figures. While Justin esteems the background dimension for its probative value, he accords it little or no independent *religious* significance. Second, Justin integrates the foreground and background dimensions of salvation history by means of his conception of the Christian church as the "true spiritual Israel," a term that he was the first to apply to the Christian church (*Dial.* 11).[12] In this way, Justin makes supersessionism crucial to his conception of the canon's narrative unity.

Justin gives special prominence to the cosmic dimension of salvation history in his writings for pagan audiences. While not one to make compromises with the truth for short-term apologetic gain, his emphasis on the cosmic dimension of salvation history serves a clear apologetic purpose: it helps demonstrate to skeptical pagans how God's action in Christ has significance for everyone, including those who are not Jews. Justin gives special prominence to four key episodes: God's creation of humankind for the sake of blessedness (*1 Apol.* 10, 28; *2 Apol.* 4, 5, 7), humankind's freedom to choose between good and evil (*1 Apol.* 10, 28; *2 Apol.* 4, 5, 7) the incarnation of the Logos in Jesus Christ (*1 Apol.* 13, 23, 46; *2 Apol.* 6, 10), and final judgment and final consummation (*1 Apol.* 10, 11, 12, 19, 28; *2 Apol.* 8, 9). In addition, he carefully points out that each of these teachings has parallels in pagan belief (*1 Apol.* 18, 20, 21, 22).

Justin's key concept for locating Jesus Christ in cosmic context, of course, is the Logos, a term with complex roots in Greek, Jewish, and early Christian literature. By Justin's time, the idea of the divine Logos was already something of a "fashionable cliché."[13] For Justin, the Logos is the principle of divine reason that sprang forth from the absolutely transcendent God at the time of creation and that has since mediated between God and the world, especially the rational world. Human beings have a germinal share in the divine Logos

(*logos spermatikos*) by virtue of their rational nature, and this enables them to have knowledge of God (*2 Apol.* 8, 13; see also *1 Apol.* 46; *2 Apol.* 10). Before Christ's advent people who lived according to reason achieved a partial knowledge of God and were in effect Christians before Christ (*1 Apol.* 46; see also 5; *2 Apol.* 10). The eternal Logos, however, was present not in germinal fashion but whole and entire in Jesus Christ, in whom the Logos "assumed a human form and became man" (*1 Apol.* 5). Christ liberates humankind from ignorance and error by revealing to all what is eternally right and acceptable before God (*2 Apol.* 9, 10). In addition, Christ by his death on the cross procures remission from sin. Followers of Christ are guilty of no ethical or theological trespass, but simply adhere to the moral law that has been present to all in every time and place.

Justin's emphasis on Christ's place in cosmic history allows him to show his pagan audience how God's action in Jesus Christ is significant for "everyone." The difficulty, however, is that Justin's apologetic strategy largely circumvents God's identity as the God of Israel and God's history with the Jewish people as related by the Hebrew Scriptures. This is not to say that in his writings for pagan audiences Justin simply disregards Israel's history. Quite the contrary. After discussing the cosmic dimensions of salvation history, Justin devotes almost the entire second half of the *First Apology* to a detailed discussion of passages from the Hebrew Scriptures. Nevertheless, Justin's purpose in this section is no longer to set forth the content and universal significance of Christian belief. Rather, his purpose is to adduce evidence that Christian belief is true. He informs his readers that "there were certain men among the Jews who were Prophets of God, through whom the Prophetic Spirit predicted events that were to happen, before they actually took place" (*1 Apol.* 31). These men foretold in detail what would come to pass in Jesus Christ, the church, and the eschaton. This proves the truth of Christian belief. Such proof is necessary, Justin acknowledges, for "why should we believe a crucified Man that He was First-begotten of an Unbegotten God, and that He will pass judgment on the entire human race, unless we had found testimonies concerning Him foretold before He came . . . ?" (*1 Apol.* 53). Thus Justin reduces the great body of the Hebrew Scriptures to prophecy of Christ, and prophecy of Christ to historical evidence for Christian doctrine in its universal and enduring significance.

In his writings for pagan audiences, Justin clearly tends to divide the content of Christian belief into two parts of unequal significance. One part (creation-for-consummation, fall, redemption in Christ, and final judgment) is of interest to all because it directly determines the being and destiny of all persons as rational creatures. The other part (God's history with the Jews construed as prophecy of Christ) is also of interest to all, not however because of its direct spiritual significance but because of its probative power.

In addition to his writings for pagan audiences, Justin authored a major apologetic dialogue that defends Christian faith against the objections of a certain Jew, Trypho. Justin's *Dialogue with Trypho* purports to record a two-day conversation that he held with Trypho, who had recently fled from the Roman suppression of the Bar Kochba revolt. As one would expect, Justin's apologetic task differs from what it was in the *Apologies.* Unlike Justin and his pagan audience, Justin and his Jewish interlocutor share the fundamental premise that God is the One "who, with a strong hand and outstretched arm, led your forefathers out of the land of Egypt . . . the God of Abraham, and of Isaac, and of Jacob" (*Dial.* 11). Now Justin's task is to demonstrate that this same God has acted in Jesus Christ and—so Justin holds—that henceforth the God of Israel is found among the church rather than among the Jews.

Justin addresses this task by taking what had been a subordinate theme in the *First Apology* and making it the center of the *Dialogue:* the Hebrew Scriptures point beyond themselves at every point to Christ and the church, the new spiritual Israel. To establish this claim, Justin employs a variety of exegetical methods, including proof from prophecy, allegory, and typology. Once again, however, Justin's solution depends less on the details of his exegesis than on his larger grasp of the narrative unity of the Scriptures. For Justin, God's history with the carnal community of the Jews is merely a passing episode within God's more encompassing purposes for creation, which are universal and spiritual in nature. As the Hebrew Scriptures themselves testify, Christ is the climax of God's spiritual purposes for creation. Christ therefore ends God's transient relationship with Abraham's physical descendants and initiates God's enduring relationship with the church, the spiritual community of salvation. Henceforth, the God of Israel is to be found with "the true, spiritual Israel."

As in the *Apologies,* Justin's account of salvation history in its universal and spiritual dimensions is based upon four chief episodes: creation-for-consummation in Adam, Adam's fall, redemption in Christ, and final consummation. God's history with humankind is inaugurated by God's initial consummating purpose for humankind and its abortive outcome in Adam. God created humankind with free will in order that they might do those things that were pleasing to God and prove themselves worthy to be called God's children. In return, God would preserve them free from suffering and death. But Adam proved disobedient to God and fell under the power of death, and since Adam, all have likewise sinned and become vulnerable to God's punishment (*Dial.* 88, 124).

For Justin, God's redemptive action in Christ is directly motivated by the wretched outcome of God's initial consummating plan. Christ did not condescend to be born and to die upon the cross "because He was in need of birth or crucifixion; He did it solely for the sake of man, who from the time of Adam had become subject to death and the deceit of the serpent, each man having sinned by his own fault" (*Dial.* 88). The Father of the Universe "willed that His Christ should shoulder the curses of the whole human race, fully realizing that He would raise Him up again after His crucifixion and death" (*Dial.* 95). As Savior of the human race, Christ introduces "an everlasting and final law" and a "trustworthy covenant" for the salvation of all (*Dial.* 11). Indeed, Christ himself is this new covenant and new law (*Dial.* 11; see 24, 34, 122). The law embodied by Christ enjoins precepts that "God knows to be eternal and fit for every nationality" (*Dial.* 67). It corresponds to what has been "universally, naturally, and eternally" done by the righteous people of every age (*Dial.* 45).

Salvation history will be concluded by Christ's second coming, an event on which Justin lays great emphasis. Upon his return, Christ will judge all men according to whether they have believed in him and lived "according to His principles" (*Dial.* 45). Then "some will be condemned to suffer eternally in the fires of Hell, while others will be eternally free from suffering, corruption, and sorrow" (*Dial.* 45). Thus salvation history is resolved when the followers of Christ attain the end that God originally foresaw for Adam.

This foreground story establishes the context in which Justin interprets the balance of the Hebrew Scriptures, and above all, God's dealings with Abraham's physical descendants, the Jews. Significantly, Justin treats this part of Scripture in a historical manner and does not simply allegorize it away. But Justin insists that God's history with the Jews never possessed saving significance in its own right. God's commerce with the Jews served either to restrain the particular wickedness of the Jewish people or to prefigure Christ.

The former purpose testifies to the uncommon sinfulness of the Jews, while the latter purpose comes to an end with Christ.

Justin's view of God's dealings with the Jews appears clearly in his account of the Mosaic law. Justin is the first Christian theologian to introduce a tripartite division into the law (see *Dial.* 44, 67).[14] Some commandments function to point to the coming of Christ. Some God ordained on account of the Jews' hardness of heart. And some are good by nature and hence are binding on all at all times.

One part of the law, then, contains precepts that prefigure Christ and the spiritual community of salvation (*Dial.* 40–42). So, for example, the Passover lamb prefigures Christ (*Dial.* 40), while the circumcision of the flesh prefigures the true spiritual circumcision of those who believe in Christ (*Dial.* 41). Justin states that such examples could be multiplied indefinitely, for in fact all of the things that Moses commanded can be interpreted as "types, symbols, and prophecies" of Christ and the church (*Dial.* 42).

God ordained a second part of the Mosaic law in order to restrain and punish the Jewish people on account of their singular wickedness (*Dial.* 21, 22, 43, 44, 46, 67, 92). Notoriously, Justin informs Trypho that God prescribed circumcision for the Jews alone in order that "you and you only might suffer the afflictions" due those who crucified Christ, since "circumcision of the flesh is the only mark by which you can certainly be distinguished from other men" (*Dial.* 16; see 19, 92). Justin has in mind the bloody aftermath of the failed Bar Kochba revolt, when Roman soldiers relied on circumcision to identify Jews for slaughter. Justin thereby chillingly transforms circumcision from a sign of election to an aid in extermination.

A third part of law consists in ethical precepts that possess universal and eternal significance and are known to all by nature (*Dial.* 45, 93). This is the part of the law that Christ confirms and perfects. In contrast, Christ brings the other portions of the Jewish law to an end. Christ's law is superior to the ceremonial law of the Jews in every respect. It is eternal rather than temporal (*Dial.* 40), universal rather than particular (*Dial.* 11). Above all, it is spiritual and inward rather than merely physical and outward as the abolition of carnal circumcision indicates (*Dial.* 41). Justin begs Trypho to recognize the obsolescence of the Old Law and the nullity of physical descent from Abraham and to join the spiritual church.

Justin's interpretive framework in the *Dialogue* organizes the

Scriptures into a narrative unity that supports the judgment that God's enduring and universal will can only be fulfilled in a spiritual community such as the church. In contrast, God's saving purpose can only be transiently concerned with a carnal family such as the Jews. This perspective is what we earlier called economic supersessionism, because it grounds Israel's transience in the very nature of God's redemptive will. Justin's economic supersessionism, in turn, sets the stage for his affirmation of punitive supersessionism. Because the Jews sinfully rejected Christ, God has rejected the Jewish people and is punishing them on account of their sin (*Dial.* 16). God's rejection of the Jews poses no theological difficulty for Justin, because God's salvation for the world was never tied directly to them but only to Christ and to "the true spiritual Israel" (*Dial.* 11).

The interpretive framework that Justin applies to the Hebrew Scriptures is the same in both the *Apologies* and the *Dialogue.* In each case, the framework unifies the biblical story by subordinating the story of Israel to the logic of the cosmic drama of creation, fall, redemption in Christ, and final consummation. The framework serves a clear though distinct apologetic role in addressing both pagans and Jews. Among pagans, the cosmic foreground emphasizes the universal relevance of God's action in Christ and underscores the analogy of Christian and pagan belief. For Jews, the Israelite background explains why the "true spiritual Israel" is not to be found among the Jews but among the Christians. By defining God's overarching purposes for creation in universal and spiritualizing terms, Justin provides a framework that makes it appear self-evident that the true Israel of God is a spiritual rather than a carnal community. Justin's accomplishment is all the more significant because, as Rowan Greer has observed, "The way the Old Testament functions for Justin is, generally speaking, the way it continues to function for the Great Church of Irenaeus and the third century, and indeed for the whole of the patristic period."[15]

IRENAEUS:
A FRAMEWORK FOR THE TWOFOLD CANON

In his great anti-gnostic masterwork, *Against Heresies,* Irenaeus of Lyon sets forth for the first time a comprehensive narrative framework for reading the church's twofold canon.[16] Although Irenaeus lived only a generation after Justin, he belonged to a different epoch of the church in one important respect. Whereas Justin's Bible was still the ancient Scriptures of the Jews, Irenaeus' Bible consisted in a twofold canon largely identical to the Christian Bible of today. The great task facing Irenaeus was to exhibit the unity of the twofold canon and on the basis of that unity to defend the "apostolic faith" against the threat of gnosticism, the third major challenge to Christian faith alongside pagans and Jews.

Irenaeus and his gnostic opponents shared the conviction that God acted redemptively in Jesus Christ. In dispute was the identity of God. The gnostics held that the Father of Jesus Christ was wholly separate from and opposed to the God of Israel. The God of Hebrew Scriptures was an inferior demiurge whose works—creation, the election of the Jews, the law—pertained exclusively to the material realm. In contrast, the God of Jesus Christ ruled the highest realm of spirit, separated from the realm of matter by many intermediate spheres and domains. The God of Jesus Christ saved the elect precisely by rescuing them from bondage to the Creator-God of the Jews and the whole material order.[17]

Irenaeus' reply to the gnostics is at heart a single massive demonstration of the claim that the God of Jesus Christ *is* "the God of Abraham, and the God of Isaac, and the God of Jacob, above whom there is no other God" (1.22.1).[18] Irenaeus vindicates this claim by building on Justin's supersessionist reading of the Hebrew Scriptures, and indeed by extending it in order to provide a framework for reading the church's twofold canon.

Irenaeus built on Justin's work at two main points. Like Justin, Irenaeus organizes the Bible in light of four key events: God's creation of the world through the Logos for the purpose of consummation, Adam's fall, redemption through the incarnate Logos, and final consummation. And like Justin, Irenaeus interprets God's covenant with the Jews as a prefiguration of God's decisive act of redemption in Christ and the church. At the same time, Irenaeus modifies both features of Justin's thought in order to confront the gnostic threat more directly. Irenaeus underscores the continuity of divine purpose that links God's initial purpose for Adam with God's redemptive work in Christ. And Irenaeus casts Israel's role in salvation history in a more positive light by portraying it as integral to God's education of the human race unto Christ and the church. Ironically, Irenaeus' modifications underscore the logic of economic supersessionism at the same time that they anchor Israel more securely into the Christian story as the prehistory of the church.

For Irenaeus, the key that unlocks the unity of the Bible and of salvation history is the church's own rule of faith (*regula fidei*). The rule of faith is a brief summary statement of Christian belief to which Irenaeus ascribes apostolic authority. When applied to the Christian Bible, the rule of faith provides a framework for interpreting the Scriptures as a whole. Irenaeus likens those who interpret the Bible apart from the rule of faith to those who take a beautiful mosaic of a king and reassemble its pieces into the image of a dog, and a poorly executed dog at that (1.8.1; see 1.9.1–4).

Near the beginning of *Against Heresies*, Irenaeus offers the following statement of the rule of faith:

> [The Church believes] in one God, the Father Almighty, Maker of heaven, and earth, and the sea, and all things that are in them; and in one Christ Jesus, the Son of God, who became incarnate for our salvation; and in the Holy Spirit, who proclaimed through the prophets the dispensations of God, and the advents, and the birth from a virgin, and the passion, and the resurrection from the dead, and the ascension into heaven in the flesh of the beloved Christ Jesus, our Lord, and His [future] manifestation from heaven in the glory of the Father "to gather all things in one," and to raise up anew all flesh of the whole human race, in order that Christ Jesus . . . should execute just judgment towards all (1.10.1).

Irenaeus' reference to "the dispensations" in the plural implies an oblique reference to God's history with the Jewish people, a point to which we will return shortly. The point to note here is that the rule of faith provides a narrative framework for reading the Scriptures that identifies God as the God of the Hebrew Scriptures (that is, maker of heaven and earth) while all but ignoring the center of those Scriptures. Following the rule of faith, Irenaeus sketches out the overarching drama of God's consummating and redemptive purposes for humankind in a way that is almost wholly uninformed by God's history with the Jews.

Irenaeus is the first Christian theologian to place God's work as Consummator at the center of the Christian story. To recall, God's work as Consummator concerns the goal and means that God appoints for the fulfillment of humankind antecedent to the calamity of sin. Irenaeus' interest in God's work as Consummator does not mean that he neglects God's work as Redeemer or the fall and the universal need for redemption that it brings in its wake. Quite the contrary, Irenaeus delights in showing point by point how God's work in Christ undoes Adam's fall and all of its destructive consequences. Still, Irenaeus places the problem of sin and redemption in the larger context of God's work as Consummator, a work that God steadfastly maintains and finally perfects despite the obstacles of sin, evil, and death.

Characteristically, Irenaeus coordinates God's work as Consummator with "the image and likeness of God" in the first parents. While Irenaeus' views are notoriously hard to pin down on this topic, it appears that he identified "the image" with the spiritual capacities of Adam and Eve and "the likeness" with the actual virtues that they might have developed over time (see 5.16.2). In any case, Irenaeus' coordination of God's work as Consummator with the image of God shapes his conception of the canon's unity in two far-reaching ways. First, Irenaeus conceives of God's work as Consummator in a manner formally independent of God's election of Israel and its life among the nations. Second, Irenaeus thinks of the human creature as the object of God's consummating grace by virtue of its specific nature as one created in the image of God: nature and grace stand in immediate relation to one another. In these two respects, Irenaeus established the parameters of most subsequent Christian thought about God's work as Consummator, at least until Karl Barth and Karl Rahner reexamined these two key Irenaean premises in the twentieth century, a point to which we shall return in chapter 4.

Irenaeus thinks of God's work as Consummator in analogy to the growth and maturation of an individual from infancy to adulthood. Just as God brings an infant from the womb into the light of the sun, God calls Adam upward from spiritual infancy into full companionship with God (2.28.1). God intends the process of growth to be ultimately perfected in the eternal vision of God, which also confers immortality on the human creature (4.38.3). Disastrously, however, Adam's first steps toward spiritual maturity led fatefully in the wrong direction. While Adam's starting point as a spiritual infant might seem to make his fall all but inevitable, it does not, in Irenaeus' view, diminish its calamitous consequences. Adam's sin despoils humankind of the Holy Spirit's "robe of sanctity" (3.23.5), forfeits the divine sonship (4.41.2,3), and subjects humankind to bondage to death (4.22.1). What is more, Irenaeus insists that it is impossible for those once conquered by sin to reform themselves or to attain salvation (3.18.2).

Nevertheless, Irenaeus makes clear that Adam's sin does not

abrogate God's intention to consummate human creation. The reason is not, as is sometimes suggested, the *anthropocentric* idea that sin is but a necessary step on the way to spiritual growth. The reason is rather Irenaeus' *theocentric* conviction that the invincible God will not give up on Adam or on God's intention to bring about the consummation of creation. To assume otherwise would be to admit that death could defeat God's will for life (3.23.1).

In fidelity to God's own purposes, therefore, God showed compassion to the first parents and their progeny and prepared them by degree for redemption in Jesus Christ. As Rowan Greer points out, Irenaeus understands redemption in Christ as *the* economy or dispensation of God.[19] Although preceded and prepared for by earlier dispensations, God's economy in Christ is *the* decisive act whereby God restores order to the household of creation. The economy encompasses God's whole activity in Christ from the virgin birth to Christ's second coming at the end of time (5.27.2; see 4.37.7). By means of the economy, God reverses the consequences of Adam's disobedience and secures the eternal communion between God and humankind that was God's original intention for humankind. This double movement of reversal and completion is what Irenaeus means by "recapitulation," his central concept for Christ's work. By his life of obedience unto death, Christ undoes the fatal consequences of Adam's disobedience to the God of life (3.18.2,6,7; 3.21.10; 5.16.3; 5.17.1). At the same time, Christ the Second Adam establishes for the first time the likeness between God and humankind that was the goal of creation from the time of Adam (3.18.1; 5.16.2).

Irenaeus can be regarded as the father of two contrasting accounts of the standard model that differ on how God's overarching work as Consummator relates to Christ's incarnation. Both versions presuppose the basic story of creation-for-consummation, fall, redemption, and final consummation, but differ on the question of whether Christ would have become incarnate even if Adam had not fallen. The question is a useful way of addressing the issue of whether Christ's incarnation is grounded solely in God's work as Redeemer or whether it is already grounded in God's work as Consummator antecedent to the catastrophe of sin and the need for redemption. One view (which we will call Scotist after its famous thirteenth-century advocate, John Duns Scotus) holds that God's work as Consummator was oriented from the very beginning toward the incarnation as the fulfillment of God's purpose for humankind. Hence the eternal Son would have become incarnate even if Adam had not fallen. The other view (which can be called Thomist after its thirteenth-century advocate, Thomas Aquinas) holds that the incarnation is grounded solely in God's work as Redeemer, and hence that Adam's sin is the necessary occasion of the incarnation. While the Thomistic account has dominated Christian theology for most of its history (both before and after Thomas), the Scotist view has become increasingly prominent in modern theology, as we shall see in subsequent chapters. As for Irenaeus himself, he undoubtedly regards Jesus Christ both in *continuity* with God's initial consummating purpose for Adam and in *opposition* to Adam's sin. Yet it is extremely doubtful that Irenaeus can be claimed with certainty for either viewpoint. The speculative question at the heart of the debate is not one that Irenaeus asked.[20]

For Irenaeus, Christ's work of recapitulation continues in the life of the church, which, like a great sun, shines everywhere and illuminates all who wish to come to knowledge of the truth (1.10.2). The church is a counterpart of paradise, a garden planted in the midst of the world into which God admits all who obey God's call. Through the church, Christ himself builds up humanity into the fullness of the image of God. Being conformed to God's image in the Son, the church will finally be brought to maturity at some future time, having been made ripe to see and comprehend God (4.37.7).

The story just outlined forms the centerpiece of Irenaeus' antignostic strategy and the core of his whole theology. Following the outline set by the rule of faith, Irenaeus identifies God the Father of Jesus Christ by referring to the Hebrew Scriptures' account of God as the Creator of heaven and earth. From this vantage point Irenaeus sketches out the majestic vision of God's consummating and redemptive purposes for humankind in a manner that firmly rebuts the gnostic heresy that separates the God who creates from the God who redeems. At the same time, however, Irenaeus construes God's overarching purposes for creation in a manner that takes little account of the *center* of the Hebrew Scriptures, this is, of God's covenant with the people Israel and its life among the nations. While Irenaeus ultimately incorporates this material into his canonical narrative, he does so by fitting it into the dominant framework already in place. In effect, Irenaeus subordinates God's identity as the God of Israel to God's identity as Creator and Redeemer of the world in Jesus Christ.

Irenaeus incorporates the story of Israel into his canonical narrative by means of the idea of preparatory dispensations. Just as the Apostolic Witness relates *the* dispensation or economy by which God reorders the household of creation, so the Hebrew Scriptures relate a sequence of prefigurative economies that prepare humanity for the incarnation. This approach allows Irenaeus to adopt Justin's view of the Hebrew Scriptures as a prefiguration of Christ while anchoring the story of Israel more securely into God's overarching plan to restore and consummate humankind in Christ. Following Justin, Irenaeus tends to view the Mosaic dispensation under a threefold aspect: as a repromulgation of natural law, as prophecy of Christ, and as punishment for sin (see 4.15.1). At the same time, Irenaeus goes beyond Justin by suggesting that God intended each of these elements to educate the Jewish people unto Christ.[21] Summing up Israel's place in God's plan of salvation, Irenaeus writes:

> Thus it was, too, that God formed man at the first, because of His munificence; but chose the patriarchs for the sake of their salvation; and prepared a people beforehand, teaching the headstrong to follow God; . . . and sketching out, like an architect, the plan of salvation to those that pleased Him (4.14.2).

In sum, Irenaeus sees God's history with Israel as an episode within the larger story whereby God prepares a fallen humanity for the incarnation. Coming between Adam's fall on one side and the incarnation on the other, Israel serves as a training ground for salvation.

One of the most significant aspects of Irenaeus' solution is the lucid account it permits of the Bible's unity. On the one hand, a single economy of redemption underlies the biblical narrative as a whole from the fall to the end of time. On the other hand, this single economy is bodied forth in two asymmetrical forms, one temporary and prophetic, the other permanent and definitive (4.9). The Old and New Covenants (Irenaeus uses these terms to refer to the Bible's *contents*, not to the collections of books themselves) are one because they come from the same God and embody God's one plan to redeem fallen humanity in Christ. They are distinct because they present the economy of salvation under different outward forms. The two covenants differ according to accident, not substance (4.9.2). The Old Covenant moves toward the incarnation in a manner congruent with humanity's immature state; the New Covenant moves from the incarnation in definitive form. The Old Covenant is suited to a spirit of bondage, the New to the spirit of freedom

(4.9.2); the old is appropriate for "one nation" only, the new for the whole world (4.9.2); the old is passing, earthly, and figurative, the new is eternal, heavenly, and unsurpassable (4.19.1). When the new comes, therefore, the old is done away with, not with respect to substance but with respect to outer form.

Later, Christian theologians applied the terms *Old* and *New Testaments* not only to the contents of the Bible but also to the two collections of writings as such. In doing so, of course, they built directly upon Irenaeus' solution to the unity of the canon. In this sense, the terms *Old* and *New Testaments* as designations for the Christian canon are part and parcel of the standard canonical narrative.[22]

Irenaeus' solution opens up two complementary perspectives on the relation of Old and New Covenants, either of which can be emphasized according to circumstances or theological predilection without threatening the solution as a whole. For example, Reformed theologians of the seventeenth and eighteenth centuries tended to emphasize the common substance that united the Old and New Testaments (the covenant of grace), while Lutheran theologians of the same period tended to emphasize the discontinuity of outer form (law and gospel). But neither party lost sight of the contrasting perspective. The two perspectives require one another and are both integral to the Irenaean solution.[23]

Curiously, Irenaeus' solution to the unity of the canon reinforces the logic of economic supersessionism at the same time that it underscores the continuity of divine purpose that unites Israel and the church, Old Covenant and New. Just as maturity is the goal of childhood training, so Christ and the church are the goals of Israel's history from the beginning. The Old Covenant is fulfilled by the New Covenant according to its inner christological substance but superseded and displaced according to its outer carnal form. Hence the whole economy of salvation is inwardly ordered to the eventual dissolution of Israel's corporate life into the life of the church. This double movement of fulfillment and cancellation appears with special clarity in Irenaeus' understanding of the law. Christ perfects and "enlarges" the natural law common to Christians and Jews but abrogates the "law of bondage" that was for the Jews alone (4.13.1; see 4.16.5). Irenaeus allows for a period during which the apostles continued to observe the Mosaic law after Christ's resurrection in order to testify to their belief that the God of Jesus Christ was the author of the Mosaic dispensation (3.12.3). Yet this period is transitional by the nature of the case, for the purpose of the Mosaic law was to prepare for the law of liberty in Christ. Once the law of liberty had been introduced, therefore, it "followed as of course that the bonds of slavery should be removed" (4.13.2; see 4.16.5). Therefore Jews who continue to follow the law of bondage do so at an unseasonable time.

Irenaeus takes for granted the fact of Israel's apostasy but gives the theme comparatively little attention. His primary interest in the overarching continuity of God's economy of redemption overshadows the lamentable fact of Israel's disbelief. God chose the Jews in order to prepare them for salvation in Christ, but at the decisive time they rejected God's son and murdered him (4.28.3; 4.18.4). Because the Jews repudiated Christ, God granted their inheritance to the Gentiles alone (4.21.3). The Jews who boast of being Israel are in fact "disinherited from the grace of God" (3.21.1).

Irenaeus' vision of the Christian story is profoundly supersessionist. There is irony in this, for Irenaeus' motive was no doubt in part to vindicate God's identity as the God of Israel. Nevertheless, the ultimate effect of his solution was to make the Israelite dimension of Christian faith indecisive for shaping conclusions about the logic of Christian doctrine. At the doctrinal level, Irenaeus' doctrine of the unity-in-difference of Old and New Covenants results in a vision of carnal Israel's obsolescence after Christ. At the structural level, Irenaeus' shapes the canon into a narrative whole only by refracting the biblical witness into two dimensions of unequal significance. One dimension, the model's foreground, delineates God's purposes for the world by linking God's redemptive work in Christ immediately with God's consummating intention for Adam, and thereby conceives of salvation history in chiefly universal and cosmic terms. The other dimension, the model's background, depicts God's dealings with Israel as historical preparation for redemption in its definitive form. As a result, the Israelite dimension of Christian faith—that is, the Hebrew Scriptures as a testimony to God's covenant with Israel and Israel's life among the nations—is rendered largely irrelevant for shaping conclusions about how God's consummating and redemptive purposes engage creation in universal and enduring ways.

THE LEGACY OF THE STANDARD MODEL

Justin Martyr and especially Irenaeus of Lyon bequeathed to the church a canonical narrative of extraordinary scope and power. On two points especially, the Irenaean solution has proved enduring. For the most part, the Christian imagination has conceived of God's works as Consummator and as Redeemer according to the story of creation-for-consummation, fall, redemption, and final consummation, just as it has conceived the relation of the Scriptures and the Apostolic Witness according to the schema of the Old and New Testaments. However widely Christian theologians have diverged from one another in detail, they have tended to do so from a common commitment to the Irenaean solution to the canon's unity. Unfortunately, however, the Irenaean solution to the unity of the canon is deeply flawed when viewed in light of the church's contemporary rejection of supersessionism. To be sure, Irenaeus' own motive was to vindicate God's identity as the God of the Hebrew Scriptures against the threat of gnosticism. Nevertheless, the Irenaean solution to the unity of the canon renders the Hebrew Scriptures largely irrelevant for shaping conclusions about God's *enduring* purposes for creation, and thereby inscribes the logic of supersessionism into the deep grammar of Christian theology.

Forgetfulness of Israel

One measure of the standard model's structural supersessionism is what can be called the Israel-forgetfulness of the model's foreground. To recall, the model's foreground is the sequence of episodes that constitute the standard model's overarching plot: God's creation of Adam and Eve for the purpose of consummation, the fall, redemption in Christ through the church, and final judgment and final consummation. Although the model's foreground is by definition not identical with the model as a whole, it does depict how God's consummating and redemptive purposes engage humankind *in universal and enduring ways*. The foreground can therefore be said to encapsulate what the standard model depicts as theologically decisive for a Christian reading of the Bible. The difficulty, of course, is that the foreground wholly omits the Hebrew Scriptures with the exception of Genesis 1–3. In proportion as Christian theology has defined its problems and solutions within the framework of the model's foreground, therefore, it has done so in an Israel-forgetful manner.

One area where the standard model's Israel-forgetfulness is especially evident is the church's classical doctrinal heritage. In principle, doctrines about the Trinity, the person of Christ, sin and salvation, and so forth presuppose the authority of the whole Christian canon, including the Scriptures of Israel. In practice, these doctrines have been shaped with almost exclusive reference to the foreground story. Not surprisingly, therefore, the doctrines mirror the foreground's emphasis upon the cosmic and universal dimensions of salvation history. The trinitarian controversy erupted over the ontological status of the pre-incarnate Word and came to be worked out protologically in terms of eternal relationship of Father and Son. The christological controversies clustered around the issue of Christ's "person" and came to be worked out in terms of Christ's divine and human natures. The Western debate about sin and salvation received its patristic resolution in Augustine's doctrine of nature and grace. In each case, the dominant categories are those of divine and human natures. By contrast, the Scriptures' testimony to God's history with the Jewish people is almost wholly absent from view.[24]

It would be absurd and ungrateful to disparage the theological accomplishment represented by the classical doctrinal tradition. Yet for some time now the weaknesses of the classical heritage have also been apparent. These include a quite particular loss of orientation toward the Hebrew Scriptures and the history of Israel, as well as a more general loss of orientation toward such "middle range" dimensions of human life as public history, economics, politics, and so on, all of which are of central concern to the Hebrew Scriptures. To cite only one example, Wolfhart Pannenberg argues that the whole edifice of classical incarnational christology is basically detachable from the Hebrew Scriptures and the history of Israel. "Jesus' relationship to Israel and to the Old Testament cannot be so fundamental for a Christology that takes its beginning point in the concept of the incarnation that such a Christology could not exist without it."[25] But much the same observation could be made about virtually every other aspect of traditional doctrine, including its keystone, classical trinitarian theology. The point I wish to underscore is simply that a connection exists between the standard model's structural supersessionism and the weakness that Pannenberg observes. The connection is the standard model's tendency to render the bulk of Israel's Scriptures indecisive for the formation of Christian doctrine. Nothing testifies to this more eloquently than the classical edifice of Christian dogmatic theology. Following the structure of the creeds, countless works of Christian theology set forth the dogmatic content of Christian belief almost wholly without reference to God's way with Israel. The first and largest part of the Bible possesses no doctrinal *locus* of its own, nor is it often materially decisive for any other *locus*.[26]

The standard model's Israel-forgetfulness can be examined from another perspective by considering God's work as the Consummator of humankind. To recall, God's work as Consummator concerns the goal and the means that God appoints for the consummation or perfection of humankind antecedent to all considerations of sin and the need for redemption. Obviously, how one conceives God's work as Consummator has enormous consequences for the shape of Christian theology. God's consummating work establishes the ultimate horizon within which God's work in Christ assumes soteriological significance. What is so characteristic of the standard model is that the crucial idea of God's consummating purpose is erected on such an extraordinarily slender basis in the Hebrew Scriptures, namely, Gen 1–2, or even more narrowly yet, Gen 1:26–27. So conceived, God's consummating work revolves around Adam as the primordial instantiation of human nature and of the image of God. To this, a Scotist account of God's work as Consummator adds the incarnation as the goal and medium of God's consummating grace to Adam.[27] In neither case, however, do the Hebrew Scriptures play a constitutive role in shaping conclusions about God's work as Consummator. In both instances, the conception of God's work as Consummator reveals a fundamental and radical neglect of the center of the Hebrew Scriptures and, above all, of their account of God's history with Israel and the nations.

There can be little doubt that the standard model's approach to God's work as Consummator has been a key point of entry for the "religious" interpretations of Christian faith that Bonhoeffer criticized while in prison.[28] Because Christian theologians coordinated God's work as Consummator with Adam and the image of God, they were perhaps too ready to conceive God's consummating work in protological and individualistic terms. Moreover, Christian theologians were forced to compensate somehow for the obvious paucity of scriptural resources for consummation, given its scanty foundation in the Hebrew Scriptures. Not surprisingly, many Christian theologians drew heavily on the philosophical resources of the day in order to give religious weight and intellectual plausibility to their account of God's work as Consummator. So, for instance, many patristic and medieval theologians organized their account of God's work as Consummator around the Neoplatonic schema of *exitus* and *reditus*, creation's emanation from and return to God. Many did not wholly escape Neoplatonism's strongly dichotomizing conception of body and soul. The point is not that Christians inevitably err by drawing on the conceptual resources of their surrounding culture, as though it were possible or desirable to do Christian theology in a vacuum. Rather, the point is that in the particular case of God's work as Consummator, the standard model fostered and supported a combination of scriptural referent and conceptual apparatus that was not an entirely happy one. By coordinating God's consummating work one-sidedly with the image of God, Christian theologians have often been inclined to think about God's work as Consummator in the "individualistic" and "metaphysical" terms whose biblical integrity and human relevance Bonhoeffer questioned.

Foreshortening the Hebrew Scriptures

Another measure of the standard model's supersessionistic structure is what might be called the soteriological foreshortening of the model's background. The raw material of the model's background, to recall, consists in all of the Hebrew Scriptures apart from the opening chapters of Genesis. The thing that strikes any reader of this material is the extraordinary range and diversity of its subject matter and interests. The Hebrew Scriptures deal with the creation of the heavens and the earth and the population of the world by animals and human beings, but also with the rise and spread of families and nations, with battles and conquest, and with marketplace, temple, and courthouse. The Scriptures touch on a virtually inexhaustible spectrum of human experience, including slavery, betrayal, migration, drought, childlessness, jealousy, theft, lust, war, infirmity, murder, and childbirth. Above all, the Scriptures are concerned with the history that transpires between the God of Israel, Israel, and the nations, a history that the Scriptures appear to regard as virtually coextensive with human history as a whole.

Characteristically, the standard model brings all of this unruly material under the hermeneutical control of the foreground story of creation, fall, redemption, and final consummation. Within this context, the background material is construed as the Old Covenant, that is, as the economy of redemption in prophetic form. As we have seen in the previous pages, one consequence of this is the logic of economic supersessionism, according to which it is Israel's destiny

to flow into the church like a river into the sea. But another consequence is what might be called the soteriological foreshortening of
Israel's Scriptures. The vast panorama of the Hebrew Scriptures is
made to unfold within the basic antithesis of Adam's sin and
redemption in Christ. This soteriological framework foreshortens
the Hebrew Scriptures both thematically and temporally. Thematically, because the Scriptures are thought to relate a story whose
fundamental presupposition is the catastrophe of sin and whose
goal is therefore deliverance from the negative conditions of existence. This perspective obscures the possibility that the Hebrew
Scriptures are not solely or even primarily concerned with the
antithesis of sin and redemption but much rather with the God of
Israel's passionate engagement with the mundane affairs of Israel
and the nations. Once again, Dietrich Bonhoeffer's reflections
from a prison cell in Nazi Germany cast a critical light on the logic
of the standard model:

> Unlike the other oriental religions, the faith of the Old Testament
> isn't a religion of redemption. It's true that Christianity has
> always been regarded as a religion of redemption. But isn't this a
> cardinal error, which separates Christ from the Old Testament
> and interprets him on the lines of the myths about redemption?
> To the objection that a crucial importance is given in the Old Tes-
> tament to redemption (from Egypt, and later from Babylon) it
> may be answered that the redemptions referred to here are *histori-
> cal*, i.e. on *this* side of death, whereas everywhere else the myths
> about redemption are concerned to overcome the barrier of
> death. Israel is delivered out of Egypt so that it may live before
> God as God's people on earth.[29]

In addition to narrowing the thematic focus of the Hebrew Scriptures to the problem of sin and redemption, the standard model
also foreshortens the Hebrew Scriptures in a temporal sense. As
perceived through the lens of the standard model, the Hebrew
Scriptures do not relate a story that extends indefinitely into the
future. They relate instead the story of one finite dispensation in the
history of God's dealings with humankind, a dispensation that
extends from Abraham or Moses to Jesus Christ but that in any case
has already come to an end. Clearly this pattern of thought creates a
gulf between the Scriptures and the Apostolic Witness by consign-
ing to the past not only God's particular concern with Israel but

also God's more general concern with humankind in all its adulter-
ous, blasphemous, and murderous ambiguity. Here too Bonhoeffer's musings can be allowed a final word:

> Why is it that in the Old Testament men tell lies vigorously and
> often to the glory of God (I've now collected the passages), kill,
> deceive, rob, divorce, and even fornicate (see the genealogy of
> Jesus), doubt, blaspheme, and curse, whereas in the New Testa-
> ment there is nothing of all this? "An earlier stage" of religion?
> That is a very naive way out; it is one and the same God.[30]

Redemption and the Flight from History

A final measure of the standard model's structural supersessionism
appears in its conception of redemption, which although anti-gnostic nevertheless entails a curious kind of flight from history. The
standard model appears in its entirety when its foreground and background are taken as complementary parts of a single comprehensive
story. The full story then consists in the sequence: creation-for-consummation, fall, Old Covenant in Israel, redemption in Christ, New
Covenant in the church, and final consummation. This story is profoundly anti-gnostic in intention, especially with respect to God's
engagement with creation. The story affirms that the God who creates and the God who redeems is one God, the Father of Jesus Christ.
Moreover, the model affirms that God's action in Christ Jesus does
not liberate humanity *from* the sphere of creation but much rather
liberates creation itself from the threat of sin and death.

When our attention shifts from God's engagement with creation
to God's engagement with the flesh of Israel, however, the story's
relationship to gnosticism appears in a different light. God's abiding
commitment to creation passes through the flesh of the people
Israel in the Old Covenant and ultimately lodges with irrevocable
finality in the one Jewish man, Jesus of Nazareth. But with that the
vocation of the people Israel reaches its foreordained goal and
comes to an end. In the process, God's commitment to Israel's flesh
is revealed as only a passing stage on the way to God's truly abiding
commitment, which is to Christ and the community of salvation in
its spiritual form. So conceived, God's commitment to creation
betrays a certain kinship to gnosticism after all. *God's work of
redemption entails liberation not indeed from creation but nevertheless
from the historical dispensation that is characterized by Israel's carnal*

election and by the distinction between Israel and the nations. This is a softened Christian gnosticism, a gnosticism not of being but of history. Humanity is redeemed not *in* history but *from* it, and above all, from a history in which God's commitment to creation goes by way of the Jewish people and its history among the nations.

Taken as a whole, the standard model embodies a vision of Christian faith that seeks to reconcile the *affirmation* of God's passionate and enduring engagement with creation with the *denial* of God's equally passionate and enduring engagement with the people Israel. The result is an evisceration of the God of Israel in Christian theology. When the question is put: is the God of Israel irrevocably bound to creation, Christians have traditionally answered with a resounding yes. But when the question is put: is the God of Israel irrevocably bound to the people Israel, Christians have equivocated. The standard model provides a framework in which it appears evident that the God of Israel's abiding commitment to creation goes not by way of the Israel of the flesh but by way of the Israel of the spirit. The upshot is a vision of the God of Israel that is internally ordered to the disappearance of the Jewish people. Yet Christians have rarely sensed any contradiction in this idea. They feel no contradiction because the standard model—while not denying God's history with the Jewish people—renders this history largely irrelevant for deciphering God's enduring purposes for creation. Because God's enduring purposes engage humankind as spirit, Israel's flesh can drop out.

Despite its quasi-gnostic character, classical Christian thought was generally unable and unwilling to consign carnal Israel's existence completely to the past. Unable, for the simple reason that the Jewish people by their survival and flourishing did not permit it. Unwilling, because the continued existence of carnal Israel demanded an explanation in theological terms. If carnal Israel was fundamentally superseded within the sphere of the church, what accounted for its continued existence outside the church? The obvious explanation, of course, was sin. Carnal Israel existed alongside the church precisely because of its disobedience to the gospel, on which account it spurned Christianity's invitation to join the spiritual church. John Chrysostom in the fourth century complained that the Jews were always perversely out of step with the times, disobeying the Mosaic law while it was in force and cleaving to it after it had been annulled. Others sought in addition to this an explanation in the providence of God. Origen, on this point as on others an exceptional voice, perceived in unbelieving Israel the unfolding of a benign providence that was ultimately directed to the redemption of Jew and Gentile alike.[31] A more influential answer was advanced by Augustine, who argued that God preserved the Jews in existence for the sake of their unwilling testimony to Christian faith. By honoring the Old Testament, the Jews demonstrated that it was no mere forgery of the church, but authentic prophecy that predicted long ago the incarnation of Jesus Christ and the rise of the spiritual church.[32]

Thus Christian theology preserved, in however backhanded a fashion, a limited theological rationale for the continued existence of the Jewish people. The rationale was not sufficient to spare the Jews from political and economic disenfranchisement after the political ascendancy of the Christian church, nor was it sufficient to spare them from murderous outbreaks of popular persecution and national expulsion. Nevertheless, it was sufficient to help spare the Jews from the programs of outright extermination that met adherents of pagan religion and to secure them a subordinate but viable niche in Christian culture. Though superseded in principle and besieged in fact, carnal Israel was permitted to exist within Christendom because of its incontrovertible connection to the God of Christian confession, the God of Israel.

3

CHRISTIAN DIVINITY
WITHOUT JEWISH FLESH
KANT AND SCHLEIERMACHER

F ROM THE PATRISTIC AGE TO THE ENLIGHTENMENT IS from one
perspective a unified period of Christian history, made so by the
relatively unchallenged role of the standard canonical narrative as
the hermeneutical foundation of Christian thought. With the
Enlightenment, Christian theology increasingly witnessed the rise
of alternative accounts of the world that competed with the standard canonical narrative as the primary depiction of reality. This
change inaugurated a prolonged revolution in Christian theology
that continues in some quarters to the present day. Christian theology more and more took shape as the comprehensive effort to
expound and justify Christian faith with reference to one or another
philosophical worldview.

The story of this development is told elsewhere and need not be
rehearsed here.[1] Our interest is to explore the development's implications for the problem of supersessionism. For this purpose we
have chosen to look at the shape of the standard model in the work
of Immanuel Kant and Friedrich Schleiermacher. In general, Kant
and Schleiermacher tried to meet the challenge of the Enlightenment by preserving as much of the standard model as seemed intel-
lectually viable and religiously relevant while jettisoning the rest as
outdated or indifferent. For us the key point is this: the operation
they undertook on the traditional body of Christian divinity cut
along the ancient line that had long distinguished the standard
model's foreground and background. Kant and Schleiermacher discovered the continuing validity of the standard model in the foreground story of creation-for-consummation, fall, redemption, and

final consummation, while they cut away the Israelite background as alien and obsolete. In this sense, the case of early modern theology confirms the analysis of the previous chapter. Early modern theology intensifies and exploits the structural supersessionism of the standard canonical narrative. Classical Christian theologians merely subordinated the Israelite dimension of Christian faith to the logic of a purportedly more basic drama between Creator and human creation. For them, God's way with Israel was *indecisive* in fact but not yet *inessential* in principle. In contrast, early modern theologians regarded the Israelite dimension of Christian faith as essentially superfluous to the nature of Christian theology. They therefore used the standard model's doctrinal foreground as a vantage point from which to expel the Jewish dimension of Christian faith altogether.

Crucial to the pruning of the standard model was the crystallization of a theological conviction of truly epochal significance. This conviction holds that the Christian conception of God can be coherently maintained in complete separation from the God of Israel as attested by the Scriptures of Israel. The conviction grows out of the standard model's traditional contrast between God's enduring spiritual purposes for creation and God's transient affiliation with the Jewish people and sharpens the contrast to the point of antithesis. The Christian God is essentially and exclusively characterized by the universality and spirituality of God's purposes for creation. The God of the Hebrew Scriptures, in contrast, is inextricably bound to Jewish flesh. While these two conceptions of God intersect in the Christian community by reason of historical accident, they have nothing to do with one another in principle. The future of Christian theology depends upon freeing the one from the other.

A key result of the new conception of God is the emergence of a characteristically modern—and more virulent—form of Christian triumphalism toward the Jews. Previously Christian theologians accorded the Jews a slender but enduring rationale for their the existence as a distinct non-Christian people in the midst of Christendom. But once Christian theologians ceased to identify God as the God of Israel, that rationale disappeared. Now the Jewish people and the Jewish religion seemed nothing more than a queer survival of an earlier age, a survival that would inevitably be absorbed into Christian culture with the passage of time. But the new conception of God brought other consequences in its wake as well. The theologies of Kant and Schleiermacher evince a further migration of Christian doctrine into the interior realm of the spirit. The result is a further loss of contact not only with the rough edges of the Hebrew Scriptures and public history but now also with the central figure of the Apostolic Witness itself, the Jew Jesus of Nazareth.

IMMANUEL KANT'S *RELIGION*

Immanuel Kant was occupied with questions of religion throughout his career, but not until the end of his life did he set forth his understanding of religion in a single work. In *Religion within the Limits of Reason Alone* (1793), Kant's purpose is twofold.[2] He wishes to sketch the religion of reason in outline and to demonstrate that it is the only true religion that humankind possesses. Yet he also wants to show that traditional Christianity can claim the respect of rational persons if and to the degree that it allows itself to be interpreted as the vehicle of rational religion. For us, the interesting question is this: what does Kant think is patient of rational interpretation in traditional Christianity, and what does he think is utterly devoid of enduring religious meaning? As we shall see, Kant's favorable vote falls entirely within the scope of the standard model's creaturely-universal foreground, while he directs his harshest criticism against the Israelite dimension of Christian faith. In what follows, we will first sketch Kant's vision of rational religion and then turn to his judgment on the enduring worth of Christianity.[3]

Kant's account of rational religion rests upon the foundation of his analysis of universal moral experience.[4] Every person has knowledge of a moral law that demands obedience for its own sake. One ought to obey this law because it is right to do so, not in order to obtain happiness. Nevertheless, everyone who does obey the moral law for its own sake *deserves* to be happy. Since common experience of the world teaches that those who morally deserve to be happy are not necessarily so, reason is led to postulate the ideas of God and immortality in order that goodness and virtue might be reconciled by a just Deity in an afterlife.

Rational religion, so conceived, simply postulates the transcendent conditions of a morally coherent world. The moral order requires a God who is both Creator and Consummator, one who is sovereign over the realms of nature and freedom and who ultimately consummates moral worth with happiness. The postulates of reason, of course, provide no knowledge regarding the actual existence of God and an afterlife. Instead they simply provide a conceptual framework that secures the intelligibility of the moral life and in this way undergirds morality with rational support. That is the sole and sufficient justification of rational religion.

Kant expounds the religion of reason in four books. Book One treats anthropology and evil, Book Two christology, and Book Three ecclesiology and the reign of God. Book Four contrasts the true versus the false service of God. In Book One, Kant argues that human nature possesses an original predisposition for the good but that this predisposition is beset by a principle of radical evil. Humanity's original predisposition for the good consists chiefly in its knowledge of and respect for the moral law and in its capacity to obey the moral law for its own sake. Humanity so endowed has everything it needs to fulfill its sublime vocation as a moral being (22–23). Yet experience teaches that, far from realizing its vocation to the good, humankind is a font of universal and incorrigible evil. The only way to account for this, Kant argues, is to posit a radical corruption of human nature's original disposition to the good (21ff.). This corruption consists in a primal reversal of the proper moral order of duty and self-interest, a reversal that corrupts every subsequent moral action from the outset (31–32). Kant holds that this reversal must be conceived as a free decision for which each person is responsible (20, 26). Yet it is a free decision unique in kind, since it precedes all subsequent free actions and corrupts them from the root (26).

Kant's moral anthropology issues in a striking vision of the human condition. Each person must obey the moral law or fall miserably short of his or her vocation as a being mysteriously endowed with duty, freedom, and dignity. Yet each person fails to obey the moral law because of the radical evil of human nature, a fact for which each person bears personal responsibility. As a result, each person must be presumed to have already forfeited what would otherwise be the rational hope of a blessed immortality from the hands of a benevolent Creator-Consummator. This hapless condition cannot be remedied by gradual moral improvement, as some moralists vainly believe. Only a revolution in humanity's moral disposition can effect the change required. As Kant explains in reliance on biblical language, "He can become a new man only by a kind of rebirth, as it were a new creation, and a change of heart" (43). Such a revolution *must* be possible for humankind, Kant declares, because it is our moral duty. Yet Kant admits that the reality of radical evil makes it impossible to conceive how such a revolution can take place.

In Book Two, Kant proposes a solution to the problem of radical evil in the form of what might be called the christology of rational religion. Kant's starting point is God's purpose for creation, which rationally conceived can be nothing other than the moral consummation or perfection of humankind. This goal can be represented to the mind by the ideal of a single morally perfect person, the archetype of a morally good humanity. The archetype so conceived is no mere creature, Kant avers, but the only-begotten Son of God who proceeds from God's very being (54). By picturing this ideal pattern as a person who encounters all our trials in their most extreme form and who victoriously overcomes them, we retain a sure guide for our own moral conduct. By practical faith in this ideal, that is, by conforming our conduct to it, we effect the revolution or rebirth necessary to fulfill our moral vocation.

But this leaves unaddressed the problem of guilt incurred before conversion to the moral archetype, a problem that Kant takes with great seriousness. To solve this problem, Kant deduces a rational doctrine of justification (70). Because Kant holds that moral debt cannot be transferred from one person to another, he reasons that each person must atone for his or her own past life. This happens when after conversion the "new creature" willingly shoulders the sufferings that inevitably accompany the moral life for the sake of the good, although these sufferings are really due as punishments to another, namely, the "old creature." In this way, each person provides "vicarious" satisfaction for his or her own previous offenses (68–69).

In Book Three, Kant considers the establishment of an ethical commonwealth and the possibility of its progress to a point where "at last the pure religion of reason will rule over all" (112). Kant holds that human reason necessarily forms the idea of an ethical commonwealth and recognizes a moral obligation to belong to it. In principle, therefore, a universal moral commonwealth should spring spontaneously into being through the free obedience of each person to the moral law. In fact, however, a peculiar weakness of human nature requires the presence of outward ceremonies to establish and maintain a visible human community (94). Such ceremonies cannot derive from reason alone because they are arbitrary and contingent in nature and therefore must be stipulated. Every viable ethical community, therefore, will possess two kinds of laws: pure moral laws dictated by reason alone and statutory laws fixed by fiat. The moral law has intrinsic worth and universal scope, while the statutory law is indifferent in itself and can possess no more than local validity.

In light of this situation, Kant foresees the necessity of a pact of cooperation between pure rational religion and the historical faiths that are based upon purported revelations.[5] The success of the pact, in Kant's view, depends upon recognition that moral religion takes precedence over statutory faith at every point. One is justified in saying that "the kingdom of God is among us" when at last a community has been established that acknowledges and teaches the supremacy of the moral law over mere statutory law. God will be "all in all" when the exclusive sovereignty of moral religion of reason will at last wholly eliminate the need for statutory faith (112).

In the last book, Kant distinguishes true from false service of religion. The false servant of religion elevates statutory religion above the claims of the moral law and thereby cripples the moral enterprise of the human race. The true servant, in contrast, subordinates statutory faith to the service of moral religion. Kant is fully aware that without an element of brute fact positive religion ceases to exist altogether. Yet the proper service of God within historical religion consists in reducing this element to the bare minimum in the interests of rational religion, and eventually in doing away with it altogether.

This then is the religion of reason, a somber but majestic edifice erected on the foundation of moral experience for the purpose of supporting the moral life. How well does traditional Christianity stack up against it? The very question, of course, reflects Kant's intention to reverse the traditional relation of philosophy and Christian doctrine in the depiction of religious and moral reality.[6] With Kant, the religion of reason declares its independence of the Christian narrative and usurps its place at the center of the religious universe. From now on, Christianity's narrative must demonstrate its enduring religious significance before the tribunal of rational religion.

Yet once this blow to Christian pride has been absorbed, Christianity does not come off too badly in Kant's account. And this is hardly surprising. For Kant's religion of reason is itself a remarkably faithful conceptual distillation of the church's standard canonical narrative, or, more exactly, of its creaturely-universal foreground. Of course, Kant erects rational religion on the foundation of universal moral experience rather than upon the church's confession of the God of Israel's action in Jesus Christ. But on this new foundation the essential episodes of the standard canonical narrative reappear as the timeless, disembodied forms of universal moral experience.

When Kant judges the moral worth of received Christian doctrine, his results fall into three broad categories: positive, neutral, and negative. There are few surprises in what Kant includes in the first category. Kant esteems that part of Christianity that can be directly interpreted to teach the moral law or to illustrate universal features of moral experience. In practice, of course, this means the story of creation, fall, redemption, and consummation, for this is the part of the traditional Christian story that concerns the creaturely-universal. Kant finds much of value in Genesis 3, not of course as a historical report but as an illustration of everyone's fall into a condition of radical evil (36f.). Likewise, he regards the Scriptures' depiction of final judgment and of heaven and hell as philosophically correct and morally useful, albeit jarring in their mode of presentation (53, 125–26). Above all, Kant honors the New Testament's record of a teacher who not only taught rational religion in its purest form but who provided an example for all by adhering to the moral law in the face of suffering and death (74–77). Finally, Kant even finds the doctrine of the Trinity susceptible of a practical interpretation, not as a statement about God's eternal being but as a summary description of God's moral relation to humanity as Legislator, Ruler, and Judge (131–32). In these respects, Kant regards Christianity as well suited to the task of providing the positive, historical vehicle for the propagation of rational religion.

Kant's verdict is decidedly more reserved regarding that part of Christian doctrine and worship that concerns the reality and appropriation of divine grace. Kant is prepared to admit these "mysteries" of Christianity only on the condition that they are firmly subordinated to the claims of the moral law. Kant does not deny that God may act graciously on humankind's behalf. But he argues that we cannot know for certain whether God so acts, and that in any case we must assume that God extends grace only to the morally worthy. Therefore the mysteries of grace may be invoked only as possible supplements to moral life and never as actual preconditions for it.

Finally, Kant rejects outright those aspects of traditional Christianity that plainly obstruct its role as the vehicle of pure moral religion. This category includes dogmas that contradict the elementary presuppositions of morality, such as the doctrine of original sin as an *inherited* condition, a teaching that obviates the role of human freedom in moral action (35). More generally, this category includes the senseless preservation of statutory belief in the church despite its purely arbitrary and contingent character.

The chief example of this last offense, for Kant, is the portrayal of the Christian religion as though it stood in a necessary relationship to Judaism and the Jewish people. The truth is that Christianity differs from Judaism essentially and from the root. As propounded by its founder, the Christian religion teaches nothing but the moral law and its universal claim upon the inward obedience of the rational creature. Judaism, in contrast, is properly speaking not even a religion at all but rather a political commonwealth based on divine legislation (116). The political character of Judaism clings to it so closely that even in its "dismemberment," that is, in its dispersal among the nations, it continues to hope for the advent of a Messiah who will restore its earthly fortunes. As further evidence for the nonreligious character of Judaism, Kant cites the merely statutory and external nature of Jewish law, the Hebrew Scripture's silence on the subject of an afterlife, and the Jewish people's understanding of itself as God's specially chosen people (116–67). Kant regards this last belief as especially obnoxious to the character of rational religion:

> Judaism fell so far short of constituting an era suited to the requirements of the *church universal* . . . as actually to exclude from its communion the entire human race, on the ground that it was a special people chosen by Jehovah for Himself—[an exclusiveness] which showed enmity toward all other peoples and which, therefore, evoked the enmity of all (117). [7]

Strikingly, Kant refers to the Deity in this context as Jehovah rather than as God. By using the transliteration of the Tetragrammaton conventional in his day, Kant clearly intends to underscore the drastic distinction between the nationalistic deity of the Jewish people and the God of rational religion. A God of mere statutory faith is "after all, not really the moral Being the concept of whom we need for a religion" (118).

For Kant, the special character of Christianity comes to light precisely in the fact that it liberated its followers from servile obedience to the arbitrary statutes of Judaism and freed them for obedience to the moral law. An emblem of this, for Kant, is the church's rejection of circumcision:

> The subsequent dispensing with the corporal sign which served wholly to separate this people [the Jews] from others warrants the judgment that the new faith, not bound to the statutes of the old, nor, indeed, to any statutes whatever, was to comprise a religion valid for the world and not for one single people (118).

By doing away with circumcision, Christianity declared itself free from any necessary connection to the Jewish people and affirmed its essentially universal and spiritual character.

In view of Christianity's essential nature as pure moral religion, no worse fate could have befallen it than for the idea to take hold that Christianity stands in essential continuity with the Jewish people. Yet this is what happened. Initially, the idea appeared only as a pedagogical tool to ease the transition from Judaism to Christianity. "To win over the adherents of the older religion to the new," Kant says, "the new order is interpreted as the fulfillment, at last, of what was only prefigured in the older religion and has all along been the design of Providence" (79). Long after the pedagogical utility of this idea had ended, however, later generations continued to affirm Christianity's essential connection with the Jews and their history. Christianity thus succeeded in freeing itself from the yoke of Jewish *law* only to remain mired in Jewish *belief*. The result, in Kant's view, was nothing short of a calamity for the Christian religion. By retaining the history of the Jews as an essential part of its doctrine, the church made itself guilty of a host of absurdities, not least in regard to Jesus himself:

> [The] procedure [of appealing to the Jewish Scriptures], wisely adopted by the first propagators of the teaching of Christ in order to achieve its introduction among the people, is taken as a part of religion itself, valid for all times and peoples, with the result that one is obliged to believe *that every Christian must be a Jew whose Messiah has come* (153, italics in original).

The preservation of Jewish belief within Christianity has led to the bizarre situation in which Christians identify themselves with reference to the Jewish people and to Jewish hope! Kant's use of emphasis clearly suggests that he can scarcely imagine anything more ridiculous than this. Another absurdity is that Christians, who ignore the statutory law of the Hebrew Scriptures, nevertheless preserve the holy book of the Jewish people as "a divine revelation given to all men." The very idea that humankind's well-being might depend upon Scriptures preserved in a poorly understood language is absurd (154–55). Finally, Kant chides the view that sees a special divine providence at work in the survival of the Jewish people despite their many adversities (127). Natural causes are more than sufficient to account for the continued existence of the Jews. In any case, Kant observes, Christians and Jews have never agreed as to what the divine intention supporting the survival of the Jews might be. Jews see a confirmation of God's faithfulness toward them, while Christians see nothing more than God's mere preservation of the Jews as a "warning ruin," partly "to preserve in memory the ancient prophecy of a Messiah arising from this people, partly to offer, in this people, an example of punitive justice [visited upon it] because it stiff-neckedly sought to create a political and not a moral concept of the Messiah" (128).

In Kant's view, Christianity's retention of the Hebrew Scriptures and all that it represents is more than a misfortune for Christian doctrine. It is a misfortune, indeed, a cataclysm, for the human race. The ills associated with Christian history are in fact the fault of the Jewish element in Christianity:

> Christianity's first intention was really no other than to introduce a pure religious faith, over which no conflict of opinions can prevail; whereas that turmoil, through which the human race was disrupted and is still set at odds, arises solely from this, that what, by reason of an evil propensity of human nature, was in the beginning to serve merely for the introduction of pure religious faith, i.e., to win over for the new faith the nation habituated to the old historical belief through its own prejudices, was in the sequel made the foundation of a universal world-religion (122).

As this astonishing passage makes clear, Kant views the preservation of Jewish thought in Christianity as the original sin of Christian history. The Jewishness of Christianity is the product of "an evil propensity of human nature," and therefore is nothing less than *the historical manifestation of radical evil*. The Jewish dimension of Christianity elevates statutory faith above the claims of moral religion and therefore stands at the source of the church's fanaticism, bloodthirsty hatreds, wars, and ecclesiastical tyranny (121–22).

Properly understood, the Christian church stands in no necessary connection to Judaism whatsoever (116). Kant elaborates this point in a footnote directed against his contemporary, the Jewish philosopher Moses Mendelssohn. In a book advocating the political enfranchisement of the Jews, Mendelssohn rebuffed the demand that Jews convert to Christianity by pointing out that Judaism is the foundation of Christian religion.[8] In reply Kant admits theologians traditionally presented Christianity as though it were grounded upon the Jewish faith. Precisely this, however, is the "weak spot" of traditional doctrine:

> Mendelssohn very ingeniously makes use of this weak spot in the customary presentation of Christianity wholly to reject every demand upon a son of Israel that he change his religion. For, he says, since the Jewish faith itself is, according to the avowal of Christians, the substructure upon which the superstructure of Christianity rests, the demand that it be abandoned is equivalent to expecting someone to demolish the ground floor of a house in order to take up his abode in the second story. His real intention is fairly clear. He means to say: First wholly remove Judaism itself out of your *religion* (it can always remain, as an antiquity, in the historical account of the faith); we can then take your proposal under advisement. (Actually nothing would then be left but pure moral religion unencumbered by statutes.) (154)

Kant's point could not be more plain. Christianity falls short of moral religion just insofar as it retains rudiments of Jewish belief, while it approximates to true religion just insofar as it breaks in principle with the Israelite dimension of traditional Christian faith. The true service of religion in the Christian church, therefore, consists in expelling the vestiges of Judaism from the body of Christian divinity. The task begun by the abolition of circumcision, the mark of Jewish flesh, must be completed by the abolition of the Hebrew Scriptures, the mark of the Jewish spirit.

It is tempting to try to separate Kant's account of Christianity from his negative view of Judaism and the Jewish dimension of Christianity. Yet, ironically, to do so would be to fail to recognize fully the brilliance of Kant's interpretation of Christian doctrine. Kant has put his finger on the critical fault line that runs through the center of the standard model of Christian theology: the line that divides the standard model's creaturely-universal foreground from its Israelite background. By identifying this fault line and exploiting it, Kant hits upon a strategy for adapting Christian doctrine to the modern age and its canons of rationality: Christian doctrine simply *is* the story of the triumph of creaturely-universal spirit over historical-particular flesh. This triumph, paradigmatically achieved in the church's supersession of the Jewish people, is for Kant the enduring spiritual content of Christianity. Purifying Christian doctrine of its residual Jewishness is therefore no distortion of the Christian faith but the necessary expression of its basic genius.

FRIEDRICH SCHLEIERMACHER'S
THE CHRISTIAN FAITH

A generation after Kant, Friedrich Schleiermacher sought to renegotiate Christianity's relation to the spirit of the age in terms that did not require the one-sided capitulation of Christian theology. Key to Schleiermacher's solution was his description of religion as a determination of human feeling (*Gefühl*) and of dogmatic theology as the expression of religious feeling in conceptually precise language.[9] This starting point allowed Schleiermacher to defend the integrity of Christian doctrine by presenting it as the conceptual expression of that particular modification of universal religious feeling in which "everything is related to the redemption accomplished by Jesus of Nazareth."

Schleiermacher's understanding of the relation of philosophy and theology is examined in detail elsewhere and need not detain us here.[10] Our interest once again is the impact of Schleiermacher's project on the shape of the standard model. His reconstruction of Christian doctrine epitomizes the process whereby the truth of Christian faith comes to be articulated solely in terms of Jesus Christ's significance for the creaturely-universal dimension of human existence, while the Israelite dimension of Christian faith is cut away altogether. This trend is especially evident in Schleiermacher's great work *The Christian Faith*, which forms the basis of the following discussion.

The Christian Faith consists in a lengthy Introduction followed by the *Glaubenslehre* (doctrine of faith), the body of the work. Both sections bear on Schleiermacher's understanding of Christianity's relationship to the Jewish people and their Scriptures, and so both are of interest for our purposes. In the Introduction, Schleiermacher defines Christianity as a particular modification of religious feeling and in the process completely dissolves Christianity's internal or essential connection to the Jewish people and the Hebrew Scriptures. In the body of the work, Schleiermacher develops a Scotist or christocentric account of Christian doctrine that is almost wholly purified of the traditional Israelite dimension of Christian faith.

The Christian Faith: *The Introduction*

The task that Schleiermacher sets himself in *The Christian Faith* is to sort, clarify, and organize the religious expressions of contemporary Protestantism in light of Christianity's distinctive essence as a particular modification of religious feeling. By testing received Christianity against Christianity's essence, Schleiermacher proposes to bring to light the inner unity of Christian doctrine and to purify the church's language of foreign and extraneous material (§§20–21). When the task is complete, every legitimate part of Christian theology will be clearly exhibited in its relation to every other part, while everything that is essentially foreign to Christian faith will be firmly excluded. If traditional material is omitted in the process, "that omission is not an arbitrary judgment on our part but sure internal evidence that such teaching is lacking in purely dogmatic content, and for that reason possessed only of a subordinate explanatory or subsidiary value" (§91.2).

So defined, the dogmatic project depends crucially on Schleiermacher's definition of the distinctive essence of Christian faith. While Schleiermacher's Introduction need not be rehearsed in detail, it is useful to trace in a general way how he arrives at his definition of Christianity. Drawing selectively from a series of nondogmatic disciplines, Schleiermacher first defines what a religious community is, then how the various communities can be distinguished from one another, and then what is the distinctive essence of Christianity.

Schleiermacher begins by tracing all religion back to a common source in human consciousness, the feeling of utter dependence (§§3–5). This feeling is a prereflective awareness that we exist in utter dependence upon a "whence" that is the source both of ourselves and the world. This whence Schleiermacher calls God. The feeling of utter dependence is thus at once an awareness of God and of being a creature. God-consciousness and creature-consciousness correspond. God-consciousness is an essential component of all human experience, although it may remain dim and indistinct for long periods of time, both in the history of the individual and of the race. The feeling simply awaits the proper stimulus in order to grow into a dominant feature of individual and communal life.

In Schleiermacher's view, the different religions of history are various manifestations of the root feeling of utter dependence. They differ from one another because of the disparate ways in which they combine God-consciousness with "objective consciousness," that is, ordinary human awareness of the world. The different religions can be ranked in three stages according to the clarity with which God-consciousness forms the controlling moment in this union (§8). The lowest stage is fetishism, which identifies the whence of utter dependence with a particular object of sensual experience and limits its sphere of influence to a particular sensual realm. The intermediate stage is polytheism, which dimly refers the feeling of utter dependence to a single source but represents that source with reference to a plurality of sensuous objects. The highest stage of religious consciousness is monotheism, which regards the whence of utter dependence as perfectly simple and extends its power over the whole world (§8.2).

History shows only three great monotheistic faiths: Judaism, Christianity, and Islam. Of these, the first is "almost in process of extinction," while the other two still contend for mastery of the human race (§8.4). Judaism is the most primitive of the monotheistic faiths because it limits God's love to the people of Abraham and thus betrays a lingering affinity with fetishism. Islam betrays a resemblance to polytheism by the strong influence of sensuous ideas on religious emotions. Christianity, being free of both these weaknesses, is the most highly developed religion known to history (§8.4). In it, God-consciousness and creature-consciousness come to their purest communal expression. Schleiermacher further classifies the three monotheistic faiths according to whether they exhibit a predominantly moral or aesthetic character (§9). Judaism and Christianity are both religions of the moral type (Schleiermacher calls it the teleological type), since both order religious feeling toward eventual expression in moral action. Christianity is a more perfect example of moral religion than Judaism, however, because Christianity relies on spiritual influence to advance the moral life, whereas Judaism relies on sensual rewards and punishments (§9.2).

Thus Judaism and Christianity are both monotheistic faiths of the moral type, a classification they share with no other living religion. All that remains is to identify the differentia that distinguishes Christianity from Judaism, and the definition of Christianity will be complete. To prepare for this final step, Schleiermacher states that religions of the same stage and type (Christianity and Judaism) differ essentially from one another because of their diverse historical origins and because of their diverse modifications of religious feeling. In the more advanced religions, these two factors converge. That is, the historical origin itself is the factor that gives the religion its peculiar modification of religious feeling (§10). According to Schleiermacher, the individuating factor shapes the religion as a whole, so that even the most "generic" aspects of the religion bear some relation to the distinctive heart of the faith.

Now Schleiermacher is ready to define Christianity in silent contrast to Judaism: "Christianity is a monotheistic faith, belonging to the teleological type of religion, and is essentially distinguished from other such faiths by the fact that in it everything is related to the redemption accomplished by Jesus of Nazareth" (§11, Heading). Redemption in Jesus is the historical origin of Christianity and the individuating factor that gives monotheistic moral God-consciousness a distinctively Christian caste. At this point, Schleiermacher's procedure has already produced two noteworthy results. First, he has substituted the philosophy of religion for the Hebrew Scriptures as the essential context for identifying the God of the Christian confession. The God of Christian confession is the whence of absolute dependence rather than the God of Israel. Second, he has transformed Christianity's relation to Judaism from an internal to an external relation. Christianity and Judaism are no longer linked by their common reference to the God of Israel but are ranged alongside one another as irreducibly distinct instantiations of monotheistic moral God-consciousness.

Schleiermacher next takes up the question of Christianity's historical relation to Judaism. He acknowledges that Christianity originally stood in a special historical connection to Judaism because Jesus "was born among the Jewish people" (§12.1). But ultimately this connection is insignificant for the nature of Christianity. Jesus was a wholly new phenomenon in the sphere of human piety, and he founded a community that was equally discontinuous with Judaism and paganism. Even Paul, who in Galatians wrote of Abraham as the prototype of Christian faith, did not mean that Christianity was a continuation or renewal of Jewish faith. Paul's real point of view was that Jew and pagan stand equally far from God and are equally in need of Christ.

Schleiermacher puts the reader on notice that his dissolution of Christianity's special relation to the Jewish people implies two important revisions of traditional Christian doctrine. First, he indicates that the ancient Irenaean conception of a single economy of salvation from Adam to Christ must be reconstructed in such a way that no special significance is accorded to the Jewish people. In one sense, all human history may be interpreted as a striving of human nature toward Christianity. But this striving is no more in evidence among the Jewish people than among the nobler and purer pagans, and therefore the idea of a special prefigurative economy of salvation among the Jews must be discarded (§12.3; see §156.1). Second, the "Old Testament" drops out entirely as an authority for Christian theology. The Old Testament is, after all, the production of a fundamentally different form of religious consciousness. At best, it approximates only faintly to those Christian religious emotions that are rather general in character, while "whatever is most definitely Jewish has least value" (§12.3). Moreover, since the New Testament is by all accounts the definitive record of Christian consciousness, the Old Testament is superfluous as an authority for the church (§27.3). Later Schleiermacher suggests that the Scriptures of Israel be relegated to an historical appendix of the Apostolic Witness in order to make clear its lack of religious authority for Christianity (§132.3). In their present location, the Scriptures of Israel give rise to the mistaken impression that "we must first work our way through the whole of the Old Testament if we are to approach the New by the right avenue" (§132.3).

By the end of the Introduction, Schleiermacher has prepared the reader for a presentation of Christian doctrine in which Israel's Scriptures and the standard model's Israelite background have been entirely stripped away. The result, as we shall see, is a reconstruction of traditional Christian doctrine in which the standard model's creaturely-universal foreground functions as the exclusive narrative framework of Christian faith.

The Christian Faith: *The* Glaubenslehre

Schleiermacher organized *The Christian Faith* in two main parts in accordance with his definition of Christianity. Part One treats Christianity in its more generic aspects as an instance of moral monotheism. Part Two deals with the specifically Christian experience of redemption in Christ. Since this latter experience entails the antithesis of sin and redemption, Part Two is again divided into a section on sin and a section on grace. Finally, each part is presented under three aspects: as statements about the self, God, and the world. Schleiermacher designed the complex structure as a means of underscoring his conviction that all Christian doctrines, including those that are least specifically Christian, are related in some way to the consciousness of redemption in Christ.[11]

Surprisingly, Schleiermacher's account of Christian doctrine is as simple at the narrative level as it is complex at the organizational level. The Christian story is about God's consummation of the human race through the perfection of humanity's natural capacity for God-consciousness. The center and pivot of this story is Jesus Christ, the Second Adam, in whom God's creative intention for humankind is fully realized for the first time and through whom the power of perfect God-consciousness is mediated to the church and world.

In Part One, Schleiermacher treats Christian consciousness in its more generic aspect as a form of monotheistic God-consciousness. Here the central datum of Christian consciousness is simply self-awareness as a creature in dependence on a Creator (§34). Like all basic forms of religious experience, Christian creature-awareness expresses itself in three different forms: as statements about the self, God, and the world. Formulated with reference to the self, creature-awareness expresses itself, naturally enough, in the doctrines of creation and preservation (§36). Formulated with reference to God, creature-awareness comes to expression in the affirmation of God's eternity, omnipresence, omnipotence, and omniscience (§50–55). Formulated with reference to the constitution of the world, creature-awareness manifests itself in the affirmation of the original perfection of the world and of humankind (§§57–60).

The doctrine of original perfection is worth dwelling on because it bears directly on the narrative logic of the dogmatic system. For Schleiermacher, original perfection does not refer to an actual state of affairs at the beginning of history and therefore has no necessary connection with the book of Genesis. Instead original perfection refers to the *perfectibility* of creature-awareness as a mode of human existence in the world. Humanity's original perfection refers to humankind's innate capacity to unite God-consciousness with every possible moment of sensuous experience. The world's original perfection affirms the world's suitability as a habitat and medium for the full development of the God-consciousness. This account of original perfection sets the stage for a vision of the Christian story in which the movement from creation to consummation is central, and in which consummation means the perfect actualization of humanity's innate capacity for God-consciousness. In addition, it prepares for Schleiermacher's christology of Jesus as the Second Adam, in whom we see "everything that can develop out of such original perfection all together in a single human instance" (§61.5).

In Part Two of the *Glaubenslehre*, Schleiermacher presents the more distinctively Christian experience of redemption in Christ. The negative condition from which Christ redeems the Christian is nothing other than the radical weakness of the God-consciousness, its incapacity to dominate every moment of self-consciousness due to the recalcitrance of our sensuous nature. This weakness takes shape as a distinctively Christian experience through encounter with the Redeemer, in relation to whom the weakness is experienced as pain. Formulated with reference to the self, the painful frailty of the God-consciousness is expressed in the doctrines of original and actual sin (§70–74). Formulated with reference to the world, it declares the world to be a source of evil that punishes sin (§§75–77). Formulated with reference to God, the consciousness of sin comes to expression in the affirmation of God's holiness and justice (§§79–84).

The positive side of redemption consists in the decisive reversal whereby God-consciousness gains dominance over sensuous consciousness and thereafter extends its dominion throughout the whole of human experience. Christians ascribe this process of reversal and growth to the power of Jesus' own perfect God-consciousness. Jesus is the first person in whom God-consciousness comes to perfect expression, and he communicates the power of his God-consciousness to others through the corporate life that he founds.

From the very beginning of his discussion of Christ, Schleiermacher signals his intention to shape Christian doctrine in what we previously called a Scotist direction.[12] To recall, a Scotist account of the standard model holds that God's work as Consummator is oriented from the very beginning toward the incarnation. Schleiermacher's Scotist posture becomes clear in his preference for the title Second Adam over Redeemer as the most fitting term for Christ's person and activity. Schleiermacher's failure to give priority to the title of Redeemer may seem surprising in view of his definition of Christianity as a religion centered on the experience of redemption. Nevertheless, Second Adam is in fact much more characteristic of Schleiermacher's vision of Christ's basic role in human history. While Redeemer is not incorrect, it suggests that Christ's religious significance is ultimately contingent upon sin. In contrast, the term Second Adam exhibits Christ's significance in God's plan in a more comprehensive and positive way by locating him in the context of God's work as the Consummator or Completer of creation:

> Jesus [is] the One in whom the human creation is perfected . . . .
> For this Second Adam is altogether like all those who are descend-
> ed from the first, only that from the outset He has an absolutely
> potent God-consciousness. With this He enters the existing his-
> torical order of human nature, in virtue of a creative divine
> causality. It follows that, according to the law of this order, His
> higher perfection must work in a stimulating and communicative
> way upon the nature which is like His own . . . . (§89.2)

As the Second Adam, Christ is the one in whom "the conception of man as the subject of the God-consciousness comes to completion" (§93.3). Christ's significance does not reside only or even chiefly in the fact that he rescues humanity from the plight of sin. More basically, Christ completes the creation of the human race and inaugurates the final stage of humanity's spiritual development.[13]

Schleiermacher's depiction of Christ as Second Adam reinforces the impression that for him the basic trajectory of the Christian story is from creation to consummation. But it also reveals his conception of consummation as extremely simple. Consummation— like christology—is wholly regulated by the concept of humankind's natural spiritual capacities. Consummation—like christology—is creature-awareness in full blossom.   This simplification of the Christian story corresponds to Schleiermacher's simplified conception of God, whose sole and exclusive activity consists in the work of creation (§100.2). In effect, Schleiermacher makes the correlation of God's creative action and human creaturely capacity absolutely central and regulative for the whole of Christian doctrine.

Schleiermacher's elevation of the Creator-creature relation to the exclusive context and content of christology entails a corresponding de-emphasis of Jesus' Jewishness. Jesus is significant because he instantiates creature-consciousness in an ideal way. If Jewishness were constitutive of Jesus' consciousness, his ideality would be threatened. Christianity would be "nothing but a new development of Judaism," and Jesus would be "nothing but a more or less original and revolutionary reformer of the Jewish law" (§93.2). In fact, however, Jesus' Jewishness determines merely his "organism," not his spiritual self-activity. Accordingly, the Christian norm of life is indifferent to "all that is simply Jewish in His life" (§93.5). Schleiermacher underscores Christ's transcendence of all that is merely Jewish in his discussion of Christ as Prophet, Priest, and King (§§102–105). The whole point of this material, in Schleiermacher's view, is to exhibit the essential contrast between the Old Covenant and the New, between Jewish theocracy and the Christian community. In each instance, Christ brings the corresponding Jewish institution to an end in its narrow nationalistic and particularistic form and replaces it with the community-forming power of his own ideal God-consciousness.

After Christ's death, the church continues to mediate the power of Christ's God-consciousness to the world in undiminished form. Although each Christian falls short of Christ's absolutely powerful God-consciousness, the Christian community as a whole preserves the ideal power of his piety. Schleiermacher represents final consummation as the time when the church will finally achieve the "spiritual fecundation" of the whole human race. So understood, final consummation entails the hope that Christianity will attain geographical mastery of the world and that no other religions will survive as organized fellowships alongside it (§157). Final consummation, therefore, implies the non-existence of Judaism:

> As long as these antiquated and imperfect forms of religion persist alongside of Christianity, striving to maintain themselves side by side with the Church, their character will be so deeply impressed on their adherents that when these have been captured by Christianity, whether individually or in the mass, they will (even if it be unconsciously) carry over many corrupting elements, which must prove a source of division and error (§157.1).

Yet even after the church attains geographical mastery of the world, the task of eradicating sin will arise again with each new generation. Hence final consummation cannot be conceived as an actual future state of affairs but only as an ideal toward which history continually approximates.

Schleiermacher completes the dogmatic system by taking up the doctrine of God for a third and final time, this time as perceived in light of the Christian consciousness of redemption. Here Christian consciousness affirms God's love and wisdom. God's love is manifested through the person of Jesus and God's wisdom through the governance of the world in behalf of Christ's ever-expanding spiritual influence (§164). As for the doctrine of the Trinity, Schleiermacher excludes it from the dogmatic system proper and relegates it to an appendix on the grounds that it is not a direct expression of Christian consciousness, which experiences God as utterly simple and unitary, but merely a synthesis of several aspects of Christian experience for the purposes of instruction.

Surveying *The Christian Faith* as a whole, one cannot but be impressed by two things. The first is the remarkable consistency with which Schleiermacher reconstructs Christian doctrine around a Scotist or christocentric understanding of Christ as the Second Adam. The second is the remarkable thoroughness with which Schleiermacher rids Christian doctrine of all lingering reference to Jewish flesh. While these two aspects of Schleiermacher's work are seldom brought into connection with one another, I think there is in fact an important link between the two. *Christocentrism represents Schleiermacher's strategy for maintaining the doctrinal integrity of Christian theology after its internal reference to the God of Israel has been wholly cut away.* At the very least, Schleiermacher demonstrates that a Scotist christology makes an admirable vehicle for bringing the logic of structural supersessionism to its final conclusion.

Schleiermacher's reconstruction of Christian doctrine is justly called christocentric because in it every aspect of Christian faith—even God's work as Consummator—is related in some way to the consciousness of redemption in Christ.[14] Whatever its substantive merits, Schleiermacher's adoption of a christocentric account of God's work as Consummator serves an important strategic function. It allows him to introduce his religious anthropology (God-consciousness as a universal determination of human nature) into the very center of Christian teaching while still preserving (at least nominally) the regulative role of christology for the whole of Christian doctrine. By defining God's work as Consummator in christocentric terms, Schleiermacher is able to guard against the objection that he, like Kant, simply subordinates the distinctive claims of Christian faith to a neutral or generic account of human religiosity.

Nevertheless, it is highly questionable whether Schleiermacher's Scotist christology is sufficient to clear him of the charge that he makes a general religious anthropology the final arbiter of Christian theology. For Schleiermacher's christocentric reconstruction of Christian doctrine is ultimately subservient to an even more basic reconstruction of Christian doctrine that he undertakes, namely, his rationalization of Christian divinity in terms of a single regulative concept: the human creature's natural capacity for consciousness of God. To be sure, Jesus Christ stands at the center of Schleiermacher's account of Christian doctrine. But Schleiermacher's conception of human consciousness stands at the center of his depiction of Jesus Christ. In this respect, Schleiermacher's theology represents the apotheosis of human consciousness—conceived as spiritual potency for relationship with God—to systematic centrality within the standard model of Christian theology.

As we shall see, Schleiermacher's greatest heirs honored his theology's christocentrism but lamented its loss of contact with the living God of the Bible. They therefore tried to reinvigorate the former while overcoming the latter. Yet whether such an effort can succeed so long as Christian theology remains committed to the logic of supersessionism, is a question we will have to examine.

DISEMBODIED GOD

Kant and Schleiermacher epitomize the process whereby the standard model of Christian theology is outfitted for life in the modern era through a process of de-Judaization. What enters the process of dogmatic reflection is a received Christianity with a heavy investment in what we have called the Israelite dimension of Christian faith. What emerges at the end is a Christianity that has been purified of the same. Key to this whole development is the rosy confidence that the Christian conception of God can be coherently maintained in separation from the God of Israel. So long as Christians identified the Creator with the God of Israel, it could not occur to them to seek to expel the Jewish dimension of Christian faith in the name of the creaturely-universal. But once this identification was denied, Christians inevitably experienced the Jewish aspects of Christianity as foreign and unassimilable.

However much Kant and Schleiermacher depart from traditional Christian thought, there is a real sense in which they continue and intensify the apologetic strategy already inscribed into the standard model at the time of its emergence during confrontation with pagans, Jews, and gnostics. Kant and Schleiermacher emphasize the universality of God's purposes by correlating them with a spiritual potency for communion with God that is ingredient in human nature; they thereby continue the strategy marked out by Justin in his writings for pagans. Kant and Schleiermacher emphasize the sole legitimacy of the church by contrasting its spirituality with the carnal community of the Jews; they thereby continue Justin's strategy in his polemic against Trypho the Jew. Finally, Kant and Schleiermacher emphasize God's identity as Creator and Redeemer by underscoring God's abiding commitment to God's spiritual purposes for creation; in this way they continue Irenaeus' strategy in his conflict with the gnostics. In each case, Kant and Schleiermacher exploit the structure of the standard model in order to consolidate the victory of creaturely-universal spirit over historical-particular flesh.

Yet by continuing and intensifying these trends, Kant and Schleiermacher also exacerbate the standard model's supersessionism and flight from history. So long as the standard model merely *subordinated* God's fidelity to the Jewish people to God's spiritual purposes for creation, the Jewish people retained a slender yet ironclad rationale for their corporeal existence in a predominantly Christian culture. This changes once God's fidelity to Jewish flesh is no longer simply subordinated but rather *expelled* from the body of Christian divinity like so much indigestible matter. Now the logic of Christian doctrine provides a rationale not for the continued existence of the Jews as a disenfranchised group but rather for the gradual disappearance of the Jewish people from human history. The new situation is graphically but not unjustly captured by Mark C. Taylor in the form of a question, "Is Abraham, father of the Jewish faith, a shit, perhaps *the* shit that the System proper must flush away?" Taylor poses the question in the context of a discussion of Hegel's philosophy, but it might just as well be put to the theology of Kant and Schleiermacher.[15]

The standard model's heightened supersessionism goes hand in hand with a further migration of Christian doctrine into the interior world of the spirit. More than ever, redemption means deliverance from a history in which the Jewish people have a role to play. As God's consummating and redemptive purposes for creation are rationalized ever more strictly in terms of humanity's natural potency for God, the central drama of Christian faith comes increasingly to be interpreted as one that transpires in the domain of human consciousness. Christian doctrine evinces a palpable shift of attention away from the biblical narratives about Jesus and the public world that they presuppose and reflects instead an increasing preoccupation with Jesus' inner life and consciousness. The result is a further loss of contact with the central figure of the Apostolic Witness itself, the Jew Jesus of Nazareth.

4

CONSUMMATION AT THE END
OF CHRISTENDOM
BARTH AND RAHNER

T HE MIDDLE OF THE TWENTIETH CENTURY WITNESSED an extraordinary flowering of Christian theology, represented most prominently perhaps in the works of the Reformed theologian Karl Barth and Roman Catholic theologian Karl Rahner. Although Barth and Rahner may represent irreconcilable alternatives in certain respects, they are curiously symmetrical figures in many important ways. Both theologians sought to overcome the doctrinal reductionism of early modern theology by drawing on the scholastic thinkers of their respective traditions. And both men sought to rejuvenate scholastic tradition by tapping the theological imagination of early modern theology. In the process, both theologians gave fresh and innovative expression to the narrative coherence of the Christian faith.

In this chapter, our interest in Barth and Rahner focuses on the oddly parallel way in which they criticize and revise the traditional narrative logic of the standard model. Prompted in part by dissatisfaction with the doctrinal reductionism of early modern theology, Barth and Rahner question—albeit from different perspectives—certain hidden premises basic to the narrative logic of the standard model in both its early modern and its classical forms. In the process, Barth and Rahner expose and correct aspects of the semignosticism latent in the deep structure of the church's standard canonical narrative. By incorporating these anti-gnostic insights into their own constructive work, Barth and Rahner go some distance toward providing genuinely post-Christendom accounts of the narrative coherence of Christian faith.

Nevertheless, Barth and Rahner ultimately fail to transcend the semignosticism implicit in the narrative structure of the standard model. Indeed, the semignosticism of the standard model ultimately avenges itself in the work of Barth and Rahner in especially egregious form. The reason for this, I argue, is the failure of both Barth and Rahner to overcome the logic of supersessionism. While supersessionism is undoubtedly an overdetermined feature of their work, one of its clearest sources is the theology of Friedrich Schleiermacher. Our discussion of Barth and Rahner begins, therefore, with their complex relation to Schleiermacher.

BARTH AND RAHNER ON SCHLEIERMACHER

One significant way in which Barth and Rahner exhibit a curious kinship is in their similarly ambivalent postures toward the great pioneer of modern liberal theology, Friedrich Schleiermacher. Both theologians are sympathetic to key aspects of Schleiermacher's thought, and above all, to Schleiermacher's vision of the christocentric coherence of Christian doctrine. At the same time, both theologians reject Schleiermacher's doctrinal reductionism and seek fresh engagement with the classical dogmatic tradition.

The complex relation of Barth and Rahner to Schleiermacher appears with special clarity in their posture toward his theology of consummation. In certain respects, Barth and Rahner are in full agreement with it. They follow him in insisting that God's primordial consummating will for creation is centered in Jesus Christ. By affirming the christomorphic character of God's work as Consummator, Barth and Rahner follow Schleiermacher in giving a generally Scotist cast to the traditional story of creation-for-consummation, fall, redemption, and final consummation. In other respects, however, Barth and Rahner are implacable foes of a theology of consummation such as Schleiermacher's. Against Schleiermacher and the whole tenor of early modern theology, Barth and Rahner insist that God's work as Consummator cannot be understood as the actualization of the human creature's natural spiritual potency for God. For Barth and Rahner, such a position makes the creature rather than the living God the tacit measure of consummation. God is reduced to being the condition for the creature's fulfillment *qua* rational nature. As a result, the God of the philosophers eclipses the God of Abraham, Isaac, and Jacob.

Positively, Barth and Rahner champion an understanding of consummation as God's utterly free self-bestowal to human creation, which wholly transcends the human creature's natural good and dynamism. God's self-bestowal summons the creature beyond its natural being to responsible encounter with God and fellow creatures in the "supernatural" medium of "covenant history." God's covenant history with humankind presupposes the gift of rational nature but cannot be reduced to it or to its fulfillment. Covenant history is driven by the living God's self-bestowal to humanity, a reality that catches up and transcends the human creature's own natural dynamism.

In the course of developing these insights, both Barth and Rahner proposed highly original accounts of God's consummating work and how it engages human creation. They are of special interest to us for the critical light they cast on certain questionable premises that inform the church's standard canonical narrative in both its classical and modern forms.

Karl Barth's theology of consummation is remembered by the slogan "creation and covenant." In developing the theology of creation and covenant, Barth was especially concerned to overcome one aspect of Schleiermacher's reductionism, namely, his loss of engagement with the Bible, and above all, the Scriptures of the Jewish people. However, in the course of pursuing this theme, Barth found it necessary to critique and revise not only Schleiermacher's extreme Israel-forgetfulness but also the narrative logic of the standard model more generally. Barth identifies and rejects the standard model's unstated premise according to which the center of the Hebrew Scriptures is indecisive for shaping conclusions about how God's work as Consummator engages creation. In place of this latent premise, Barth advances the innovative thesis that God's work as Consummator engages human creation in and through the covenant that God initiates, sustains, and ultimately completes with the Jewish people. As we shall see, this proposal marks a significant break with the structural supersessionism of the standard model and points the way toward a nonsupersessionist account of Christian doctrine.

Karl Rahner's theology of consummation is associated with the concept "the supernatural existential." The idea grew out of Rahner's desire to show how God's consummating grace engages humankind in the depths of its existence as a specifically *historical*—in contrast to merely natural—being. Yet in pursuing this theme, Rahner, like Barth, found it necessary to critique and revise a hidden premise of the standard model. In particular, Rahner identifies and rejects the tacit assumption that God's consummating grace engages humankind with immediate reference to its specific nature as a rational being. Against this, Rahner insists that God's work as Consummator engages humankind with reference to a contingent, historical feature of its identity that is both supernatural in origin and prior to every act of human freedom.

No doubt Barth's creation and covenant and Rahner's supernatural existential are the products of very different theological imaginations. They reflect different confessional allegiances, different postures toward the Bible and toward philosophy, and—in considerable measure—different substantive theological concerns. Despite these weighty differences, there is a marked kinship between Barth's creation and covenant and Rahner's supernatural existential on one crucial point. Both concepts articulate the conviction that God's all-embracing work as the Consummator of creation cannot be understood to engage humankind simply with reference to its specific nature as a rational creature. Rather, God's work as Consummator engages humankind in and through irreducibly contingent, historical, and particular features of human history and human identity. In this key respect, Barth's creation and covenant and Rahner's supernatural existential share a common anti-gnosticizing desire to ground God's free and gracious work as Consummator in the texture of human history.

Yet despite their best efforts, Barth and Rahner ultimately fail to give convincing shape to covenant history as the medium of God's consummating work. The reason is their continued allegiance to a christocentric account of consummation and the economic supersessionism it entails. Like Schleiermacher, Barth and Rahner insist that God's work as Consummator is mediated to humanity in and through the person of Jesus Christ. They thereby assimilate God's consummating work to the relationship that obtains between the particular person Jesus Christ and certain universal features of the human condition. Unfortunately, the result of this exigency is that covenant history as the medium of God's consummating work ultimately collapses into one of the two poles of Schleiermacher's original christocentric paradigm. In Barth's case, covenant history collapses into the particular figure of Jesus Christ. In Rahner's, it collapses into the dynamism of the human creature. In both cases, covenant history as an identifiable feature of the public world disappears.

In the following pages, we will examine Barth and Rahner in turn, first treating each man's innovative account of God's work as Consummator *remoto Christo* and then turning to how their conceptions are assimilated to—and ultimately undermined by—the traditional logic of the standard model. Admittedly, the resulting exposition labors under some degree of artificiality. By first presenting each man's account of consummation apart from consideration of Jesus Christ, the exposition separates what in the intention of both men cannot be separated. The artificiality seems justified, however, because it helps to clarify the contribution these theologians make to our constructive argument.

BARTH ON CONSUMMATION
Creation, Covenant, and the People Israel

Although Karl Barth's theology of God's work as Consummator is vast in execution, its basic shape is easily summarized.[1] Barth understands consummation as the covenantal relationship that God freely initiates, sustains, and ultimately completes with human creation. According to Barth, God's covenant with creation is the supreme good for the sake of which God creates in the first place. As Creator, God endows what is not God with being and existence. As Lord of covenant history, God summons the human creature beyond the dynamism of its natural being into a wholly new relationship of covenantal encounter and responsibility with God. God thereby bestows upon humanity a new identity above and beyond its identity as God's creature. The human creature's new identity consists in its determination to be God's freely elected covenant partner.

Barth's theology of creation and covenant can be summarized in two propositions, "Creation is the external basis of the covenant," and "Covenant is the internal basis of creation" (*CD* III/1, 103, 258).[2] The sentences encapsulate the fundamental distinction yet mutual relation of creation and covenant in God's eternal decree. Yet for Barth a general formula such as this has theological validity only to the degree that it redescribes the particular history attested by the Bible. Where, then, according to the biblical witness, does

God's consummating work engage creation concretely as a history of covenantal encounter and responsibility? For Barth, the answer is unmistakable. God's work as Consummator takes concrete shape as covenantal history in God's gracious election of the Jewish people:

> The covenant which God made with Abraham and his seed . . . was not an arbitrary invention of God and therefore something wholly new in history. It was simply the initial stage in the execution of the purpose God intended when he caused history to commence in and with creation and therefore in and with the beginning of time generally (*CD* III/2, 476).[3]

For Barth, God's covenant with Israel marks the point at which God's work as Consummator initially engages humankind in concrete, historical form.

We do well to underscore immediately the significance and boldness of Barth's proposal. As noted in previous chapters, Christian theology typically shapes its conclusions about God's work as Consummator with reference to Genesis 1–3, the story of Adam, and the concept of the image of God. To this, a Scotist theology adds reference to Christ as the original goal of God's consummating work. In either case, the traditional view assumes that God's consummating work engages certain universal structures of human being that are ingredient in humankind's specific nature as rational or spiritual beings, structures that are of course in place apart from and prior to the fall and to God's covenant with Israel.[4] Barth, however, is critical of traditional method on precisely this point:

> The whole force of the truth and validity of what is said generally in this account [in Genesis 1–3] depends on the fact that it is said primarily with God and Israel in view. According to the tenor of the Old Testament as a whole, the covenant which God formed with all flesh on earth in the person of Adam and later again in that of Noah was actualized in and through the medium of this covenant [with Israel]. It is here that we have the promise of life, but also the threat of death for the sake of the promise of life (*CD* III/1, 273).

By coordinating God's consummating work with Adam and the general structures of human existence, traditional theology privileges the general and abstract over the particular and concrete. Barth revises the traditional pattern of dogmatic thought by making the center of the Hebrew Scriptures decisive for shaping conclusions about God's work as the Consummator of creation. "The history of Israel controls in certain respects the problem of the covenant between God and man indicated in the story of Paradise" (*CD* III/1, 275). With this, Barth breaks with one of the key aspects of the standard model.

Barth's decision to coordinate God's consummating work with God's covenant with Israel has wide-ranging consequences not only for Barth's theology of Israel but for his grasp of the biblical story as a whole. By making covenant with Israel constitutive of God's work as Consummator, Barth fundamentally reconceives the sense in which God's covenant with Israel is a covenant of "grace." God's covenant with Israel is no longer gracious primarily as an expression of God's *redemptive* activity, whereby God enters into conflict with sin and evil on behalf of the fallen creature. Rather, God's covenant with Israel is supremely gracious in its own right antecedent to sin and the need for redemption. Israel's election is the gracious *presupposition* of God's work as Redeemer, not God's redemptive work itself (*CD* IV/1, 27). The essential content of God's consummating work is summed up in God's declaration to Israel, "I will be your God, and ye shall be my people" (*CD* IV/1, 22). God's covenantal promise initiates a relationship of mutual responsibility that is supremely good in itself, quite apart from the antithesis of sin and redemption. God unilaterally resolves to be Israel's God in a sovereign act of freedom and love. Simultaneously, God summons Israel to accept the yoke of election by responding to God's faithfulness with praise and thanksgiving. The covenant so established is, Barth insists, eternal. It cannot be abrogated or set aside (*CD* IV/1, 23).

For Barth, God's eternal covenant of grace is the fundamental presupposition of God's whole history with Israel, from the calling of Abraham, to the wandering in the wilderness, to the settling of the promised land and beyond (*CD* IV/1, 22–23). Above all, God's granting of the Mosaic law from Mt. Sinai must be understood within the horizon of God's positive will for covenant relationship. The law's claim to obedience is not antithetical to the covenant of grace but its fit and congruent counterpart. Barth wholly does away with the ancient motif of the law as an image of servitude and interprets it instead as a call to freedom (*CD* IV/1, 102). The law summons the Israelite to respond to God's act of grace with the corresponding acts of praise and thanksgiving (*CD* IV/1, 42f.).

Barth's decision to link God's all-embracing work as Consummator with God's particular covenant with Israel also informs his understanding of what it is to be a Gentile. For Barth, being a Gentile does not simply coincide with being a creature. Creaturely identity as such does not imply actual participation in covenant history. In principle, God could have created the world without summoning it into covenant history (*CD* IV/1, 9). In contrast, the term *Gentile* implies actual participation in covenant history because it conceives of (non-Jewish) humanity within the horizon of Israel's particular election:

> In themselves and as such they [the gentile nations] lack what this people [Israel] has. Or rather they have it only in their co-existence with this one people, as marginal peoples. They have it as that which applies to it is first and finally aimed at them; only as in terms of Genesis 12:3 they may seek blessing in its name; only as that which takes place to this people in demonstration of the goodness and severity of God also applies to them. In themselves and as such, however, they are *goyim,* even in the sense of "heathen." But this means that there is an irreversible way from the many peoples, not back to the one pre-Noachic humanity of creation . . . but forward to the one people of the one God, which is no mere figment but has become a historical reality as the one people of the Jews which is so curious a nation among the nations. . . . But this means that it is not any other people, not the totality of others, but the Jews who are the universal horizon of each and all peoples (*CD* III/4, 319).

It is only apparently true that the gentile nations lack a positive determination in the context of God's consummating work. If Gentiles existed alone, they would indeed lack such a determination. But the Gentiles do not exist alone! They exist alongside Israel, whose election, precisely in its particularity, is the medium of God's consummating work for all creation. Hence Israel's very existence entails a positive determination of the Gentiles above and beyond the good of human creaturehood. Because the Gentiles exist within the universal horizon of Israel's election, they are included rather than excluded from God's work as Consummator.

Thus far we have stressed the link Barth forges between God's work as Consummator and God's election of Israel, while leaving to one side the topics of sin and redemption. This is hardly to suggest that Barth has nothing to say about these latter themes. Nothing could be further from the truth. Barth, like few theologians before

him, vigorously describes Israel's history as one of disobedience
and rebellion against God's covenant (see *CD* II/2, 195f.). This, of
course, is hardly an original theme in Christian theology. Nevertheless, Barth's decision to locate Israel's covenant in the context
of God's work as Consummator places even the familiar theme of
Israel's disobedience in a distinctive light.[5] On the one hand,
Israel's sin becomes a matter of utmost gravity. Israel's rebellion
strikes not against an ancillary part of God's design but rather
against the heart of God's consummating work for all creation. In
this sense, the fall does not lie *behind* God's history with Israel
but *within* it (*CD* III/1, 276f.). On the other hand, the significance
of God's *fidelity* toward sinful Israel is also vastly magnified. By
acting as the Redeemer of Israel, God demonstrates fidelity
toward God's work as the Consummator of all creation. For
Barth, the world's redemption is conceivable only as an event that
confirms and vindicates God's promise to be "the God of Abraham, of Isaac, and of Jacob."

On the basis of what we have seen so far, Barth would seem to
have gone a considerable distance toward overcoming the standard
model's structural supersessionism and latent semignosticism.
Barth identifies and rejects the hermeneutical premise that regards
the Israelite dimension of Christian faith as indecisive for shaping
conclusions about God's consummating purpose for creation. Con-
fronting the issue head-on, Barth insists that God's universal consummating work engages creation for the first time historically and
concretely in God's particular election of the people Israel. This
judgment represents a genuine innovation in the history of Christian theology. What is more, it appears to prohibit the subordina-
tion of the Israelite dimension of Christian faith to the logic of a
purportedly more basic drama between Creator and creature. For
Barth, God's works as Consummator and Redeemer of creation
unfold within God's covenant with Israel, not outside or beyond it.
For Barth, therefore, God's fidelity to the consummation of the
world can be nothing other than God's fidelity to God's eternal
covenant with the people Israel.

Barth's Christocentric Concentration

The previous account of Barth's theology is true enough as far as it
goes, but it omits a crucial aspect of his thought. Ultimately, Barth
regards God's covenant with Israel as only the provisional form of a
more basic covenant that God has established with human creation

as a whole, namely, God's eternal covenant with creation in Jesus Christ. As he writes, "The covenant relationship between Yahweh and Israel . . . without denying its exclusiveness . . . points to a covenant which was there at the beginning and which will be there at the end, the covenant of God with all men [in Jesus Christ]" (*CD* IV/1, 31f.). Once the Scotist or christocentric shape of Barth's theology of consummation is taken into account, the innovative features of his theology of Israel are quickly assimilated to the economic supersessionism of the standard model. God's covenant with Israel is fulfilled in Jesus Christ's life, death, and resurrection. At that point Israel's distinctive role comes to an end in principle, and its place is taken by the church.

In Barth's view, God's work as Consummator is joined primordially not to the people Israel as a whole but to the one Israelite Jesus Christ (*CD* II/2, 94ff.). God elects Jesus Christ before the foundation of the world so that in and through him God may freely and graciously enter into covenant with the rest of human creation. God's covenant with creation is not simply undertaken *in view of* Jesus Christ. Rather, God's covenant with creation is accomplished *in* Jesus Christ. As the personal union of God and humanity, Jesus Christ *is* the covenant between God and creation. Covenant fellowship and hypostatic union coincide. Accordingly, humanity's gracious determination to be God's covenant partner consists simply in the reality of Jesus Christ (*CD* III/2, 132). Covenant identity refers not to a reality intrinsic to the human creature but rather to the extrinsic reality of Jesus Christ as God's Word to and for humankind. Since God's Word in Christ is for everyone, covenant identity is a universal determination that applies to every human creature in the same way.

What then becomes of the link that joined God's consummating plan—not to the rest of human creation as a whole—but quite specifically to the Jewish people? Barth's answer is that Israel is the place where God's definitive covenant with creation first comes to light in "provisional and provisionally representative" form (*CD* IV/1, 28). God's particular covenant with Israel is the promissory sign of God's universal covenant with creation in Jesus Christ (*CD* III/2, 580–81). From the beginning, Israel's history rushes toward its *telos* in the personal history of Jesus Christ, who enacts and reveals God's eternal covenant with humankind. At that point Israel's history comes to an end, and its place is taken by the church, the New Israel (*CD* III/3, 180f.). Like Israel, the church is a sign of humanity's universal election in Jesus Christ. But unlike Israel, the church is a final and definitive sign, at least so far as this is possible under conditions of time and space.

Barth accords only anticipatory significance to God's covenant with Israel for several interrelated reasons (see *CD* II/2, 194ff.). In Israel, God's covenant takes the form of promise, whereas in Jesus Christ it takes the form of promise fulfilled. In Israel, God's promise encounters disbelief and sin, whereas in Jesus Christ it encounters faith and obedience. In Israel, the penalty of sin is borne by the people, whereas in Jesus Christ it is borne by God. Finally, in Israel God's covenant is limited to the stock of Abraham, whereas in Jesus Christ it is enacted for the whole human race. At each of these points, the church supersedes Israel as a community of witness by testifying to God's covenant in its definitive christological form. In contrast to Israel, the church proclaims God's promise as fulfilled for all in Christ's obedient sacrifice on the cross.

Barth vigorously insists that Christ does not destroy God's covenant with Israel but fulfills and confirms it. Employing the formula devised by Irenaeus and later employed by John Calvin, Barth holds that the Old and New Covenants differ not according to inner substance but only according to accidental form (*CD* IV/1, 32). Yet for Barth the accidental form of the Old Covenant includes Israel's vocation as a natural people. In principle, at least, Israel's carnality belongs to the passing form, not the enduring substance, of covenant history:

> The first Israel, constituted on the basis of physical descent from Abraham, has fulfilled its mission now that the Savior of the world has sprung from it and its Messiah has appeared. Its members can only accept this fact with gratitude, and in confirmation of their own deepest election and calling attach themselves to the people of this Savior, their own King, whose members the Gentiles are now called to be as well. *Its mission as a natural community has now run its course and cannot be continued or repeated* (*CD* III/2, 584, emphasis added).

Christ's death and resurrection bring Israel's career as a natural people to an end. Thereafter Israel's sole legitimate destiny is to be taken up into the church, the new and true Israel, where the significance of its identity as a carnal people is permanently transcended.

Barth's unusually rigorous statement of economic supersessionism appears with special clarity in his doctrine of the human creature. According to Barth, the intrinsic goodness of the human creature consists in its suitability for covenant partnership, a capacity that Barth finds embodied in humanity's fundamental orientation toward sociality, or what Barth calls co-humanity (*CD* III/2, 222–324). In the context of God's covenant with Israel, Barth interprets co-humanity to include not only the relation of male and female but also the relation of one generation and the next. In this way, Barth makes provision for the characteristic way in which Israel participates in covenant history, namely, as a natural family over time. Ultimately, however, Barth redefines the essential content of human creatureliness to exclude intergenerationality, on the grounds that fellowship with Christ does not presuppose the relation of one generation and the next. The necessity of procreation was imposed upon Israel only in view of the coming Messiah. After Christ's birth, the importance of the sequence of generations is eclipsed (see *CD* III/4, 142–43, 266). Once again, Christ's coming entails the obsolescence of the very preconditions of Israel's existence as a carnal people.

A final striking instance of Barth's economic supersessionism appears in his understanding of Christ as the end of history. For Barth, history means the unfolding of God's covenant with creation (*CD* III/2, 160). But since this unfolding takes place in Jesus Christ, Barth holds that history in the strict sense comes to its conclusion in Christ's crucifixion and resurrection. "Human history was actually terminated at this point" (*CD* IV/1, 734). Christ's resurrection inaugurates not a further stage in covenant history but rather "fulfilled time." According to Barth, history is the characteristic temporal medium of Israel's existence before Christ, while fulfilled time is the characteristic temporal medium of the church after Christ. Strictly speaking, therefore, Christ's coming means the end of history in general and Israel's history in particular (*CD* III/2, 582). With this judgment, Barth carries the logic of economic supersessionism through to its precise gnosticizing conclusion. Redemption in Christ means the church's deliverance from history and above all from that particular history in which the Jews have a decisive role to play (see *CD* III/2, 584).

Despite its innovative features, Barth's theology of consummation embodies the logic of economic supersessionism as clearly as any in the history of the church.[6] The incarnation brings Israel's history to a conclusion in principle, after which Israel's sole legitimate destiny is to be absorbed into the spiritual church. If nevertheless the Jewish people paradoxically survive the end of their own history, then this can only be ascribed to their blind rejection of the gospel. In one important respect, however, Barth differs significantly from most of his predecessors. While Barth embraces the logic of economic supersessionism, he refuses to deduce from it punitive supersessionism, that is, the view that God has abrogated God's covenant with Israel on account of its unbelief. With an eloquence that has few parallels in Christian theology, Barth insists upon God's unbroken fidelity toward the Jews despite their disbelief in the gospel, a fidelity that will endure to the end of time. Yet the fact remains that, for Barth, Israel's continued existence is a mystery, an enigmatic testimony to God's unfathomable fidelity to human creation in the face of abysmal blindness and unbelief.

The Christological Collapse of Covenant History

Much of the vigor and plausibility of Barth's response to Schleiermacher turns on Barth's discovery of covenant history as the medium of God's work as the Consummator of creation. Barth uses covenant history to reassert the freedom and graciousness of the living God and to block the naturalization of grace. Likewise, Barth uses the category of covenant history to rejoin christology with the Scriptures of Israel and to reaffirm the particularity and concreteness of God's consummating work. Ultimately, however, Barth subordinates his unprecedented vision of covenant history to a christocentric account of Christian doctrine that stands in direct continuity with Schleiermacher and, through Schleiermacher, with the standard canonical narrative in its classical form. One result of this, as we have seen, is Barth's reproduction of the traditional logic of economic supersessionism. But another result is that Barth fails to give convincing shape and content to covenant history itself as the medium of God's consummating work for creation. Barth's embrace of Schleiermacher's christocentric version of the standard model leads him to depict covenant history as a drama that is ultimately played out between humankind and the one particular person Jesus Christ. Every "chapter" of the Christian story is referred again and again to some dimension of humanity's relation to this person. The result is that Jesus Christ alone becomes the locus of particularity, concreteness, and historicity in Barth's vision of the

Christian story. The interface between covenant history and humanity in its concrete historical location is constantly proclaimed but little exhibited. Covenant history becomes a reality that exists extrinsically to human history in Jesus Christ alone. In the end, covenant history seems to collapse and disappear into the figure of Jesus Christ.

There is a final irony that clings to the christological collapse of covenant history in Barth's theology. By insisting upon Jesus Christ as the climax and completion of God's covenant history with Israel in particular and with humankind in general, Barth brings the latent historical gnosticism of Christian doctrine to its purest possible expression. As we have seen, Barth holds that covenant history in the strict sense comes to an end with the crucifixion and resurrection of Jesus Christ. Thereafter the church quite literally has history at its back. For the Christian, history is over! Only time—a curiously metaphysical category—remains. No wonder Barth can only look upon the stubborn historicality of the Jewish people as an extraordinary riddle.

RAHNER ON CONSUMMATION
Nature, Grace, and the Supernatural Existential

Karl Rahner is remembered even more than Karl Barth for his contribution to the theology of consummation, a contribution rightly associated with his concept of the supernatural existential.[7] Like Barth's account of consummation as covenant, Rahner's supernatural existential is intended to vindicate the gratuity, contingency, and particularity of God's work as Consummator. But whereas Barth attempts to do so by concentrating God's work as Consummator in the single human figure of Jesus Christ, Rahner draws the moment of gratuity, contingency, and particularity into the immanent structure of human religious identity. By so doing, he, like Barth, intends to articulate "covenant history" as the medium of God's work as the Consummator of creation. Yet whether Rahner's vision of covenant history is ultimately any less prone to collapse is, as we shall see, an open question.

The general shape of Rahner's theology of consummation resembles Barth's at many points. Rahner holds that consummation consists in God's self-bestowal to the creature and that God creates the human creature for the sake of this self-bestowal from the very first. As God's *self*-bestowal, consummation is a gift that infinitely surpasses the good that is congruent with the creature's natural spiritual dynamism. Human nature does not possess an intrinsic capacity for consummation but must receive this capacity as a gift from "outside." Finally, Rahner holds that because grace is the greater reality for the sake of which nature exists, a proper theological understanding of nature is possible only on the basis of a prior understanding of grace. On all of these points, Rahner and Barth stand in firm agreement.

Where Rahner differs is in his sensitivity to a concern almost wholly alien to Barth's theological sensibility. In effect, Rahner is troubled by the very feature of God's consummating work that Barth celebrates, namely, its concentration in a particular reality extrinsic to the creature.[8] For Rahner, such an understanding of consummation is not so much wrong as one-sided and incomplete. It fails to show how the human creature can receive God's consummating grace as something that corresponds to his or her own immanent spiritual dynamism. If the human creature possesses no intrinsic dynamism toward consummation, then is there not the danger that the human creature will simply be indifferent to the offer of divine grace? Similarly, will not the grace of consummation itself appear as insuperably alien, embodied in a hodgepodge of disparate facts perhaps, but with no real power to engage and transform the creature's innermost identity?[9] Against all of this, Rahner counters with the following premise. It simply must be the case—and our experience confirms that it is so—that the human creature possesses a positive orientation toward God's consummating grace that is more than a mere nonrepugnance to grace. Put another way, personal intimacy with God is a goal that is not foreign or extraneous to the human condition but rather is congruent with the human creature's innermost identity and the deepest longings of the human heart.

The trouble, of course, is how to make this last conviction cohere with the initial set of convictions sketched above. For the first position stipulates that human nature *cannot include* an active dynamism toward consummation, and in this way guards the gratuity of God's consummating grace. But the second position stipulates that the human condition *must include* an active potency for consummation, or else God's consummating grace becomes merely extrinsic. How then can one do justice to both concerns? How can one reconcile the absolute gratuity of God's consummating grace with the creature's active dynamism toward personal union with God?

Rahner's answer is both original and extraordinarily simple. Might it not be the case, he asks, that humanity possesses an active potency for consummation, but that this potency belongs to the human condition not by nature but by grace? In that case the two positions could be reconciled. The human *condition* would include an active dynamism toward consummation, but human *nature* would not. Humanity's orientation toward consummation would be a gratuitous, contingent, and in this sense "historical" gift to humanity above and beyond its created nature grounded in God's consummating will for creation.[10]

In developing this original insight, Rahner freely draws upon concepts and patterns of argument found in Thomas Aquinas and Martin Heidegger. From Thomas, Rahner borrows the realistic axiom of the ontological creativity of divine love.[11] According to Thomas, both God's work as Creator and God's work as Consummator are ontologically creative. God's love as Creator finds outward embodiment in the being of creation, while God's love as Consummator finds outward embodiment in the gift of created grace, a supernatural quality that inheres in and transforms the natural being of the human creature. Rahner simply applies Thomas' axiom to a "middle case" that arises "between" the advent of God's love as Creator and the advent of God's love as Consummator. This middle case consists in the divine *intention* to consummate creation. For Rahner, this intention can also be presumed to be ontologically creative, leaving the world other than it would have been had God not chosen to consummate creation. In this middle case, the "ontological echo" of God's love is the creature's active potency for consummation. From Heidegger, Rahner borrows the concept of the existential.[12] For Heidegger, existentiality refers to the total fabric of those underlying structures or determinations of human being that permanently shape the distinctively human experience of existence.[13] An existential refers to any one of these permanent, underlying structures, such as "being-unto-death."

Drawing on these two families of concepts, Rahner proposes the idea of a supernatural and yet permanent and underlying structure of existence whose content is a "being-unto-consummation." This Rahner calls the supernatural existential. Being-unto-consummation is supernatural because it is not part and parcel of humanity's created nature but rather is the contingent gift of God's free and unexacted desire to consummate creation. Yet being-unto-consummation is an existential because it is part of the permanent, underlying structure of human existence that sets the stage for every possible act of human freedom. As Rahner summarizes the concept:

> If one understands by 'existential' an enduring, continuing condition of a finite spiritual person, that which enables and is the ontological predetermination of personal behavior (that which, therefore, is involved in the free acts of a person), then I think one can signify well what is meant here by 'supernatural existential.' This existential is supernatural not only because it directs men toward the supernatural goal, but also because it is unowed. It is existential because it does not . . . stem from the free act of the person, but rather is its presupposition.[14]

Rahner's supernatural existential, we must immediately note, revises a central premise of traditional theology in an important way. Theologians who have interpreted the Bible in light of the standard model have generally assumed that humankind figures in the Bible's overarching narrative chiefly by virtue of its status as a creature endowed with a certain specific rational or spiritual nature. The human creature as the possessor of such a nature is thus the immediate agent or subject of the Christian story: God's consummating grace engages human nature as such, the fall distorts human nature as such, etc. Had Rahner simply accepted the standard model on this score, he would never have been able to solve the dilemma that concerned him. For by the terms of the standard model, either humanity's specific nature possesses a dynamism toward consummation or it does not. A third alternative does not exist.

Rahner, however, dissolves the dilemma precisely by rejecting the tacit assumption that humankind figures in the biblical story chiefly as the possessor of rational nature. According to Rahner, nothing in Christian theology or human experience forces us to make this assumption. To the contrary. Bearing in mind the axiom of the ontological creativity of God's love, one is justified in viewing the Christian drama as one that unfolds between God and a humanity that possesses—in addition to its specific nature—a purely contingent and gratuitous dimension of religious identity rooted in creation's supernatural vocation to personal intimacy with God. Within this imaginative framework, Rahner is able to reconcile the two propositions that the standard model depicts as mutually exclusive.

Curiously, Rahner's supernatural existential modifies traditional understandings of God's work as Consummator in a manner that shares a certain formal similarity with Barth's thought. Like Barth, Rahner insists that God's work as Consummator is inconceivable apart from an essential reference to certain historically contingent features of the human condition. Nevertheless, the two conceptions differ in significant ways. Barth's idea of covenant identity has the status of a christological declaration outside ourselves. Its priority to human freedom is analogous to the way in which an accomplished deed is prior to its acknowledgment. In contrast, Rahner's supernatural existential determines human identity from within. Its priority to human freedom comes from "behind" or "below." Furthermore, the supernatural existential secures covenant identity not in the form of an incontrovertible declaration but in the form of an ever-present offer, promise, or invitation that is configured into the innermost secret of human identity. For Rahner, covenant identity is a mystery posed in the depths of the human heart, a mystery that can be unraveled only through an outward journey of discovery and assent in the medium of public history.

A striking feature of Rahner's supernatural existential is its frontal contradiction of a common assumption about human identity: who we really are is determined by that which is most natural to us, most deeply ingredient in our own natural being. Rahner insists to the contrary that human identity is constituted at the innermost level by a moment of gracious contingency:

> The nature of the spiritual creature consists in the fact that that which is "innermost" to it, that whence, to which and through which it is, is precisely *not* an element of this essence and this nature which belongs to it. Rather its nature is based upon the fact that that which is supra-essential, that which transcends it, is that which gives it its support, its meaning, its future and its most basic impulse.[15]

What is most important and central about the human creature, its being-unto-consummation, is present not as a part of its nature but as a contingent determination of its identity. Accordingly, the attempt to live a "purely natural" existence amounts to a sinful rejection of God's self-offer and of one's own innermost identity. "When indeed one seeks to realize the 'purely natural' in the concrete order in a way that is merely 'pure,'" says Rahner, "what results is not the purely natural, but rather the *guilty* natural that closes itself to grace to its own damnation."[16] The supernatural existential makes a purely natural existence impossible for the human creature. A person who accepts his or her vocation to consummation may initially ascribe this vocation to his or her natural being. But that person will ultimately come to a moment of self-discovery in which he or she perceives that the orientation toward consummation was itself an unowed gift of God, above and beyond the good of created nature.[17]

Rahner ascribes a similarly "supernatural" journey of discovery and assent to human history as a whole. Human history is never at any point driven forward solely by the intrinsic dynamism of human nature. Rather it is always and everywhere informed "from below" by human creation's supernatural orientation toward consummation:

> Notwithstanding its supernaturality and unmeritedness, [God's universal salvific will] can certainly be seen as a permanent existential of man, of mankind and its history, always and everywhere present, as permanently present possibility of a salvific relationship of freedom to God, as innermost entelechy of this history of the individual and of mankind as a whole, in which the unmerited gracious self-communication of God to the world is the ultimate finality and dynamism of the world and world history, whether the human freedom of any particular individual accepts this innermost entelechy or closes itself up against it.[18]

In Rahner's view, God's gracious self-offer to humanity determines not only the inward dynamism of the individual's history but also the inward dynamism of human history as a whole. Accordingly, the individual's hope for the future is embedded in and inseparable from God's work as the Consummator of world history in its entirety.

The Shape of the Christian Story

Given the importance Rahner accords the supernatural existential, one might reasonably expect it to shape Rahner's conception of the Christian story in decisive ways. And, in a certain sense, it does. Rahner gives a distinctive shape to the Christian story by insisting that each episode presupposes the presence of the supernatural existential. In this way, he tries to give content to his conviction that God's grace engages the human creature as a specifically historical being, that is, as one whose innermost identity has been contingently shaped by the ontological creativity of God's free decision to consummate creation. God's grace engages the creature as one who is always already *more than* and *other than* the mere possessor of rational nature.

Yet the supernatural existential notwithstanding, in a real sense Rahner simply recapitulates Schleiermacher's christocentric version of the standard model with only the most formal modifications.[19] To be sure, Rahner, as a faithful interpreter of the Roman Catholic tradition, vindicates a host of dogmatic claims that Schleiermacher felt free to reject, such as the historicity of the state of original righteousness, the virgin birth. In many of these areas Rahner made independent contributions of great creativity and power. All in all, however, Rahner's overarching conception of the Christian story follows closely on Schleiermacher's simplified version of the standard model. Like Schleiermacher, Rahner organizes the Christian story in terms of humankind's universal capacity for consummation, a capacity realized for the first time in Jesus Christ. Consequently the supernatural existential exercises little if any critical leverage against the standard model's structural supersessionism, that is, its privileging of the creaturely-universal foreground and its marginalization of the Israelite dimension of Christian faith. What is more, the supernatural existential itself comes to occupy a mainly formal place in Rahner's system, largely devoid of material contact with the biblical texts or public history.

According to Rahner, God created the first parents with a dynamic orientation toward personal union with God as mediated through the incarnation of the eternal Son, Jesus Christ. Rahner distinguishes two aspects of this dynamic orientation. First, God created the progenitors of the human race in an actual state of grace, a state that, however, could be lost through sin. Here Rahner adheres to traditional scholastic teaching. Second, God created the first parents with an inward orientation toward the goal of personal union with God.[20] Unlike the state of grace, this orientation belongs to the permanent and universal structure of human existence and therefore cannot be forfeited through sin. This second point allows Rahner, like Schleiermacher, to organize the Christian story around the central axis of humankind's creaturely-universal potency for consummation. At the same time, Rahner avoids Schleiermacher's dangerous naturalization of grace by insisting that humankind's orientation to consummation is a gift not of nature but of grace. The orientation is, in short, a supernatural existential.

Turning to the fall, Rahner holds that the disobedience of the first parents resulted in the loss of sanctifying grace but not in the loss of humanity's fundamental orientation toward consummation. Once again, the first insight follows traditional scholastic theology while the second represents Rahner's special contribution. While sin culpably disrupts humankind's actual fellowship with God, it cannot destroy humanity's fundamental orientation toward consummation with God in Christ.[21] This is true not because this orientation belongs to human nature, as Schleiermacher simply assumed, but rather because it is an unexacted but irrevocable gift of God. A child of Adam can say no to God but cannot undo its identity as one whose specific nature has always already been transformed by the contingent offer of God's consummating grace.[22]

For Rahner, Jesus Christ's centrality to human history is not contingent on sin but instead reflects God's original consummating intention for human creation. Jesus Christ embodies God's consummating self-offer to humankind both "from above" and "from below." From above, because Jesus Christ is God's own eternal Word bodied forth in finite human nature. From below, because Jesus Christ is that particular human being who not only receives God's self-offer in the form of the supernatural existential but also sinlessly accepts God's self-offer throughout the totality of his life, even unto the acceptance of death. By personally uniting God's self-offer to humanity both from above and from below, Jesus Christ ensures the ultimate victory of God's consummating work.

If the incarnation is the center point of God's original desire to consummate human creation, the cross is the place where this plan is irrevocably established and confirmed in the face of human sin. Because of sin, God's self-offer in Christ takes the form of an act of forgiving and redeeming love. Yet in contrast to Barth, Rahner does not claim that Jesus Christ marks the conclusion of covenant history, after which only time remains. Rather, Rahner presents the incarnation, cross, and resurrection as the decisive turning point in God's supernatural history with creation, but not as the completion of that history itself:

> In the incarnation and cross God has decided the history of the world as a whole—history which—without detriment to human freedom—in favor of a world and nature which is to be saved, transfigured, and made blessed through victorious grace. The drama of world history is no longer simply open in equal measure to salvation *and* damnation, but is at bottom already decided, and indeed, to salvation.[23]

In Jesus Christ, God's self-offer to humanity and humanity's acceptance of God's self-offer reaches an unsurpassable high point. The incarnation ensures the "irreversibility" of God's history with humankind as a history of grace. Because of this event, it is now certain that the history of God's self-offer to creation will reach its culmination in the final consummation of humankind.

Unlike Barth, Rahner apparently discerns no connection whatsoever between his attempt to rethink the Christian story as covenant history and the testimony of the Hebrew Scriptures to God's history with Israel and the nations. Taken all in all, Rahner's theology is a remarkably pure instance of the kind of theology that is so exclusively concerned with the standard model's creaturely-universal foreground that it omits the Israelite dimension of Christian faith altogether. When from time to time Rahner does acknowledge the Hebrew Scriptures and Israel's history as internal aspects of Christian faith, he does so in formulas that encapsulate the logic of economic supersessionism. So Rahner writes, "The 1500 years of the real history of the Old Testament covenant with Moses and the prophets, with all their differences and all their dramatic changes, are still only a brief moment in the history of preparation for Christ."[24] Or again: "The whole biblical age from Abraham to Christ shrinks into the brief moment of the inauguration of the event of Christ. Moreover, insofar as we are Christians we have the right and the obligation to see it . . . as the final moment before the event of Christ and as forming a unity along with this event."[25] Or Rahner can say simply that God's dealings with the Jewish people constitute the "immediate historical prelude" to the incarnation.[26] More commonly, however, Rahner simply omits any reference to the Scriptures of Israel and to God's history with the Jewish people. For all practical purposes, Rahner's dogmatic interest is focused exclusively on the creaturely-universal foreground of creation, fall, redemption, and consummation.

The previous sketch barely hints at the unusual richness of Rahner's theology. But it should be sufficient to indicate how Rahner incorporates the supernatural existential into his larger vision of the Christian story. Clearly, Rahner structures his theology around the standard model's creaturely-universal foreground, that is, the story of creation-for-consummation, fall, redemption in Christ, and final consummation. Like Schleiermacher, Rahner organizes this story in Scotist fashion around humankind's active potency for consummation, a potency decisively realized in Christ. The supernatural existential permits Rahner to conceive this potency in a way that formally preserves divine freedom and that prevents the naturalization of grace. Capacity for consummation is a gift not of nature but of grace! At the end of the day, however, Rahner's crucial insight remains surprisingly formal in nature, with few implications for the ultimate shape of the Christian story.

The Anthropological Collapse of Covenant History

Rahner's vision of the Christian story, like Barth's, can be viewed as an extraordinarily creative attempt to recast Schleiermacher's version of Christian doctrine into the "higher key" of covenant history. Yet granting this, there can be little doubt that in the end Rahner's theology reproduces the narrative logic of Schleiermacher's theology with only relatively formal modifications. Like Schleiermacher, Rahner structures the Christian story around the idea of Christ as the person in whom a universal human potency is realized. The difference is simply that Schleiermacher ascribes this potency to nature, while Rahner ascribes it to grace. In both cases, what results is a view of the Christian story that lopsidedly emphasizes the standard model's foreground at the expense of the Israelite dimension of Christian faith.

So what becomes of covenant history? What becomes of the supernatural yet historical medium of God's intercourse with humankind? The fact is that for all practical purposes, it collapses and disappears. In this respect, too, Rahner's theology forms a curious parallel to that of Karl Barth. But whereas Barth's analysis of covenant history disappears into the particular figure of Jesus Christ, Rahner's analysis disappears into the universal dynamism of the human creature. Although Rahner distinguishes the supernatural existential from humankind's natural being, Rahner's distinction has a largely formal quality that remains devoid of material content. The supernatural existential is, as it were, a stipulated theological concept whose purchase in the realm of public history and biblical testimony is precariously thin.

A further irony is how astonishingly little public or biblical history actually penetrates Rahner's theology, despite the extraordinary earnestness with which the centrality of history is discussed. The whole theology seems remarkably immune from the accidents of history, even such catastrophic accidents as the Holocaust. One student of Rahner's who makes the connection between the absence of history in Rahner's theology and the absence of Jews is Johann-Baptist Metz:

> I had the good fortune to learn that Catholic theology which in my eyes was the best of that time. . . . I mean the theology taught by Karl Rahner. To be sure, gradually, much too gradually, it dawned on me that even in this theology Auschwitz was not mentioned. Thus, in confrontation with this catastrophe, I began to ask critical questions and to look for additional viewpoints of theological identity. Were we still caught in a kind of historical idealism? . . . . This was perhaps the reason why (especially immediately after the war) we talked so much about the 'historicity' of faith and theology in order to cover up the real contradictions of historical experience through this formalism . . . . Didn't we know, ahead of any Christian practice, too much about the sense of history, which makes every catastrophe merely appear like the echo of a departing thunderstorm? It seems that we did not know that for the understanding of our own history and our own promises we had to depend on a non-Christian partner, on our victims, in short on the Jews of Auschwitz.[27]

COVENANT HISTORY AT AN IMPASSE

If one had to identify just one rock-ribbed conviction that motivated Karl Barth's and Karl Rahner's rebellion against Schleiermacher in favor of covenant history, it might be the belief that Schleiermacher's God was ultimately incapable of doing "a new thing" and hence was ultimately more akin to the God of the philosophers than to the living God of Israel. Yet if this conviction is central, others also played a role. Barth's desire was to reorient theology on God's revelation in Christ as attested by the totality of the biblical witness, as well as to renew the Reformation's understanding of the *ec-centric* structure of Christian life. Rahner's desire was to show how humankind is predisposed for God's consummating grace not only as a natural being but quite specifically as an historical one.

For our purposes, the noteworthy fact is that in the process of giving coherent shape to these disparate concerns, Barth and Rahner do not merely transcend Schleiermacher's reductionistic understanding of consummation. They also transcend and in some measure counteract certain faults inherent in the structural logic of the standard model. Barth does so when he seeks to make the Israelite dimension of Christian faith decisive for shaping conclusions about God's consummating purpose for creation. This decision comes to its high point in the affirmation that God's all-embracing work as Consummator engages creation in and through God's particular election of the people Israel. Taken with utmost seriousness, this linkage would block the standard model's tendency to subordinate God's election of Israel to a more basic drama. God's history with Israel simply *is* the form of God's consummating work! There is no story more basic than this! In a curiously parallel way, Rahner also parts with the ancient logic of the standard model by suggesting that our permanent disposition for consummation encompasses not only our natural being but also an absolutely contingent moment of historical identity. Taken seriously, this idea strives against the traditional logic of the standard model insofar as it prohibits an end-run around history, which would appeal to a more basic drama that unfolds between God and human creaturehood as such.

Ultimately, however, neither Barth nor Rahner arrives at genuinely new models for Christian theology. The reason, quite simply, is that both theologians assimilate the category of covenant history to Schleiermacher's christocentric version of the standard model. As heirs of Schleiermacher (and, through him, of the whole history of the standard model), Barth and Rahner link God's consummating purpose from the very outset to the person of Jesus Christ. For them, Jesus Christ is the person in and through whom God's original consummating purpose for humankind is mediated to creation. As a consequence, both men are forced to make covenant history a function of the particular relationship that exists between the God-man Jesus Christ and human creation as a whole. Unfortunately, the result is that covenant history as the medium of God's consummating work tends to collapse into one of the two poles of Schleiermacher's original christocentric paradigm. In Barth's case, covenant history collapses back into the particular figure of Jesus Christ. In Rahner, it collapses into the dynamism of the human creature. In both cases, covenant history disappears as an identifiable feature of the common world. The irony of this collapse is that both theologians remain bound to Schleiermacher at precisely the point where one might have expected them to transcend him. Despite Barth's recovery of Israel for Christian faith, he recapitulates Schleiermacher's supersessionism. And despite Rahner's discovery of the historicity of God's consummating work, he absorbs the detail of the biblical story and public history into the dynamism of the human creature.

Could Barth and Rahner have avoided the collapse of covenant history? Perhaps. They might have done so by exploring the possibility that God's work as Consummator engages creation in the total, open-ended, and still ongoing history that unfolds between the Lord, Israel, and the nations. Such a view would have been no less grounded in the particularity of the biblical story than Barth's view. It would have been no less universal and grounded in the contingency of human existence than Rahner's. But to have pursued such a possibility, Barth and Rahner would have had to break radically with the ancient logic of supersessionism. This they saw no compelling reason to do.

PART TWO

THE UNITY OF THE CANON
AFTER CHRISTENDOM

5

THE BLESSING OF AN OTHER
A PROPOSAL

Part One examined the logic and limitations of the church's standard canonical narrative. The standard model provides a narrative construal of the Christian Bible that gives powerful expression to the church's central confession: the God of Hebrew Scriptures acted in Jesus of Nazareth for all the world. Nevertheless, we have seen that the standard model does this in a manner that is profoundly supersessionist in both doctrinal and structural ways. Doctrinally, the model depicts carnal Israel's role in the economy of redemption as essentially transient by virtue of the spiritualizing and universalizing impetus of God's salvific will. Structurally, the model renders God's identity as the God of Israel largely indecisive for shaping theological conclusions about how God's works as Consummator and as Redeemer engage creation in universal and enduring ways. The result is an interpretive framework for reading the Christian canon that is both triumphalist toward Jews and latently gnostic in its approach toward history.

Now in Part Two I want to propose an alternative way of conceiving the narrative unity of the Christian Bible, a way that I believe overcomes the doctrinal and structural supersessionism of the standard model while continuing to construe the canon as a coherent witness to the church's basic confession. The proposal seeks not to break haphazardly with the standard model but rather to carry through more consistently the implications of the Christian confession of the God of Israel.

Systematically considered, the standard model embodies an incomplete conversion toward the God of Israel because it embodies an incomplete repudiation of gnosticism. The standard model rejects gnosticism at the level of ontology but not at the level of covenant history. Gnosticism drives an *ontological* wedge between the gospel and the God of Israel *by collapsing creation into the fall.* Gnosticism thereby nullifies the intrinsic goodness of creation and misinterprets redemption in Christ as deliverance from the created order. The standard model drives an *historical* wedge between the gospel and the God of Israel *by collapsing God's covenant with Israel into the economy of redemption in its prefigurative form.* The standard model thereby fatally undercuts the theological significance of God's way with Israel and misinterprets redemption in Christ as deliverance from God's history with Israel and the nations.

Christians can better confess their faith in the God of Israel by giving more consistent expression to the anti-gnostic impulse that the standard model only incompletely embodies. Just as the standard model repudiates Gnosticism at the ontological level by affirming the integrity of creation antecedent to sin and evil, so Christians can overcome the standard model's latent historical gnosticism by affirming that God's way with Israel possesses a theological integrity and significance antecedent to the economy of redemption in its prefigurative form. This entails, as Karl Barth correctly saw, locating God's election of Israel in the context of God's work as Consummator, for it is precisely God's work as Consummator that provides a context of divine purpose antecedent to the crisis of sin and evil. But this move alone is not sufficient to overcome the logic of supersessionism, as Barth's own theology ultimately demonstrates. In addition, Christians should acknowledge that God's election of Israel possesses a significance within God's work as Consummator that is not merely preparatory and prefigurative in nature. In short (and this is my proposal in the briefest possible compass), Christians should acknowledge that God's history with Israel and the nations is the permanent and enduring medium of God's work as the Consummator of human creation, and therefore it is also the permanent and enduring context of the gospel about Jesus. Unpacking the implications of this proposal for a Christian reading of the Bible is the task of the next three chapters.

One way of approaching the present proposal is to consider the possible Christian significance of an *economy of consummation.* In principle, the idea of a divine economy (meaning God's providential management of and care for the households of creation) seems equally applicable both to God's work as Consummator and to God's work as Redeemer. In practice, however, Christians have commonly limited the notion of a divine economy to God's work as Redeemer and specifically to the work by which God redeems creation in Christ and the Holy Spirit from the threat of sin, evil, oppression, and death. In this sense, Christians can be said to have submitted the concept of divine economy to a consistent soteriological reduction. By largely restricting the concept of divine economy to God's work as Redeemer, Christians have tended to imply that God's work as Consummator is in itself devoid of economy, that is, of God's care and providential management of the households of creation. Conversely, they have implied that God's "economic" engagement with the households of creation is contingent upon the catastrophe of sin. The concept of an economy of consummation directly challenges both of these latent assumptions. It affirms that God's work as Consummator is itself intrinsically economic, that is, God consummates human creation in and through God's providential management of and care for the households of creation. And it implies that God's work as Consummator economizes the human condition in a manner logically antecedent to the crisis of sin and therefore logically antecedent to the economy of redemption itself.

In chapter 6, I sketch a Christian reading of the Scriptures of Israel focused on God's overarching work as the Consummator of creation. God's work as Consummator, I argue, is essentially economic in nature; it is characterized by God's providential management of and care for the households of creation. In particular, God's work as Consummator economizes or distributes the one human family into relationships of mutual blessing, relationships that entail difference and reciprocal dependence within and between the households of creation. As attested by the Scriptures, God's work as Consummator engages the human family in a historically decisive way in God's election of Israel as a blessing to the nations. The resulting distinction and mutual dependence of Israel and the nations is the fundamental form of the economy of consummation through which God initiates, sustains, and ultimately fulfills the one human family's destiny for life with God. So conceived, God's economy of consummation is essentially constituted as *an economy of mutual blessing* between those who are and who remain different.

Thus interpreted, God's work as Consummator is inseparable from the open-ended history that unfolds between the God of

Israel, Israel, and the nations. This history is not a more or less unfortunate consequence of sin, nor is it a merely prefigurative economy that prepares the way for something much higher and grander. Rather, God's history with Israel and the nations is the enduring form of God's gracious work as Consummator, apart from which the realization of the final end of human life is inconceivable. On this view, God's primordial work as Creator is oriented from the outset toward God's history with Israel and the nations, just as God's history with Israel and the nations is oriented at every point toward God's eschatological reign of *shalom*, where God's work as Consummator will finally be fulfilled.

Chapter 7 continues the discussion of the Scriptures of Israel by turning from God's work as Consummator to God's work as Redeemer. The occasion of God's work as Redeemer is the fact that the economy of consummation is vulnerable to devastating injury whenever the human family proves unready to accept the blessing of an other. Sin, evil, and oppression (and the corresponding need for redemption and liberation) are undeniable dimensions of God's history with Israel and the nations as it actually unfolds. Still, the antithesis of sin and redemption is not the central theme of the Hebrew Scriptures, nor is it an object of concern in its own right. Rather, liberation from powers that destroy is a matter of utmost urgency precisely because such powers threaten to cut humankind off from God's economy of consummation, where God's blessings are bestowed. In this sense, God's work as Redeemer confirms rather than supplants the centrality of God's work as Consummator in a Christian reading of the Scriptures.

Turning to the Apostolic Witness in chapter 8, I examine the gospel as good news about the God of Israel's coming reign. The gospel proclaims Jesus' life, death, and resurrection as the proleptic enactment of God's eschatological fidelity to the work of consummation, that is, to fullness of mutual blessing as the outcome of God's economy with Israel, the nations, and all creation. Understood in this way, the gospel is by nature "good news about the kingdom of God and the name of Jesus Christ" (Acts 8:12). In Jesus, an answer is given in the present to the question of whether God's work as Consummator will prove ultimately victorious on behalf of all creation over all the powers that destroy. The gospel summons all who receive it to enact their trust in the ultimate victory of blessing over curse by conforming themselves in the present to the way of

Jesus' cross. Through cruciform discipleship, followers of Jesus manifest their faith in the ultimate victory of the God of Israel.

The present account of the Bible's narrative unity entails an important revision of how Christians understand the hermeneutical center of the Christian canon. Traditionally, Christians have assumed that the hermeneutical complexity of the Christian canon is sufficiently addressed by positing Jesus Christ as the ultimate unifying center of both parts of the Christian canon. The present account, in contrast, suggests that the Christian canon possesses an irreducibly double focus. The hermeneutical center of the Scriptures is the God of Israel's eschatological reign, conceived as the final outcome of God's work as the One who consummates the human family in and through God's history with Israel and the nations. The hermeneutical center of the Apostolic Witness is "good news about the kingdom of God and the name of Jesus Christ" (Acts 8:12). These twin *foci* of the Christian canon are related like two concentric circles. The eschatological reign of the God of Israel provides the indispensable hermeneutical context for the center of Christian faith, namely, the gospel about God's kingdom and the name of Jesus Christ.

6

THE SCRIPTURES
THE ECONOMY OF CONSUMMATION

The Scriptures are concerned throughout with the character, purposes, and actions of the Lord.[1] The Scriptures portray the Lord with reference to two chief objects of divine concern: God's creation, which forms the central theme of Genesis 1–11 and which thereafter remains the constant presupposition of the biblical story; and God's covenant with the people Israel in the midst of the nations, a theme introduced in Genesis 12 and sustained throughout the rest of the Bible. Despite all provisional twists and turns, the Scriptures portray the Lord as one who maintains "steadfast love and faithfulness" (Gen 24:27; Exod 34:6; Ps 36:5), both to creation and to Israel and its role among the nations.

If this is so, then an important question arises: what is the relationship between God's work as Creator and God's covenant with the people Israel? Put another way, what is the narrative logic that joins Genesis 1–11 to Genesis 12 and beyond? If it is true, as Jews and Christians have commonly affirmed, that the Lord's purposes are coherent, or, in the words of David, "ordered in all things and secure" (2 Sam 23:5), then this question cannot really be avoided.

One familiar answer to this question is summarized in the following passage:

> The story of creation, fall and primordial history sets the stage for the national history by dramatizing the fundamental conflict between the Creator and his human creatures; the call of Abraham, which promises him that he will be a blessing to the nations, is the beginning of the resolution of the conflict.[2]

In this view, the Bible's narrative unity consists in the history of God's mighty acts of redemption or, in more classical terms, in the economy of redemption. God's original purpose for creation is disrupted by an event known as the fall, which introduces fundamental conflict between Creator and creation. Thereafter the central theme of the Bible is God's work as one who redeems, delivers, and rescues the threatened and sinful creature. The turning point in the economy of redemption is God's calling of Abraham. God's history with Israel moves toward the restoration of God's original purpose for creation, which was interrupted by the fall. Israel is the instrument by means of which God heals the fundamental conflict between God and creation.

However, another, quite different point of view is also possible. This second view does not deny that the movement from Genesis 1–11 to Genesis 12 and following concerns the antithesis of sin and redemption *as a secondary matter*. It sees this antithesis, however, within a more basic narrative context, namely, the unfolding of God's work as the Consummator of human creation. In contrast to God's work as Redeemer, God's work as Consummator concerns not God's power to deliver the creature from sin, evil, and oppression, but rather the ultimate good that God intends for human creation antecedent and subsequent to the calamity of sin. As represented in the Scriptures, God's work as Consummator revolves around God's blessing and its power to communicate life, wholeness, well-being, and joy to that which is other than God. Genesis 1–11 depict how God prepares for the work of consummation by bestowing and sustaining God's blessing in the sphere of the natural world (Gen 1:22, 28; 5:2; 9:1). Genesis 12 and beyond tell how God initiates the work of consummation proper by promising to bless Abraham and "in him" all of the nations of the earth (Gen 12:1–3; 18:18). While judgment and deliverance become part of God's history with creation as it actually unfolds, they presuppose rather than supplant the Scriptures' central narrative vector, which is God's work as the Consummator of creation.

Construed in this way, the canon's overarching plot revolves chiefly not around an "economy of redemption" contingent on sin but rather around an antecedent economy of consummation based on the Lord's blessing. Through the economy of consummation, the Lord blesses the human family and brings it to fullness of life through the providential care and management of the households of creation. While this reading departs from many traditional Christian accounts of the Scriptures' unity, it is consonant with Bonhoeffer's observation from prison, "Unlike the other oriental religions, the faith of the Old Testament is not a religion of redemption."[3] Moreover, this reading makes allowance for the presence throughout the Scriptures of a theology of God's *blessing* alongside the more familiar theology of redemption.[4] Whereas the theology of redemption is centrally concerned with God's saving intervention through particular events and circumstances, the theology of blessing concerns a divine work that does not "belong to just one time and place, for example, exodus deliverance from enemies and the like. Rather, the blessing which persons seek from God and which he promises to provide belongs to all times and places, to the continuity of life (birth, fertility, health, peace, prosperity, the presence and favor of God, a place to live, means of life, protection, and care)."[5] Bonhoeffer, too, recognized that concern for God's blessing is one of the Hebrew Scriptures' defining themes:

> You think the Bible hasn't much to say about health, fortune, vigor, etc. I've been thinking over that again. It's certainly not true of the Old Testament. The intermediate theological category between God and human fortune is, as far as I can see, that of blessing. In the Old Testament—e.g. among the patriarchs— there's a concern not for fortune, but for God's blessing, which includes in itself all earthly good. In that blessing the whole of the earthly life is claimed for God, and it includes all his promises.[6]

As Bonhoeffer correctly perceived, God's blessing is the crucial category that mediates between God's fullness of life and the fullness of human life on earth.

Significantly, the Scriptures consistently portray the Lord's blessing in inextricable connection with relations of difference and mutual dependence among God's creatures. In the primeval sagas (Gen 1–11), God's blessing is connected with difference and mutual dependence within the natural world. This is evident in the relation of the human family and the rest of the created realm, and then again within the human family itself in the relations of male and female, of parents and children, of one generation and the next. In the sphere of covenant history (Gen 12 and forward) , God's blessing is connected with the difference and mutual dependence of Abraham and Sarah's chosen children and all the other families, clans, and nations of the earth. *God's work as Consummator, it seems, consistently presupposes and entails economies of mutual blessing between those who are different.* The centrality of mutual relation to the biblical view of reality is aptly summarized as follows:

From its very beginning the Bible sees human life in terms of relationships. There is no attempt to strip away the accidents of history in order to find the real essence of what it is to be human. Human life is seen in terms of mutual relationships: first, the most fundamental relation, between man and woman, then between parents and children, then between families and clans and nations. The Bible does not speak about "humanity" but about "all the families of the earth" or "all the nations." *It follows that this mutual relatedness, this dependence of one on another, is not merely part of the journey toward the goal of salvation, but is intrinsic to the goal itself.* For knowing God, for being in communion with him, we are dependent on the one whom he gives us to be the bearer of this relation, not just as a teacher and guide on the way but as the partner in the end.[7]

Difference and mutual dependence are not extrinsic to the supreme good that God appoints for creation but are "intrinsic to the goal itself." The Lord's blessing is available only through through the blessing of an other.

Crucially, when the canon's unity is grasped in light of God's economies of difference and mutual dependence, the distinction between Israel and the nations cannot be viewed as a mere instrument God employs to overcome conflict with creation, an instrument that becomes obsolete once the conflict is decisively resolved. Rather, the distinction of Israel and the nations, of Jew and of Gentile, is intrinsic to God's overarching purpose and work as Consummator of the world. God promises to bless the human family with fullness of life in and through an historical economy of difference and mutual dependence between Israel and the nations. God's work as Consummator will first be completed at the end of history when God's "faithfulness to the house of Israel" (Ps 98:3) redounds in definitive and unsurpassable fashion to the blessing of Israel, the nations, and all of creation (including the generations before Abraham).

BLESSING AND CREATION

The Book of Genesis frames the biblical narrative within two great economies of divine blessing: God's blessing on creation (Gen 1–11) and God's promise to bless Abraham and "in him" all the families of the earth (Gen 12–50). The majestic priestly account of creation (Gen

1–2:3) anticipates both economies of divine blessing and thereby provides a programmatic overture to the Scriptures as a whole.

God pronounces God's blessing three times in Gen 1–2:3. God bestows the first two blessings during the six days of creation. Here God's blessing concerns the fertility, abundance, and well-being of animals and humans in the natural world (Gen 1:22, 28). In contrast, God pronounces the third and final blessing after the six days of creation are over. This blessing concerns God's hallowing of the seventh day (2:3). When the sequence of these blessings is taken into account, it is hard to conclude that the account turns on the declaration that God created humankind "in the image and likeness of God" (1:26). Rather, the passage views the entire six days' work in light of God's Sabbath blessing. God's Sabbath blessing forms the true climax of the passage and simultaneously points forward to God's history with Israel, for it is there that God's Sabbath will first be commanded and observed (Exod 16:23; 20:8–11). The relation of the three blessings anticipates the contents of the canon as a whole: God's blessing as Creator prepares for God's blessing as Consummator. God's blessing as Consummator crowns God's blessing as Creator.

God's six-days' blessing on the human family is summed up in the phrase: "be fruitful and multiply and fill the earth" (Gen 1:22, 28). From the outset, this blessing is bestowed and received through economies of difference and mutual dependence, economies embodied in the distinction of humankind and the natural world, of male and female, of parents and children, of one generation and the next. Both accounts of God's creation of the human family underscore the essential connection between blessing and difference. According to Gen 2:18–25, God saw that it was not good for the man to be alone, and therefore God created a "partner" from the man's side, not merely as his double, but as female, that is, as different (Gen 2:18). The priestly creation account (Gen 1:26–31) underscores the concomitance of blessing and difference even more emphatically by stating that God created humankind (*'adam*) "male and female" from the outset (Gen 1:27; 5:2). As Bruce Birch notes, nothing in this witness suggests anything less than absolute equality of men and women in creation.[8]

In a real sense, the great theme of Genesis 2–11 is genealogy, for it is through genealogy that God's blessing to "be fruitful and multiply" and "to fill the earth" is fulfilled. At the same time, the genealogies signal by their structure the fact that God's intention for the human family is not exhausted by the economy of God's six-days' blessing alone. As Brevard Childs has pointed out, the genealogies of Genesis 1–11 are of two different kinds, vertical and horizontal. The vertical genealogies (5:1ff., 11:10ff.) focus on the chosen line by tracing a direct line of descent from Adam to Abraham. In contrast, a horizontal genealogy (10:1ff.) traces in a more leisurely way all of the various subgroups that stem from Noah's three sons and that populate the earth after the flood. In this way, the genealogies anticipate the future distinction between Israel and the nations.[9] Thus even in Genesis 2–11, the economy of creation is viewed in the light of the coming economy of consummation.

Genesis 10–11 sets the stage for God's election of Israel by introducing a world populated by a great diversity of families, clans, and nations. Far from lamenting the new development, the genealogical tables depict it in a positive light.[10] The diversification of the human family stands in continuity with God's blessing to "fill the earth" (9:1, 7) and reflects a world blessed by God. In contrast, the story of Babel (11:1–9) seems to place the diversity of nations and languages in a negative light. Yet on closer examination, the story depicts the human family's diversification as the outworking of God's blessing "to fill the earth." The builders of Shinar seek to "make a name" for themselves by building a tower. Their motivation is the fear that "otherwise we shall be scattered abroad upon the face of the whole earth" (11:4). But this fear reflects a failure to trust that God's blessing will come through "filling the earth." By confusing their languages and scattering the people "over the face of all the earth," God brings about the end originally foreseen by God's blessing.[11] Like the narrative of God's creation of woman from man's side, the story of Babel portrays the movement from sameness to difference as mandated by the logic of divine blessing.

Certainly, Genesis 1–11 frankly acknowledges the catastrophic power of sin, evil, and oppression and the corresponding need for God's deliverance, a point we will take up in the next chapter. Yet while the theme of sin and deliverance complicates the basic plot established by God's economies of difference and mutual blessing in Genesis 1–11, it does not supplant it. Even in the story of the flood, the high point of God's struggle with wickedness in the creation sagas, the narrative's prime concern remains God's blessing and the economies of created difference it entails. God's dealings with Noah's household and the animals are directed toward the preservation of God's blessing to "be fruitful and multiply" (9:1, 7). This blessing is the true cargo of the ark.

BLESSING AND COVENANT

At the beginning of Genesis 12, God's blessing engages the human family in a new way that proves decisive for the rest of the Scriptures:

> Now the Lord said to Abram, "Go from your country and your kindred and your father's house to the land that I will show you. I will make of you a great nation, and I will bless you, and make your name great, so that you will be a blessing. I will bless those who bless you, and the one who curses you I will curse; and in you all the families of the earth shall be blessed. (Gen 12:1–3)

Contrary to a common Christian assumption, nothing about this passage or its immediate context suggests that God's primary motive in calling Abraham is any special concern with the problem of sin, evil, or wickedness. To the contrary, God's motive seems chiefly to be the sheer fecundity and capaciousness of the divine good pleasure. While God's call of Abraham does indeed interrupt previous cycles of curse, this interruption appears to serve a more basic divine purpose. The same God who freely created the human family and blessed it with increase and growth (Gen 1–11) now graciously promises to bless the world ("all the families of the earth") in a new way that presupposes God's previous activity but cannot be reduced to it.

The best analogy for God's promise to bless Abraham in Gen 12:1–3 is God's hallowing of the seventh day after the work of creation (Gen 2:2–3). Both passages presuppose the presence and operation of God's six-days' blessing in the natural world, while nevertheless announcing the advent of God's blessing in a new and supremely gracious and intimate way. Moreover, both passages relate God's new blessing quite specifically to the temporal order: Gen 2:2–3 with reference to "the seventh day," Gen 12:1–3 with reference to God's "promise." God's promise places the entire history that is about to unfold between the Lord, Israel, and the nations under the programmatic sign of God's covenant blessing.

The Distinction between Israel and the Nations

Curiously, God's promise to bless Abraham, like God's blessing on creation, entails an inescapable moment of difference. On one side stand Abraham, Sarah, and their chosen descendants, on the other "all the families of the earth" (Gen 12:3; 28:14). The resulting distinction between Israel and the nations runs through the rest of the Scriptures like a golden thread.

Of course, the golden thread is also an elastic one. The distinction between Israel and the nations assumes an enormous variety of shapes over the course of the biblical story. Before Abraham's calling, the distinction is present only as anticipated in the contrast of vertical and horizontal genealogies. After Abraham's calling, the distinction undergoes a constant process of formation and reformation. The distinction takes an intimate, familial form in the stories of Abraham and Lot, Sarah and Hagar, Ishmael and Isaac, Isaac and Rebecca, Jacob and Esau. The distinction takes another form altogether in the harrowing stories of the conquest of Canaan. At times the distinction stands at the very center of the biblical narrative, as in God's deliverance of the Israelites from captivity in Egypt or the story of Ruth and Naomi. At other times the distinction recedes into the furthest background, as in the book of Job. Strikingly, the distinction even retains its validity in the context of the end times, as the prophets and psalms frequently suggest. In the meantime, the Scriptures do not shy away from placing the distinction in an ironic light, as in the story of Jonah.

Yet however varied its shape, the distinction between Israel and the nations is an inescapable fact of the biblical narrative. Indeed, Friedrich-Wilhelm Marquardt has suggested that the distinction between Israel and the nations constitutes the basic structure of an ontology in Israelite idiom.[12] In this he is undoubtedly correct. Marquardt's appeal to the term *ontology* is appropriate because the Scriptures view the distinction between Israel and the nations as a part of the abiding constitution of reality in God, anticipated from the beginning and present at the end of all things. At the same time, his observation can be made more precise. Viewed in light of the distinction between Israel and the nations, biblical ontology takes the concrete form of economy, that is, of God's providential care and management of the households of creation. More particularly still, biblical ontology takes the form of an economy of mutual blessing, in which God summons the households of creation to receive God's blessing in the company of an other. Because it belongs to the glory of the biblical God to love the human family in a human way, in the fullness of its corporeality and concreteness, God's economy of mutual blessing exhibits a certain order or taxis, a taxis summarized by a first-century Jew in the phrase, "to the Jew first and also to the Greek" (Rom 1:16).

The God of Israel and the Israel of God

By electing Abraham, Sarah, and their chosen descendants, God inaugurates a new economy of difference and mutual blessing that encompasses the whole future of humankind, an economy to be enacted between God and the households of creation and between the households of creation and one another. The heart of the new economy is the covenant between the God of Israel and the Israel of God. As the famous Aaronic benediction richly indicates, God's covenant blessing on Israel is inseparable from the proximity of God's countenance and God's name:

> The Lord spoke to Moses, saying: Speak to Aaron and his sons,
> saying, Thus you shall bless the Israelites: You shall say to them,
>> The Lord bless you and keep you;
>> the Lord make his face to shine upon you, and be
> gracious to you;
>> the Lord lift up his countenance upon you, and give
> you peace.
>> So they shall put my name on the Israelites, and I will
> bless them. (Num 6:22–27)

The presence of God's name draws Israel into a peace (*shalom*) that is essentially constituted by relations of difference and mutual blessing. The qualitative distinction between God and Israel is inscribed into the *shema*, Israel's central confession of faith: "Hear, O Israel: The Lord is our God, the Lord alone" (Deut 6:4). The Lord alone can bless Israel with life and fullness of life because the Lord is God and "not a human being" (Num 23:19). Through God's blessing, God gives Israel a share in God's own vitality and everlasting life (Ps 133:3). In return, Israel blesses the Lord in the only way it can, with thanksgiving, song, worship, and praise (Neh 9:5; Ps 34:1; etc.). The economy of mutual blessing between the Lord and Israel is encapsulated in the briefest possible compass in Psalm 134:

> Come, bless the Lord, all you servants of the Lord,
>> who stand by night in the house of the Lord!
> Lift up your hands to the holy place,
>> and bless the Lord.
> May the Lord, maker of heaven and earth,
>> bless you from Zion.

Over time, God's economy of mutual blessing with Israel assumes three enduring features: people, Torah, and land. Each of these dimensions of Israel's life is not chiefly or primarily concerned with the dramatic antithesis of evil and deliverance. Rather, each is a concrete way through which God blesses Israel with life and the fullness of life.

People. Of the whole panoply of God's blessings on Israel, none is more basic than Israel's sheer existence as a human family sustained by God from generation to generation. Beginning with Sarah's conception of Isaac in her aged womb, Israel's corporeal existence is not merely the presupposition of God's blessing but, in large part, its very content. Each Israelite newly born into the world receives not only the blessing of creation but also the blessing of covenantal relation to God transmitted from parent to child. That is why Israel's story turns time and again on themes such as the plight of the barren woman, childbirth, genealogy, and national survival.

As Michael Wyschogrod notes, there is something scandalous about a God who elects a carnal family. Yet by choosing to be identified as the God of a particular family, and by promising to sustain and care for it over time, God in fact makes the human condition God's own in a particularly deep and irrevocable way. By electing Israel as a people, God inextricably intertwines God's work as Consummator with God's work as Creator. For better or for worse, God's consummating work must now engage the totality of the human condition, including its most private and its most corporate dimensions. Moreover, God's election of Israel as a family makes it all but impossible for either Israel or the nations to slough off God's supreme engagement with human history.

Torah. God blesses Israel in a second decisive way through God's gift of Torah, properly understood as instruction or guidance and embodied above all in the commandments given by God to Israel through Moses at Mt. Sinai. God's granting the Torah at Mt. Sinai forms the climax of the story of Israel's deliverance from Egypt, and at the same time goes beyond the theme of deliverance from bondage to the more basic and encompassing theme of God's positive blessing on the house of Israel. The Torah is never merely a bulwark against sin. It is much rather a medium of blessing and life, the divinely prescribed form of Israel's existence as a people chosen and blessed by God (Deut 30:16):

> See, I am setting before you today a blessing and a curse: the bless-
> ing, if you obey the commandments of the Lord your God that I
> am commanding you today; and the curse, if you do not obey the
> commandments of the Lord your God, but turn from the way that
> I am commanding you today, to follow other gods that you have
> not known. (Deut 11:26–29)

By walking according to the Torah, Israel says yes to God's election and to the fullness of God's blessing that God has promised. By
turning away from Torah, Israel turns away from God and from
God's blessing and invites God's curse. Torah is never merely a
means to the end of God's blessing. For Israel, life lived according to
God's instruction is itself in large measure the content of the blessed
life (Ps 119).

Land. From the first moment, God's promise to bless Abraham is
tied to "the land that I will show you" (Gen 12:1). Thereafter, as
Walter Brueggemann notes, the Scriptures are to a remarkable
degree "the story of God's people with God's land."[13] Land, alongside posterity and Torah, is an indispensable component of the relationship between the Lord and Israel. God, who holds ultimate title
to the land, promises and then gives it to Israel as an "inheritance"
that Israel may enjoy so long as Israel in turn cares for the land in
accordance with God's requirements of justice. This requires,
among other things, that Israel treat justly the aliens and tenants
within its borders, for the Israelites themselves are "aliens and tenants" before God (Lev 25:23).

There can be no gainsaying the fact that the theme of land makes
Christians uncomfortable and uncertain, especially in view of the
justified concern for the well-being of all the inhabitants of Israel
today, both Jew and Arab. Yet it seems that Christian discomfort
with the land also reflects a predisposition to overlook that dimension of the biblical testimony that is chiefly concerned with God's
blessing in contrast to God's redemption. For God's gift of land is
above all a life-giving embodiment of God's promised blessing on
Israel (Deut 28). As Brueggemann observes, the land is not merely
the neutral staging ground for dramatic acts of deliverance and salvation. Life in the land is an enduring, sustained gift of God, a gift
measured out in brooks and fields and in the continuities of seasons, planting, harvest, and rain. The land is not merely empty
space, to be filled at will by the "autonomous individual," but partic-

ular *place,* rich with the memory and hope of life lived in covenant-
ed fellowship with God, and in peace and justice with household,
neighbor, and stranger.[14] By electing Israel and blessing it "in the
land," God elects Israel together with the whole human family in all
its time-, place-, and season-bound earthiness as the object of God's
consummating work. At the same time, God subjects human history to an economy of mutual blessing that infinitely transcends any
mere natural law alone.

Thus God blesses Israel through the life-giving continuities of
people, Torah, and land. By blessing Israel in this way, God sanctifies
her. God distinguishes her from the other nations and makes her a
"treasured possession," a "priestly kingdom," and a "holy nation"
among all the nations of the earth (Exod 19:5, 6). By blessing God in
return, Israel praises God's name before the nations and calls upon
the nations to sing God's praises as well. From the outset, therefore,
the economy of mutual blessing between God and Israel is ordered
to the inclusion of the other households of creation as well.

The God of Israel and the Nations

The Gentiles stand on the other side of God's schismatic choice.
"Gentiles" are the whole of non-Israelite humanity, both before and
after the calling of Abraham.[15] The Scriptures' approach to non-
Israelite humanity is peculiarly two-sided. On the one hand, the
Scriptures are fully aware that the story of God's interaction with
the human family is not only the story of God's relationship with
Israel. Israel's God is the Creator and Ruler of all creation, including
the totality of non-Israelite humanity. Israel is so intensely aware of
this that it prefaces the story of God's relation to Israel with an
account of God's relation to primordial humanity, long before Israel
had come on the scene. On the other hand, the Scriptures never
treat non-Israelite humanity as though it constituted an independent realm of creation in its own right. The Scriptures view everything, including the totality of non-Israelite humanity both before
and after Abraham, from the perspective of the story that unfolds
between God and the people Israel. The Scriptures concern themselves with non-Israelite humanity precisely in light of God's relation with the people Israel.

In this context, the question is not, "Who are the Gentiles?" but
rather, "Who are the Gentiles in light of God's election of Israel?"
Formulated in this way, the question answers itself. To be a Gentile

is to be the other of Israel and as such an indispensable partner in a single economy of blessing that embraces the whole human family. This does not mean that Israel alone will bless the nations or the nations alone will bless Israel. God is the ultimate source of blessing for both. But God blesses both as the God of Israel, and hence in the context of the history that unfolds on the basis of the distinction between Israel and "all the families of the earth."

Many passages point to the fundamentally positive significance of gentile identity within the single differentiated economy of covenant history. One need only think of Melchizedek, king of Salem and "priest of the God Most High," who at the very outset of Israel's history offers Abraham bread and wine and blesses him (Gen 14:17–20); of Abimelech, the upright king of Gerar, who protects Sarah the matriarch of Israel (Gen 20:1ff.) and who later concludes a covenant of peace with Isaac (Gen 26:26ff.); of Jethro, the Midianite father-in-law of Moses who offers him wise counsel in judging the people (Exod 2:16ff.; 18:1–24); of Balaam, the seer from the Euphrates who blesses Israel against the will of its enemies (Num 22–24); of Rahab the prostitute of Canaan who risks her life for the spies (Josh 2:1–20); of Ruth, the Moabite grandmother of David to whom an entire book is devoted; of Ittai the Gittite, who refuses to abandon David and his small band of loyalists during Absalom's revolt (2 Sam 15:19–23); of Hiram, king of Tyre, who blesses the Lord for Solomon's wisdom and provides all the timber for the temple in Jerusalem (1 Kings 5:1–12); of Naaman, the commander of Aram's army who is healed of leprosy by Elisha and who then confesses the Lord as God of all the earth (2 Kings 5:1–19); of Cyrus, king of Persia and ruler "of all the kingdoms of the earth," who proclaims liberty to the exiles in the Lord's name (2 Chron 36:23; see Isa 45:1–3; Ezra 1:1–3).

From the many possibilities, we select two stories for closer attention: the story of Abraham's circumcision of Ishmael and the story of Jacob's household and the land of Egypt. Both possess emblematic significance for the relation of Israel and the nations.

The story of Abraham's circumcision of Ishmael is extremely instructive in this connection (Gen 16, 17, 21).[16] After many years in the land of Canaan, the aged Abraham and Sarah were still childless. God had not yet provided the child of promise. Desiring an heir of her own (for Abraham's heir at this time was Eliezer of Damascus), Sarah instructed Abraham to sleep with her maid, Hagar. Abraham did so, and Hagar conceived. But immediately Sarah was displeased and, dealing harshly with Hagar, drove the pregnant woman into the wilderness. Yet the Lord refused to let Hagar be separated from the household of promise. Although Hagar's child was not the child of promise, the Lord instructed her to return to the household of promise and to call the child Ishmael, "God has heard." There Hagar bore Abraham a son, and Abraham called him Ishmael.

Hagar's and Ishmael's continued presence in the household of promise, though ultimately temporary, is extremely important. For it provides the basis for the surprising fact that Ishmael is included in the covenant of circumcision, which seals God's covenant with Abraham, Sarah, and their chosen descendants. When Ishmael is a young man, God announces again the everlasting covenant that God will establish with Abraham and his children, and this time commands circumcision as the sign of the covenant (17:9–14). Over Abraham's objection, God insists that his covenant will not be with Ishmael, but with Sarah's son, as yet unborn (17:15–21). Then Abraham seals the covenant, circumcising Ishmael first of all (17:23).

The surprising result is that Ishmael, though "rejected," is explicitly included in the covenant that God establishes with Abraham and Sarah through Isaac, the child of promise. Indeed, Ishmael bears the mark of the covenant first of all, before Isaac is even conceived. As Paul van Buren has written:

> Surely the conclusion to be reached from this strange text . . . is that election is for the sake of God's purpose for all those who are not the elect. Ishmael in particular, standing perhaps for all the nations of the world, although not to be the bearer of the covenant, is intimately and concretely touched by it. Its mark is left also on him.[17]

Later, after the birth of Isaac, Hagar and Ishmael are forced to leave Abraham's household, this time permanently (21:8–14). The distinction between the chosen and the unchosen becomes public and irrevocable. But by this time it is clear that Ishmael's "rejection" does not entail his exclusion from the blessings of God's covenant concern for the human family. Ishmael, touched by God's covenant with Abraham and Sarah, remains the object of God's passionate concern and also receives a promise (21:15–21).

The story of Ishmael's circumcision suggests that gentile identity arises from the center of God's covenant with creation. Gentile identity is a category of covenant history every bit as much as Jewish identity. Ishmael, like Isaac, is included in God's covenant plan, albeit in a distinctive way. Though not chosen to be the bearer of the covenant, Ishmael is one whose own story originates in the household of promise, and he bears the mark of that promise all his days.

Throughout the Scriptures of Israel, God's blessing regularly falls to the younger brother rather than to the older, yet not in such a way that the older is excluded from God's favor. The elder brother, simply because he already exists and is active in the world, shapes his surrounding world according to his intentions and his plans and sets up a realm of facts and expectations in which he proposes to acquire whatever blessing the world affords. The younger brother comes into the world after the older brother and must therefore come to terms with the existence and plans of his older brother. Nevertheless, God's blessing falls to the younger brother rather than the older. The blessing of the younger does not exclude the older. It encompasses him. But it does so in such a way that the older brother is required to make room for the younger and the blessing that he brings.

The wonderfully intricate story of Jacob's household and the land of Egypt (Gen 37–50) provides a second model for understanding gentile existence in the context of God's election of Israel. Joseph, hated by his brothers for his special place in their father's esteem, is sold into slavery in the land of Egypt (37). But Joseph's Egyptian master, unlike his brothers, "saw that the Lord was with Joseph, and that the Lord caused all that he did to prosper in his hands" (39:2–3). Eventually, Joseph comes to the attention of the Pharaoh himself. He calls upon Joseph to interpret his foreboding dream. Frightened by the prospect of famine that Joseph lays before him, Pharaoh appoints Joseph governor of all Egypt and commissions him to do all that is necessary to save the country from ruin. When the years of famine come, Egypt's storehouses are full (41).

Then "all the world came to Joseph in Egypt to buy grain, because the famine was severe throughout the world" (41:57). And so it happened that the sons of Israel went to Egypt to buy grain. On the brothers' first visit, Joseph tests his brothers without revealing himself to them, and they interpret their misfortune as recompense for their sin against their brother Joseph (42:21–22). But when the brothers return to Egypt a second time to buy grain, Joseph reveals his identity to them, and the brothers are reconciled (45). When

Pharaoh and his servants heard the report, they were glad and directed Joseph to settle his father and his brothers in the best land of Egypt (45:18). In an especially moving episode, Joseph presents his father to Pharaoh; and Jacob, the aged nomadic herdsman, bestows his blessing upon the powerful ruler (47:7–10). And so when Jacob at last died, he was mourned not only by his own household, but "by all the servants of Pharaoh" and "all the elders of the land of Egypt," so that the Canaanites, seeing the mourning, said, "This is a grievous mourning on the part of the Egyptians" (50:7, 11). And when Joseph himself died, being one hundred ten years old, he was embalmed and placed in a coffin in Egypt (50:26). On this note of blessing fulfilled, the book of Genesis ends.

The Joseph cycle is a particularly rich indication of how God's providential care for the house of Jacob unfolds in a way that simultaneously brings blessings to the Gentiles. "The Lord blessed the Egyptian's house for Joseph's sake" (Gen 39:5). The key point is that God nurses God's covenant with Israel—in this case by reconciling Jacob's estranged children—in a way that weaves the story of Israel into the story of the nations in a single pattern of mutual blessing. The central point of the story is not deliverance but blessing. Of course, deliverance also takes place. But deliverance serves the cunning of God's blessing, which from the outset drives toward overflowing *life*.

Once again, gentile identity is depicted positively in light of an economy of mutual blessing that ties the nations to God's covenant with Israel. This understanding of gentile identity is also clearly articulated by the rabbis:

> "A land which the YHWH your God cares for" (Deut 11:12). Does he really care for it alone? Does he not care for all the lands, as it is written, "To bring rain on a land where no man is, . . . to satisfy the waste and desolate land" (Job 38:26f.). What, then, does Scripture teach by saying: "A land which YHWH your God cares for"? That he does not care but for this one, but because of the care with which he cares for it, he cares for all the lands together with it. In the same way, you read: "Behold, he who keeps (guards) Israel will neither slumber nor sleep" (Psalm 121:4). Does he not keep the whole universe, as it is said: "In his hand is the life of every living thing and the breath of all mankind" (Job 12:12)? What does Scripture teach by saying: "He who keeps Israel"? That he does not keep but Israel, but because of the keeping with which he keeps them, he keeps the universe together with them. (Sifre Deut §40)[18]

God's election of Israel does not pass over the rest of the human family, abandoning them like the people left behind by Noah's ark. This would be the case only if Israel's election were not linked to the blessing of the nations. Because God cares for one family as Israel, God cares for the others as precious children as well and thereby embraces both in a single economy of blessing.

Indeed, the intimate connection between God's election of Israel and gentile identity can be taken one step further, as in the following rabbinic passage:

> Israel is compared to the dust of the earth, without which the world could not abide. Without dust there would be no trees and no produce from the earth; so if it were not for Israel, the Gentiles would not exist, for "in thy seed shall all the Gentiles be blest" (Gen 22:18). (Pesichta Rabbati 45b)[19]

Apart from Israel, Gentiles would not exist. Upon consideration, this is not hyperbolic speech but a sober statement of theological reality. A Gentile is by definition a non-Jew. At a semantic level, therefore, there could be no Gentiles without Jews. This linguistic reality points to a more basic theological truth. The Lord's election of Israel is a situation-creating reality that determines the existence and identity not only of Israel, but also of the rest of human creation. Gentile identity is a category of covenant history just as certainly and irrevocably as is Jewish identity. To be a Gentile *means* to be the other of Israel and as such a full participant in a single economy of mutual blessing anchored in God's carnal election of the Jewish people.

BLESSING AND ESCHATOLOGY

What is the final goal of the Lord's work as Consummator? Throughout its many strands and layers, the Hebrew Scriptures consistently envision the goal of God's works as that future wherein the blessing promised by God in the past is finally realized in all its fullness. The future fulfillment of God's blessing is envisioned in progressively more encompassing terms until it ultimately embraces not only the entire human family but the whole of creation as well. Perhaps the term that most aptly summarizes the eschatological fullness of God's blessing is *shalom* (Isa 11; 52:7; 54:10; Ezek 37:26).[20] *Shalom* entails wholeness, righteousness, harmony, and joy, not only between God and creation but within the created order

as well. *Shalom* is that realization of God's economies of difference
and mutual blessing that brings fullness of life to all (Job 5: 22–24;
Ps 29:11; Ps 128). As such, consummation/*shalom* stands in strong
continuity with the corporeal, communal, and historical dimensions of the world, including the covenantal distinction between
Israel and the nations (Ps 122:6–8; Zech 9–10).

In sum, the goal of God's work as Consummator is that future
reign of *shalom* in which the economy of difference and mutual
dependence initiated by God's promise to Abraham and Sarah is
fulfilled in a way that brings fullness of life to Israel, to the nations,
and to all of creation. Three strands of biblical testimony combine
to illuminate this vision of final consummation.

A first strand of testimony makes clear that God's *shalom* concerns Israel, the Jewish people. Indeed, God's reign of peace is nothing other than the fulfillment of the blessing that God promised to
the patriarchs and their descendants from of old. Ezekiel foresees
God's kingdom of peace in this way:

> They [the Israelites] shall live in the land that I gave to my servant
> Jacob, in which your ancestors lived; they and their children and
> their children's children shall live there forever; and my servant
> David shall be their prince forever. I will make a covenant of peace
> with them; it shall be an everlasting covenant with them; and I
> will bless them and multiply them, and will set my sanctuary
> among them forevermore. My dwelling place shall be with them;
> and I will be their God, and they shall be my people. Then the
> nations shall know that I the Lord sanctify Israel, when my sanc-
> tuary is among them forevermore. (Ezek 37:25–28)

The passage draws together God's blessings of land, progeny,
and temple and views them as integral parts of a single, eternal
"covenant of peace" between God and Israel. The center of the
covenant of peace is God's dwelling in the midst of the people.
Final consummation, far from annulling God's self-identification
with the Jewish people, confirms it and manifests it before the eyes
of the nations.

A second strand of testimony makes clear that God's *shalom* with
Israel encompasses the well-being of the nations as well. The blessings of God's consummating work—wholeness, righteousness,
security, joy and, above all, fullness of life with God—are not
Israel's privilege alone. To the contrary, they are the blessings of

God's will and work among the nations, too:

> In days to come
>> the mountain of the Lord's house
> shall be established as the highest of the mountains,
>> and shall be raised up above the hills.
> Peoples shall stream to it,
>> and many nations shall come and say:
> "Come, let us go up to the mountain of the Lord,
>> to the house of the God of Jacob;
> that he may teach us his ways
>> and that we may walk in his paths."
> For out of Zion shall go forth instruction,
>> and the word of the Lord from Jerusalem.
> He shall judge between many peoples,
>> and shall arbitrate between strong nations far away;
> they shall beat their swords into plowshares,
>> and their spears into pruning hooks;
> nation shall not lift up sword against nation,
>> neither shall they learn war any more;
> but they shall all sit under their own vines and
> under their own fig trees,
>> and no one shall make them afraid;
>> for the mouth of the Lord of hosts has spoken. (Mic 4:1–4)

As the image of the nations' eschatological trek to Zion indicates, the act by which God fulfills God's blessing on Israel is the same act by which God fulfills God's blessing on the nations as well. God's peace with Israel comes not at the nations' expense, but to their benefit.

Finally, a third strand of testimony confirms and illuminates the essential content of the previous two. *God's history with Israel and the nations is ordered from the outset toward a final reign of* shalom *in which the distinction between Israel and the nations is not abrogated and overcome but affirmed within a single economy of mutual blessing.* "On that day," say Isaiah, "Israel will be the third with Egypt and Assyria, a blessing in the midst of the earth, whom the Lord of hosts has blessed, saying, 'Blessed be Egypt my people, and Assyria the work of my hands, and Israel my heritage'" (Isa 19:24–25). Final consummation does not mean a loss of national identity on the part of Assyria, Egypt, or Israel. Rather, Israel and the nations—for in this passage Assyria and Egypt stand as parts for whole—retain their distinctiveness within a single community of blessing that God establishes "in the midst of the earth." Excluded is the enmity that have long set Israel, Egypt, and Assyria in bloody antithesis, opposition, and discord. Preserved is the distinctive identity of each in a single economy of mutual blessing that originates from and returns to the Lord. How else, indeed, could God's covenant with *Israel* prove to be a blessing to the *nations?*

Taken together, these strands of biblical testimony confirm the view that God's work as Consummator is ordered toward the fulfillment of God's original promise to bless Abraham and "in him" all of the nations of the earth (Gen 12:1–3; 18:18; 22:18). At the same time, it seems that fulfillment of God's covenant with Abraham and Sarah entails fulfillment of the whole created order. The movement from creation (Gen 1–11) to covenant (Gen 12:1ff.) at the beginning of time is balanced at the end of time by a movement from covenant to new creation. God's eschatological *shalom* encompasses not only Israel and the nations and all who have died, but animals, mountains, streams, and indeed, a new heaven and a new earth (Isa 11; 65:17ff.; 66:22).

Accordingly, it seems appropriate to distinguish between the "historical" and the "cosmic" dimensions of God's one eschatological blessing. The historical dimension of final consummation concerns the climax of the history that unfolds between the Lord, Israel, and the nations. The cosmic dimension concerns God's establishment of a new heaven and a new earth, in which God will dwell in glory. The rabbis operated with a similar distinction in their understanding of "the world to come" (*olam haba*). The phrase may refer to the days when Israel shall live in prosperity and righteousness, at peace with the nations. But this age is not to last forever: it is followed by the revivification of all creation and the inauguration of God's own reign in creation.[21]

We arrive then at a two-stage picture of final consummation. The fulfillment of God's covenant with Israel is the historical side of the new creation, and the new creation is the cosmic side of the fulfillment of God's covenant fidelity toward Israel. For our purposes, the key point is this: *God's historical fidelity toward Israel is the "narrow gate" that opens on the new creation.* There is no shortcut to the eschaton that bypasses or overrides God's fidelity toward Jewish flesh and the permanent historical distinction between Jew and Gentile. Certainly human creation is the object of God's work as

Consummator. What else would God consummate, if not God's creation? But God's consummating work does not engage the human family "immediately." God's consummating work engages the one human family in its covenantal identity as Jew and Gentile, as Israel and the nations, and *in this way* engages the human creature and human creation as a whole. The path from creation to new creation goes by way of the open-ended story that unfolds among God, Israel, and the nations.

SYSTEMATIC REFLECTIONS
Two Dimensions of Human Identity

I have argued that the central theme of the Scriptures is the God of Israel's work as Consummator and that God's work as Consummator engages the human family by opening up an "economy of mutual blessing" between those who are and who remain different. God consummates the human family by electing it into an historical and open-ended economy of difference and reciprocal dependence, the identifying characteristic of which is the divinely drawn distinction between Israel and the nations. Jewish and gentile identity are not basically antithetical or even "separate but equal" ways of relating to God. They are, rather, two mutually dependent ways of participating in a single divine *oikonomia* of blessing oriented toward the final consummation of the whole human family in God's eschatological *shalom*.

But why, one may ask, has God chosen to tie the consummation of the world to the distinction between Israel and the nations? After all, it was Jean-Jacques Rousseau who asked why, if God had something to say to Rousseau, he could not say it directly but had to go through Moses to say it.[22] In reply, one might observe that a blessing is by its very nature something imparted from one to an *other*. As such, blessing presupposes difference. When difference disappears, so too does the possibility of genuine blessing. Christians have always recognized the paradigmatic instance of this truth in the relation of Creator and creature. The difference (not distance!) between Creator and creature is the basis for the blessings that creation enjoys from God: that it is, that it is good, that it is preserved, and that it is adequate to God's covenant purpose. Furthermore, Christians have long affirmed that nothing poses a graver threat to God's blessings on creation than the creature's

misguided attempt to overcome or erase the difference that distinguishes Creator and creature.

As we have seen, the link between blessing and difference is also
mirrored within the textures of the created realm itself. The creation stories underscore the concomitance of God's blessing and
the difference between female and male, parent and child, and one
generation and the next. Indeed, the concommitance of difference
and blessing is so marked that it suggests a possible solution to the
meaning of Gen 1:26, according to which God created humankind
in the "image and likeness" of God. In what sense is the human
family created in God's image? In the sense that God creates the
human family with the capacity to mirror God's own activity as
one who blesses what is other and who is blessed in return. So
understood, the image of God presupposes not only the difference
of male and female (1:27c) but also familial and social differences
more generally, as well as the difference between the human family
and the natural world (1:28–31). Whether or not this interpretation corresponds to the intention of the text's author or editors,
the passage does underscore the concommitance of blessing and
difference and in this way suggests that creation is a mirror of
God's own creative activity.[23]

Now we can ask again why God has chosen to consummate the
human family through an economy of difference and mutual
dependence between Israel and the nations. The difference
between Israel and the nations belongs to a different level of divine
intention than the differences intrinsic to the created order. The
latter differences arise from God's work as Creator, whereas the
former difference arises from God's election of Abraham, Sarah,
and their chosen children. Yet the order of covenant history
exhibits an analogy with the order of creation. God intends the
human family to learn to give and receive blessings in the company
of an other. God wishes to bless Israel in the company of the
nations, and the nations in the company of Israel.

In light of these considerations, it seems appropriate and necessary to draw a distinction between two different dimensions of
human identity: creaturehood in God's image and partnership in
covenant history. The necessity of this distinction arises from the
freedom of the living God, who as the Consummator of creation
summons the human family beyond the dynamism of its natural
being into the open-ended arena of covenant history.

A first dimension of human identity consists in creaturehood in God's image. This encompasses, at the very least, our constitution as embodied rational agents. As embodied rational agents, human creatures have their own finite reality that is other than God's, and they are capable of being called by God to responsible participation in God's covenant with creation. Yet embodied rational agency alone is an incomplete account of human creaturehood in God's image. It could apply just as well to immortal, sexless beings far removed from the mundane reality of human life. The picture becomes more complete only when one adds that the human family possesses embodied rational agency only in matrices of corporeal difference and mutual dependence. These relationships are given along distinct yet interrelated axes: the difference of the natural world and the human family, of female and male, of parents and children, of one generation and the next. These differences are not accidental to our condition as embodied rational agents but constitutive of it. They provide the fit and congruent form for our lives as those whose supreme good and final end consist in the exchange of blessings with those who are other.

A second dimension of human identity arises from God's vocation of the human family into covenant history. Since God promises to bless Abraham and "in him" all the families of the earth, the human family participates in covenant history in a particular way, namely, as Israel and the nations, as Jews and as Gentiles. Covenant history encompasses but does not derive from God's work of creation. Rather, God's election of Israel, and therefore Jewish and gentile identity, is a "new creation" above and beyond creaturehood in the image of God. Just such a recognition informs the following passage from the rabbinic text, *Pirqe Abot:*

> [Rabbi Aqiba] would say, "Precious is the human being, who was created in the image [of God]. It was an act of still greater love that it was made known to him that he was created in the image [of God]. As it is said, 'For in the image of God he made man' (Gen 9:6).

> "Precious are Israelites, who are called children to the Omnipresent. It was an act of still greater love that it was made known to them that they were called children to the Omnipresent, as it is said, 'You are the children of the Lord your God'" (Deut 14:1). (*Pirqe Abot* 31:14 A and B)[24]

The text extols two gifts of God: creaturehood in God's image and Israelite identity as children of God. While both are precious, the covenant identity is the greater benefit since on its account humans are called the children of God. Remarkably, the text also distinguishes an ontic and a noetic side to each benefit. It is a boon to receive creaturehood and election as God's child, but in each case it is an act of still greater love to know that it is so.

Israel's unique place in God's consummating plan means that it not only receives the gifts of creaturehood and childhood but also learns directly from God that this is so. This is the privilege that comes with Israel's identity as God's specially beloved child. In contrast, Gentiles receive the same benefits but come to know about them through contact with the Jewish people. This poses a challenge, of course, for Gentiles must learn about their own childhood from the specially beloved child. Given the frailty of human nature, not surprisingly Gentiles have sought to identify themselves primarily with God's first blessing, creaturehood in God's image, while rejecting God's greater blessing or redefining the terms on which it is offered. Like Joseph's siblings, Gentiles would prefer to do away with God's special fatherly love altogether, even at the cost of rending the father's heart, rather than see it go first of all to another. Nevertheless, God's special love for Israel is the guarantee that God has elected the whole human family into the economy of consummation as God's beloved children. When this is recognized, then Gentiles can receive the news of gentile identity with joy.

Ultimately, both dimensions of human religious identity—creaturehood in God's image and partnership in the economy of Israel and the nations—are necessary to account for the human condition in the context of God's work as the Consummator of creation. Neither aspect of human identity can be sacrificed to the other. As creatures in God's image, all human beings, from conception to death, are subjects of sacred worth and dignity. As Jew or as Gentile, all human beings are responsible participants in God's covenant with creation. Creaturehood is the "outer basis" of covenant identity in the difference of Jew and Gentile. Covenant identity as Jew or as Gentile is the "inner basis" of human creaturehood.

Barth and Rahner Revisited

I have suggested how Christians might make the center of the Scriptures of Israel decisive for a Christian understanding of God's work
as the Consummator of creation. Such a reading, I believe, works
against the structural supersessionism of traditional Christian
thought, together with its latent semignosticism. Far from breaking
completely with mainstream Christian thought, such an interpretation of God's consummating work picks up and continues the anti-
gnosticizing themes identified previously in the work of Karl Barth
and Karl Rahner.

Barth, I would argue, is exactly right to insist that Christians
make the center of Israel's Scriptures decisive for understanding
God's work as the Consummator of creation. Barth correctly sees
that when Christians do so, God's consummating work must be
described as covenant history and, in particular, as the covenant
history that God initiates and sustains with Abraham's children
after the flesh in the midst of, and for the sake of, humankind as a
whole. Barth errs, it seems, only when he tries to force this fundamentally anti-gnostic conception of God's consummating work into
the procrustean bed of the Old Covenant/New Covenant schema.
This leads Barth to declare that God's covenant history with Israel
and the nations has come to a premature conclusion in Jesus Christ
and that only time remains. However much one may honor the
boldness and consistency of Barth's claim, it seems in the end to
represent an especially egregious example of the semignosticism
latent in much traditional Christian thought.

The necessary correction is a frank reorientation of the
hermeneutical center of the Scriptures from the incarnation to the
reign of God, where God's reign is understood as the eschatological
outcome of human history at the end of time. On this view, God's
covenant with Israel in the midst of the nations does not come to an
end with Jesus Christ's resurrection, nor indeed with any event
prior to the eschatological consummation of God's reign. Rather,
God's history with Israel and the nations remains the constant and
universal medium of God's ongoing work as the Consummator of
the human family in the midst of creation.

Similarly, I believe that Karl Rahner is substantially correct in the
theological reasoning he adduces for the supernatural existential. To
recall, Rahner starts with the axiom of the ontological creativity of
divine love. Rahner holds that God's love is intrinsically creative

even in the case of God's *intention* to consummate human creation. As a result, the human condition is *other than* and *more than* what it would have been had God freely chosen *not* to consummate the world. What human creation possesses that it otherwise would not have is an active orientation toward participation in God's own eternal life. This orientation consists in a supernatural determination of created nature that is at once supremely historical and contingent yet antecedent to every act of human freedom. On all these points, Rahner's argument seems to me wholly persuasive. Yet as we saw in a previous chapter, Rahner's own use of the supernatural existential ultimately collapses. What has gone wrong?

The problem, I suggest, is that Rahner *misidentifies* the supernatural existential. Rahner falls into this error because he seeks the supernatural existential in the realm of private consciousness rather than in the public arena as interpreted in light of the biblical witness. In this connection it is worth remembering Bonhoeffer's call for the nonreligious interpretation of theological concepts: "What does it mean to 'interpret in a religious sense'? I think it means to speak on the one hand metaphysically, and on the other hand individualistically. Neither of these is relevant to the Bible message or to the man of today."[25] However skillfully developed, Rahner's interpretation of the supernatural existential seems metaphysical and individualistic in just the sense Bonhoeffer criticized. As a result, Rahner leaves the supernatural existential stranded in the realm of interiority with little or no identifiable connection to the biblical narratives or public history.

Bonhoeffer believed that Christians could recover the legitimate sense of theological concepts by relocating them from the private to the public realm, from the world interpreted by metaphysics to the world interpreted by the Hebrew Scriptures. This can also be done in the case of the supernatural existential. If, as I have argued, God's work as Consummator takes concrete shape through God's election of Israel, then the legitimate sense of the supernatural existential must be sought within the triadic history that unfolds between the Lord, Israel, and the nations. In that case, the supernatural existential is nothing other than the human family's individual and corporate existence in the difference and mutual dependence of Jew and Gentile.

Upon reflection, the difference and mutual dependence of Jew and Gentile corresponds closely to Rahner's supernatural existential. From above, the economy of Jew and Gentile displays the ontological creativity of the Lord's love. God's election of the Jewish people embodies in supremely corporeal fashion God's *intention* to consummate the human family. From below, the economy of Jew and Gentile determines the identity and existence of every human being in a manner that is at once supremely historical yet antecedent to every act of human freedom. Each member of the human family finds him- or herself "always already" a Jew or a Gentile and in this way confronted in one way or another by the offer and invitation of the blessing of an other. With Rahner, moreover, we can say that the "supernatural existential" imparts a dynamic orientation not only to each human creature individually but also to human history as a whole. Nevertheless, the dynamism of human history appears rather differently than Rahner supposed. God's work as Consummator engages the entire human family from a point that falls between Israel and the nations. Consequently, the path toward the eschaton does not lead through the center of *any* community's history, not even the histories of Israel or the church. This is one reason why God's work as Consummator eludes human control.

When the supernatural existential is identified with the human family's existence in the distinction between Israel and the nations, two crucial things happen. First, the supernatural existential is rescued from the realm of interiority and situated in public history without losing its grasp on deep and universal features of human identity. Second, the distinction between Israel and the nations appears in its proper light as a sign of promise, a promise that encompasses Israel, the nations, and creation as a whole. The distinction between Israel and the nations can be ignored and assaulted. Its significance can be distorted from a sign of blessing to a source of enmity, discord, and destruction. But the distinction itself cannot be effaced or destroyed short of annihilating the Jewish people. So long as the human family lives in the problematic encounter of Jew and Gentile, of Israel and the nations, the economy of consummation remains open and full of promise.

7

THE SCRIPTURES
CURSE AND REDEMPTION

THE GREAT CENTRAL THEME OF THE SCRIPTURES, I have argued, is the Lord's work as Consummator of creation. As Consummator, God promises fullness of life to the human family and to all of creation in and through economies of mutual blessing. God's economy is inaugurated primordially through the distinction of God and creation: God blesses creation with life and the promise of fullness of life, and creation in return blesses God with thanksgiving and praise. At the same time, God summons the human family to receive God's blessing in and through finite economies of difference and mutual dependence. At the natural level, God's economy manifests itself in the creaturely difference between the human family and the natural world, between female and male, between parent and child, between one generation and the next. At the level of covenant history, God's economy takes shape in the difference between Jew and Gentile, between Israel and the nations. To the extent that the human family receives life and fullness of life as the blessing of an Other, in solidarity with the human other, the Lord promises to bring covenant history to fulfillment in the reign of eschatological *shalom*.

Yet if the great central theme of the Hebrew Scriptures is the Lord's work as the Consummator of creation, its great subordinate theme is God's work as Redeemer and Deliverer. That is the subject of the present chapter. The occasion (not cause!) of God's work as Redeemer is the appalling reality of sin, the incomprehensible fact that the human family cuts itself off from God's economies of mutual blessing and instead seeks to procure blessing on its own terms at the other's expense. Male seeks blessing at the expense of female, Gentile at the expense of Jew, Jew at the expense of Gentile.

In these ways and others, the human family turns its back on God's blessing and does violence to the human other. The economy of difference and mutual dependence becomes an economy of curse rather than blessing and is therefore overshadowed by the curse of God. God's curse is simply God's blessing as seen from the backside, that is, as seen from the perspective of the creature who has repudiated it. But from this perspective, God's curse is curse indeed.

CURSE AND THE ECONOMY OF CONSUMMATION
Curse and the Economy of Creation

The primeval history (Gen 1–11) knows nothing of a single catastrophic fall that introduces a major turning point into the biblical story.[1] On the contrary, as we argued previously, the central theme of the primeval history and of Genesis as a whole is the continuity, resilience, and growth of God's work as the Consummator of creation. Nevertheless, the creation sagas are nothing if not utterly unsentimental about the seriousness of human sin and dreadful weight of the divine curse. The creation sagas trace the human family's readiness to receive God's blessing through a series of social pairs: male and female (Gen 2–3), brother and brother (Gen 4), comrade and comrade (Gen 11). In each case, the result is distressingly negative.

The first parents of the human family stand beneath the Lord's blessing from the dawn of their existence. Nevertheless, they quickly grow impatient for the fullness of divine blessing (Gen 2–3). Rather than trust God as the source of that fullness, they seek to wrest blessing for themselves from the forbidden tree of knowledge, that is, from a creature like themselves (3:6–7). By so doing, the first parents refuse to trust that blessing is the gift of an Other. Instead, they picture the divine Other as fundamentally untrustworthy, a threat to their hope for fullness of life (3:4–5).[2] As a consequence, God's blessing is in fact overshadowed by God's curse (14–19). The first parents go on to procreate and fill the earth in accordance with God's original promise (1:28), but now these activities are accompanied by hardship and suffering (3:14–19). Above all, the man's rule over the woman is depicted as a wound in the economy of mutual blessing. "The companion of chapter 2 has become a master."[3]

The story of Cain and Abel (Gen 4:1–16) signals a further rup-

ture in God's economy of blessing. Cain and Abel both bring offer-
ings to the Lord, but the Lord has regard only for Abel and his offering. The story introduces a motif that recurs throughout the rest of
the biblical narrative: the "deflection of primogeniture"[4] or God's
preference for the younger over the older of two siblings. While
many purely human considerations might be adduced against God's
giving preference to either brother, the pattern is in fact basic to the
logic of God's blessing. By preferring Abel's offering over Cain's,
God does not spurn Cain but rather requires him to receive God's
blessing in solidarity with his brother, who receives God's favor in a
special way. God even gives Cain a special word of comfort and
warning: "Why are you angry, and why has your countenance fall-
en? If you do well, will you not be accepted? And if you do not do
well, sin is lurking at the door; its desire is for you, but you must
master it" (4:6–7). But Cain cannot master his bitterness and slays
his brother. Cain thereby cuts off a living soul from the economy of
blessing and deprives it of fullness of life. But by cutting off his
brother, Cain cuts himself off from God's blessing as well, for God's
blessing comes by way of an other. Thus Cain brings God's curse
upon his own head (4:10–16). The story anticipates the future relation of Jew and Gentile by signaling both the promised blessing and
the threatened curse that attend those summoned by God to perform different tasks in a single economy of mutual blessing.

The story of Babel (Gen 11:1–9) indicates in an entirely different
way how the human family resists God's blessing as mediated
through the human other. As noted in the previous chapter, the
human family's plan to build a tower to the heavens is motivated by
the fear that otherwise "we shall be scattered abroad upon the face
of the whole earth" (11:4). This ambition stands counter to God's
original blessing to "fill the earth." In effect, the comrades of Shinar
exploit the unity of the human family in order to frustrate God's
intention to bless through difference (compare Gen 10:1–32).[5]

By the end of the creation sagas, it has become utterly clear how
resistant the human family is to receiving God's blessing in and
through economies of difference and mutual dependence. The difference of male and female becomes an occasion for deceit, shame,
and injustice; the difference of brother and brother an occasion for
hatred and fratricide; the difference of comrade and comrade an
occasion for hubris, isolationism, and confusion. At each point, sin
refuses to accept the blessing of an Other in solidarity with the

human other. Sin assaults the link that joins blessing and otherness. Sin seeks blessing apart from its source in the divine Other and apart from life with the human other. As a consequence, sin transforms the divine blessing into curse and the relationship with the human other into a source of enmity and discord.

Curse and the Economy of Covenant History

God inaugurates the work of consummation in its enduring historical form by promising to bless Abraham and, in him, all the families of the earth. "I will bless you, and make your name great, so that you will be a blessing. I will bless those who bless you, and the one who curses you I will curse; and in you all the families of the earth shall be blessed" (Gen 12:2b–3). The passage signals that blessing and curse are not equally weighted alternatives in God's purpose for the human family: blessing is mentioned five times, curse only twice. Nevertheless, God's blessing is available only on the condition that Israel and the nations recognize in the other their own indispensable partner in God's economy. Unless obedience to God includes openness to the other, God's history with Israel and the nations proceeds from curse to curse.

The Exodus (Exod 1–15) offers a paradigmatic account of how the Lord's history with Israel and the nations can be distorted from an economy of mutual blessing to an economy of one-sided exploitation and devastating curse. After Joseph's death, Jacob's descendants continue to flourish in Egypt, becoming "fruitful" and "prolific" and growing "exceedingly strong" (1:7). An earlier generation of Egyptians had learned that God's providential care for Egypt was inextricably intertwined with God's care for Jacob's family. But "Now a new king arose over Egypt, who did not know Joseph" (1:8). The new king sees in Israel's flourishing not a confirmation of God's blessing but a threatening other (1:9). Therefore the Pharaoh seeks to constrain the increase of the Israelites by taskmasters, oppression, forced labor and bitter slavery; and when all of these fail, by instructing the midwives to kill Israelite males at birth (1:16). The plan fails, but Pharaoh and his successors continue to oppress the Israelites. Even when Moses and Aaron perform a wonder before Pharaoh and his magicians that testifies to the Lord's presence with the Israelites, Pharaoh refuses to relent (7:8–13). Pharaoh's heart is "hardened," that is, closed to the blessing of Israel and Israel's God. "Who is the Lord, that I should heed him and let Israel go? I do not know the Lord, and I will not let Israel go" (5:2).

Pharaoh has scorned God's economy of blessing. As a result, a land that had been fruitful for Egypt and Israel alike is shattered by a series of plagues. The land and rivers are filled with blood, decay, pestilence, and stink, culminating finally in the death of every firstborn, both child and chattel. In the midst of the mounting devastation, the Lord makes a "distinction" between Israel and Egypt (8:23, 9:4, 11:7). But now the distinction signals not the promise of mutual blessing but rather the reality of an opposition and antithesis that results in one-sided catastrophe for the house of Egypt. Stunned by the disaster, Pharaoh momentarily relents. "Rise up," he tells Moses and Aaron, "go away from my people, both you and the Israelites! Go, worship the Lord, as you said. Take your flocks and your herds, as you said, and be gone. And bring a *blessing* on me too!" (12:31b–32). But the minds of Pharaoh and his officials are soon changed again (14:5). The contest is not settled until the waters of the Red Sea part for the fleeing Israelites and close again on the chariots of the pursuing Egyptians, throwing "horse and rider" into the sea (15:1).

As the story of the Exodus shows, God's curse does not necessarily fall upon all parties in equal measure. God can single out the nations for curse, according to the saying, "The one who curses you I will curse" (Gen 12:3). The Scriptures return often to two negative images of the Gentiles: as idolaters and as blood enemies of Israel and Israel's God. These two negative characteristics are joined at the root, because both stem from the nation's rejection of the truth that the Lord, the God of Israel, is God. Because this truth is manifest for all to see in the works of the Lord on Israel's behalf and in creation (see Psalms 117, 126), the Gentiles are without excuse. They cannot claim to be idolaters and enemies of Israel "by nature." Rather, the nations become these things historically because of their unwillingness to accept God's blessing in solidarity with the people Israel.

Yet for all of its harrowing realism regarding God's judgment of the nations, the Scriptures of Israel are at least equally concerned with God's judgment of Israel. From the outset, Israel's special obligation has a shadow side, the covenant curses (Gen 17:14, Lev 26:3ff., Deut 28). The covenant curses testify to the importance that God attaches to Israel's part of the bargain in

God's covenant with creation. If Israel fulfills its obligation to be Israel, God's blessing will surely follow. But if Israel tires of this task, the result is calamity for Israel, and often enough for the nations as well.

The Scriptures are astonishingly direct in their account of Israel's repeated fall beneath the divine curses. Much of the narrative material in the Hebrew Scriptures recounts the various circumstances in which Israel by its trespasses unleashed the covenant curses (Judg 2ff., 1 Kings 11ff., 2 Kings 1ff.). Much of the prophetic material denounces Israel for its neglect of the covenant and foretells the fresh disasters that will overtake Israel if it fails to repent. Time and again the Scriptures trace back the source of Israel's failing to two interrelated faults: Israel has turned its back on the Lord, the source of true blessing, and has sought for blessing from some other quarter:

> Be appalled, O heavens, at this,
> be shocked, be utterly desolate, says the Lord,
> for my people have committed two evils:
> they have forsaken me, the fountain of living water,
> and dug out cisterns for themselves,
> cracked cisterns,
> that can hold no water. (Jer 2:12–13)

Like the nations, Israel is prone to forget that God's covenant is the only trustworthy source of benediction for Israel and for creation. But in Israel's case this forgetfulness is especially bewildering, since Israel is the bearer of God's covenant, and Israel has experienced first of all the life-giving power of God's blessing. For that reason, the Scriptures suggest that Israel's sin is more grievous to God than the sin of the nations:

> You only have I known
> of all the families of the earth;
> therefore I will punish you
> for all your iniquities. (Amos 3:2)

According to one strand of rabbinic thought, Israel's sin brings suffering not only for Israel but for the nations as well. "If the Gentiles only knew that they would suffer through Israel's sin, they would establish two armies so as to guard every Israelite from wrong-doing."[6] The world-encompassing significance of Israel's sin is the counterpoint to the world-encompassing significance of Israel's election.

Curse and Final Consummation

Not suprisingly, in view of the nations' persistent persecution of Israel, the Scriptures often picture the denouement of the Lord's history with Israel and the nations as one in which Israel alone receives the fulfillment of God's blessing, while the nations come at last to grief (Isa 30:27–28; 63:1–6; Zeph 2).[7] The prophet Haggai, in particular, pictures the climax of covenant history as a kind of Exodus writ large. God vindicates and exalts Israel but brings the nations to destruction:

> I am about to shake the heavens and the earth, and to overthrow the throne of kingdoms; I am about to destroy the strength of the kingdoms of the nations, and overthrow the chariots and their riders; and the horses and their riders shall fall, every one by the sword of a comrade. On that day, says the Lord of hosts, I will take you, O Zerubbabel my servant, son of Shealtiel, says the Lord, and make you like a signet ring; for I have chosen you, says the Lord of hosts. (Hag 2:21–23)

Such an outcome of covenant history would represent a partial failure of God's original promise as Consummator, inasmuch as God promised to bless not only Abraham but also "in him" all the families of the earth. Yet Haggai's vision of the future must not be dismissed as narrow and particularistic. On the contrary, it depicts one possible outcome of covenant history in view of the fact that the nations stand not only under the promise of God's blessing but also under the threat of God's curse.

Yet external enemies are not the only threat to God's intention to bring Israel to final consummation. There is also the fact of Israel's own sin. In view of Israel's repeated failure to obey the Lord's command for righteousness, at least one prophet depicts Israel's own future in colors of unrelieved gloom:

> Alas for you who desire the day of the Lord!
> Why do you want the day of the Lord?
> It is darkness, not light;
> as if someone fled from a lion,
> and was met by a bear;
> or went into the house and rested a hand against the wall,

and was bitten by a snake.
Is not the day of the Lord darkness,
and not light,
and gloom with no brightness in it? (Amos 5:18–20)

REDEMPTION AND THE
ECONOMY OF CONSUMMATION

At the deepest level, the catastrophe of sin raises the question of the future of God's work as Consummator. Given the human family's recalcitrant opposition to the Other's blessing, might God abandon the economy of mutual blessing altogether and simply permit covenant history to end in well-deserved curse?

The Hebrew Scriptures answer the question of the future of God's work as Consummator by testifying to a second way in which God engages human creation, namely, as Redeemer. As Redeemer, God acts in fidelity to God's work as Consummator by refusing to let curse have the last word. God enters into conflict with sin, evil, and violence on behalf of the economy of blessing but especially on behalf of those who are threatened with being cut off from the promise of life.

At times the bitter conflict of sin and deliverance swells until it almost fills the entire canvas of the Hebrew Scriptures. This is true, for example, in the story of God's deliverance of the Israelites from Egypt, Israel's birth-narrative as a nation among the other nations of the earth. Yet even in the Exodus, the conflict of sin and deliverance never eclipses the memory and hope of God's antecedent work as Consummator.

Exodus: Redemption for Consummation's Sake

The story of the Exodus occupies a central place in Israel's memory, in large part because it testifies to God's power to deliver Israel from destruction at the hands of its enemies. How far will God go to preserve Israel from annihilation by the nations? Remembering the Exodus, Israel answers: very far indeed. For Israel, this is no idle matter, for over the millennia Israel has faced repeated threats of extermination by the nations. According to the Passover Haggadah, "Not in one generation alone but in every generation they have risen up against us to destroy us. . . ." Yet time and again the "horses and chariots" of Israel's foes have failed to extinguish Israel's life or (what is the same thing) to eradicate its corporate body. For Israel, this fact is clear testimony to God's fidelity to God's promises, and by no means the least of God's works as Redeemer.

Yet deliverance from destruction is only one dimension of the significance of the Exodus cycle. Equally fundamental is the fact that God liberates Israel from slavery *in fidelity to God's intention to consummate Israel, that is, to bless Israel's life in this world.* Dietrich Bonhoeffer clearly grasped this point in his reflections in prison:

> Unlike the other oriental religions, the faith of the Old Testament is not a religion of redemption . . . . To the objection that a crucial importance is given in the Old Testament to redemption (from Egypt and later from Babylon, cf. Deutero-Isaiah) it may be answered that the redemptions referred to here are *historical,* i.e., on *this* side of death, whereas everywhere else the myths about redemption are concerned to overcome the barrier of death. *Israel is delivered out of Egypt so that it may live before God as God's people on earth.*[8]

Bonhoeffer's remark is borne out by Claus Westermann's observation that the whole pentateuchal history of deliverance (Exodus through Numbers) is framed by two books in which God's blessing is the dominant theme, namely Genesis and Deuteronomy.[9] But Bonhoeffer's point is also confirmed by the details of the Exodus itself. The crucial turning point of the story comes when God heard the "groaning" of the Israelites and "remembered" God's covenant with "Abraham, Isaac, and Jacob" (Exod 2:24). God's memory of God's obligation as Consummator prompts God's work as Redeemer in the present. Later God reassures a discouraged Moses with the words, "I have remembered my covenant" (6:5). God then immediately instructs Moses to say to the Israelites not only that "I will redeem you with an outstretched arm" (6:6) but moreover that "I will bring you into the land that I swore to give to Abraham, Isaac, and Jacob" (6:8). The story makes clear that God *delivers* Israel in order to *bless* it, that is, to make Israel a great nation, to sanctify it through God's own good precepts, and to lead it eventually into the promised land.

When the Exodus is viewed in the broader context of God's work as Consummator, certain details reveal a significance that might otherwise be overlooked. Chief among these are clues that suggest a glimmering recollection and hope that the economy of Jew and

Gentile is properly one of mutual blessing, not curse. Within the canvas of the Exodus cycle as a whole, no fact is more startling than that Moses, the deliverer of Israel, should himself be delivered by Pharaoh's daughter and raised in Pharaoh's household (2:1–10). The incident might seem a mere curiosity were it not for the epic background of the Joseph cycle, in which the interlocking destinies of Egypt and Israel is a central theme. Later a fugitive Moses is adopted a second time into a gentile household, that of Jethro, priest in the land of Midian. After defending Jethro's daughters against thieves, Moses marries Zipporah, Jethro's daughter, and Zipporah gives birth to a son (2:15–22). When God commands Moses to return to Egypt to lead the Israelites out of slavery, Zipporah remains in Midian with her children. The family is reunited only after the victory at the Sea of Reeds, when Jethro, having heard of what the Lord had done, leads his daughter and grandchildren into the wilderness to join Moses and the Israelites at camp. There Jethro declares, "Blessed be the Lord, who has delivered you from the Egyptians and from Pharaoh" (18:10). Thus in the person of Jethro the nations join in praise of God's work as the Redeemer of Israel, and in doing so hint at the all-encompassing scope of God's work as the Consummator of creation. Finally, there is the terse reference to the "mixed crowd" that went out from Egypt at the time of the Exodus together with the Israelites (12:38). The throng of liberated captives consisted of more than the descendants of Jacob. *Like the story of the ark, the Exodus remembers that the Lord delivers the human family in the company of an other.*

Jubilee and the Restoration of the Whole

The institution of Jubilee (Lev 25) offers another vivid instance in which redemption clearly serves a more comprehensive vision of wholeness and blessing. Here redemption concerns households that had been compelled through hardship to sell land or even family members. The Jubilee declared amnesty on all previous debts and thereby restored the threatened households to full participation in the life-giving economies of family, land, and harvest.

A year of Jubilee was to be announced by the blowing of rams horns on the Day of Atonement at the end of every cycle of seven sabbatical years. The horns proclaimed liberty to Israelites who had become enslaved for debt and the restoration of land to families who had been forced by economic distress to sell during the previous fifty years. In addition, the Jubilee mandated that the regular Sabbath year ordinances be observed. Fields were to be left fallow, producing only what grew without sowing or pruning, and everyone was to be permitted to eat of the land regardless of rights of ownership.

The year of Jubilee presupposes God's readiness to bless Israel in and through the life-giving economies of land, family, and harvest. Here, to redeem means to restore those in danger of being cut off from God's life-giving economies to a position in which they can receive and enjoy God's blessing. Just this is the point of the Exodus, for God delivered Israel from Egypt "to give you the land of Canaan, to be your God" (Lev 25:38, cf. 42, 55). Jubilee envisions redemption as the restoration of the whole, where the whole means the open-ended economies of difference and mutual blessing between God and people, people and people, people and land.[10]

Redemption and Eschatology

Ultimately Israel's eschatological hope concerns not redemption but wholeness, not deliverance but fullness of life and blessing.[11] Moreover, Israel's hope concerns wholeness, life, and blessing as realities of this world, manifested in peace between God and Israel, between Israel and the nations, between the human family and the natural world. Yet Israel's prophets recognized with extraordinary sobriety and rigor that, in the wake of sin, wholeness and fullness of life were simply unavailable in any direct or unmediated way. On the contrary, God's reign of *shalom* can eventually be established only through a struggle with the powers that destroy. Final consummation can come only through an act of *restoration,* where restoration does not mean a return to the *status quo ante* but rather the fulfillment of God's original purpose through the defeat of dangerous powers.

The prophets envisioned God's eschatological act of redemption in a variety of ways, as indeed one might expect in view of the many ways in which the human family closes itself to God's consummating work. The vision of God's final work as Redeemer takes one shape when the economy of blessing is threatened by the nations' malice toward Israel. It takes another shape altogether when the sin in question is Israel's own failure to live up to its vocation. It takes yet another shape in the face of Israel's and the nations' collective repudiation of God's consummating purpose.

God's judgment upon Israel, real though it is, is rarely the prophets' last word regarding God's attitude and action toward Israel.[12] The prophets also regularly pronounce a word of hope and promise. The prophetic word of both judgment and promise is meant to lead Israel to repentance and to restoration of right relation to God. However grievous Israel's sin, God remains ready to take her back. The reason for this, at times, seems simply to be that God cannot bear the thought of life without Israel:

> How can I give you up, Ephraim?
> How can I hand you over, O Israel. . . .
> My heart recoils within me;
>   my compassion grows warm and tender.
> I will not execute my fierce anger;
> I will not again destroy Ephraim;
>   for I am God and no mortal,
>   the Holy One in your midst,
>   and I will not come in wrath. (Hos 11:8–9)

Precisely with regard to God's readiness to redeem Israel from its sins, it appears impossible to set limits to how far God is prepared to go.

SYSTEMATIC REFLECTIONS

The Scriptures testify amply that the Lord's work as Consummator is vulnerable to damage and distortion whenever the human family proves unready to accept the blessing of an other. Sin, evil, oppression, and the corresponding need for God's liberation are undeniable aspects of God's history with Israel and the nations as it actually unfolds. Still, the antithesis of sin and redemption is not the central theme of the Scriptures, nor indeed is it an object of concern in its own right. Rather, liberation from the powers that destroy is a matter of utmost urgency precisely because these powers threaten to cut off the human family from the arena in which God's blessings are bestowed. The antithesis of sin and redemption is misunderstood if it is torn from its context in God's work as Consummator and from the economies of mutual blessing that God establishes and sustains.

Under the influence of the standard model, Christian theology has traditionally devoted enormous attention to the antithesis of sin and redemption. For this it can hardly be faulted. The weakness of the traditional approach, however, is that it has often considered sin and redemption in the context of an abstract account of God's antecedent work as Consummator. According to the biblical witness, God's work as Consummator takes enduring shape in the history that unfolds between the Lord, Israel, and the nations. Accordingly, human sin is never merely the sin of the creature against the Creator-Consummator. Human sin is also always the sin of Jew and Gentile, of Israel and the nations, against the Lord, the God of Israel.

Once again, Karl Rahner's concept of the supernatural existential provides useful orientation:

> Our actual nature is *never* "pure" nature. It is a nature installed in a supernatural order which man can never leave, even as a sinner and unbeliever. It is a nature which is continually being determined (which does not mean justified) by the supernatural grace of salvation offered to it.[13]

According to Rahner, the proper context for considering sin and redemption is the human condition *insofar as it has been concretely transformed by God's intention to consummate.* We have already argued that Rahner in fact misidentifies the supernatural existential. If the Lord consummates creation through the history that unfolds between Israel and the nations, then the supernatural existential consists in the human family's existence in the difference and mutual dependence of Jew and Gentile. This is the gracious determination of human identity that is at once utterly historical and yet prior to the exercise of human freedom. Yet once allowance is made for this fundamental revision, Rahner's basic point stands. If the human family says no to God, it does so in the context of its concrete location in the supernatural order, an order that entails a gratuitous determination of human identity above and beyond its being and existence as God's creature.

To recall, Rahner holds that one way in which the human being may close itself to grace is by attempting to live merely according to its created nature. "When indeed one seeks to realize the 'purely natural' in the concrete order in a way that is merely 'pure,' what results is not the purely natural, but rather the *guilty* natural that closes itself to grace to its own damnation."[14] When the concrete content of the supernatural existential is borne in mind, the gravity of this observation is immediately evident. Michael Wyschogrod warns that discounting Jewish identity in favor of identity simply as a person or creature of God poses a great threat to Israel.[15] If such a program could be consistently carried out, it would result in the dissolution of the people Israel.

Is there a comparable temptation for Gentiles? On reflection, it would seem that there is. For Gentiles, the temptation to define themselves solely in terms of creaturehood arises only after confrontation with the Jewish people and their Scriptures, since it is through this confrontation that Gentiles come to know the biblical word regarding creation in the first place. The temptation then takes the form of trying to appropriate the blessing of creation while discounting the core of covenant history, that is, discounting the open-ended economy of difference and mutual dependence that unfolds among the Lord, Israel, and the nations. In fact, the standard canonical narrative embodies precisely this kind of sin in its pervasive logic of supersessionism. Gentiles have affirmed the Scriptures' witness to God's identity as Creator, for they have discerned in the Scriptures' the voice of the Living God who is the source of all true blessing. But Gentiles have used the standard model to suppress recognition that God's blessing for creation can be accepted only in solidarity with Israel.

In fact, however, there are limits to what sin in this form can do. As Karl Rahner has observed with reference to the human family's location in the supernatural order of grace:

> The state of elevated nature is man's most fundamental determination. . . . This state is unconditional and cannot be abolished by sin. Man's freedom can sinfully say no to this state but cannot abolish it any more than man's freedom can abolish his nature and existence by saying no to them.[16]

Human beings can say no to their "supernatural" identities as Jews and as Gentiles, and in this way they can close themselves to God's consummating work. In the extreme case, this no can take shape as the effort to eradicate Israel's body. But short of this, the fact of Jewish and Gentile identity cannot be effaced. The ineluctable character of these dimensions of human identity attests to the depth and resolution of God's consummating engagement with creation. As the Redeemer of Israel, God acts in fidelity not only to Israel but to the totality of the human family's created and covenantal identity. By preserving Israel's body from annihilation, God preserves the human family's existence in the difference of Gentile and Jew. In this way, God sustains the reality and promise of covenant history itself.

8

THE APOSTOLIC WITNESS
GOD'S REIGN AND THE NAME OF JESUS CHRIST

THE GOSPEL IS THE STORY OF THE GOD OF ISRAEL'S victory in Jesus over powers that destroy. Just so, God's victory in Jesus is the center but not the totality of Christian faith. Faith in the gospel presupposes the God of Israel's antecedent purpose for creation, a purpose threatened by destructive powers but vindicated by God in the life, death, and resurrection of Jesus.

Christians have almost universally assented to the truth of the previous paragraph. But, as we saw in Part One, they have commonly accounted for its truth by means of a construal of the Bible's narrative unity that—paradoxically enough—renders God's identity as the God of Israel and the center of the Hebrew Scriptures almost wholly indecisive for grasping God's antecedent purpose for human creation. As an alternative to the standard construal, I have sketched in the previous chapters one way in which God's identity as the God of Israel becomes decisive for grasping God's antecedent purpose for creation. I have argued that God's work as the Consummator of creation promises life and the fullness of life to creation and to the human family in and through earthly economies of difference and mutual dependence. In the context of God's six-days' blessing, God's economy is embodied in the distinction and mutual relation of the natural world and the human family, of female and male, of parent and child, of one generation and the next. In the context of God's crowning Sabbath blessing, God's economy is irrevocably embodied in the carnal election of the Jewish people and in the consequent distinction between Jew and Gentile, between Israel and the nations. Furthermore, I have argued that

God's work as Consummator is oriented from the outset toward God's eschatological *shalom*, where God intends to fulfill the economies of difference and reciprocity to be fulfilled in unsurpassable fashion to the mutual blessing of all in a reign of wholeness, righteousness, and peace.

Viewed within this context, the gospel can be described as follows: *the gospel is good news about the God of Israel's coming reign, which proclaims in Jesus' life, death, and resurrection the victorious guarantee of God's fidelity to the work of consummation, that is, to fullness of mutual blessing as the outcome of God's economy with Israel, the nations, and all creation.* This is the understanding of the gospel to which we now turn.

THE GOSPEL

"The gospel is good news about the God of Israel's coming reign . . ."

The gospel is news, and like all news irreducibly particular in nature. The particularity of the gospel derives in the first instance from the fact that it tells about the living God of the Scriptures, the God of Israel. The gospel does not concern a new and hitherto unknown God (as Marcion held), nor does it speak about a general God of monotheism (as Schleiermacher held). Rather the gospel says something new and good about the same One whose name, character, and works have been declared by the people Israel from the time of Sarah, Rebekah, Leah, and Rachel to the present day.

The particularity of the gospel derives in the second instance from the fact that it tells something new about the God of Israel's *coming reign.* God's reign is the place where God's work as the Consummator of creation will be resolved with eschatological finality, whether to blessing or to curse. As such, God's reign is both distinct from and related to every other work and purpose of God. God's reign is not identical with the work of creation, but it is the place where creation's future will be finally decided. Similarly, God's reign is not identical with God's covenant with Israel and, through Israel, with all of the families of the earth. But it is the place where the future of God's covenant with Israel will be decided, whether to blessing or to curse.

News about God's coming reign is good or bad depending on the outcome of God's work as the Consummator of creation. News about God's coming reign is good to the degree that it announces the fulfillment of God's original purpose for creation, that is, the bestowal of fullness of life on creation through economies of difference and mutual blessing. But the reality and ubiquity of evil mean that such an outcome of God's consummating work is anything but assured. At the very least, the fact of evil means that God's initial purpose for creation can be fulfilled—if it is to be fulfilled at all—through an act of redemption, that is, through God's struggle with and victory over powers that destroy. Even so, evil may well inflict so much damage on God's economies of difference and mutual dependence that they become irredeemable, either in part or in whole. In that event, God's initial goal of eschatological blessing for all would prove unattainable, and God would be forced to settle for some more modest outcome. So, for instance, God might consummate the natural world but not the human family, or the nations but not Israel, or the more righteous but not the less righteous, and so on. In each of these cases, God would achieve only a partial vindication of the economies of difference and mutual dependence.

Then again, evil might prove so catastrophic in scope that it rendered God's economies of difference and mutual blessing irredeemable not only with respect to one or another of its finite regions or dimensions but also with respect to its very heart, that is, the primordial and all-encompassing relation of difference and mutual blessing between God and all that is not God. In that case, the final outcome of God's work as Consummator could only be the ratification of final separation between God and creation, and hence the eschatological validity of curse.

"which proclaims in Jesus'. . ."

The gospel announces something both new and *good* about the coming reign of the God of Israel by speaking about Jesus of Nazareth. The gospel is at heart "good news about the kingdom of God and the name of Jesus Christ" (Acts 8:12). In Jesus, whose name means "YHWH saves," God gives a present answer to the eschatological question of whether God's work as Consummator will prove ultimately victorious on behalf of all creation over all the powers that destroy. The gospel summons all who receive it to enact their trust in the ultimate victory of blessing over curse by conforming themselves in the present to the way of Jesus' cross (Mark 8:34; Phil 2:1–11; 1 John 3:16). Through cruciform discipleship, disciples of Jesus prove their faith in the final victory of the blessing of the God of Israel.

"life. . ."

Like every life, Jesus' life unfolds in context. But what context? If Jesus' life is grasped solely in the context of God's work as Redeemer, its significance is foreshortened in an implicitly gnosticizing way. Instead, the gospel situates Jesus' life in the context of God's work as Consummator. Only within this ultimate horizon does Jesus' life also figure within the necessary but subordinate context of God's work as Redeemer.

Looking backward, Jesus' story is grounded in God's work as Consummator by means of *genealogy* (Matt 1:2–16; Luke 3:23–38). Genealogy binds Jesus to the corporeal sequence of generations from the patriarchs and matriarchs onward and hence to the promised blessing of progeny that inaugurates God's history with Israel and before Israel with the first parents of the human family. What is more, genealogy links Jesus to the peculiar *difference* between Israel and the nations through the gentile women Rahab and Ruth (Matt 1:5). Thus Jesus' genealogy catches up in the briefest possible compass all the manifold dimensions of God's work as Consummator—the difference of God and the human family (Luke 3:38!), of male and female, of one generation and the next, of Israel and the nations—and confirms and illuminates its divinely intended character as an economy of mutual blessing.

Looking forward, Jesus appears in the context of God's consummating work by virtue of his relation to the coming reign of God. God's coming reign is the great overriding reality that determines the whole pattern and significance of Jesus' preaching, ministry, and miracles. The Apostolic Witness hardly suggests that Jesus was the first to announce God's coming reign. On the contrary, the Gospels make clear that Jesus was preceded by John, who in turn took up the call of the ancient prophets of Israel. Yet in one crucial respect the message about God's coming reign takes on a distinctive character on Jesus' lips: it becomes *gospel*, an unambiguous proclamation of good news. Why? What did Jesus trust God's coming reign to bring? An answer can be suggested by distinguishing two different dimensions of Jesus' expectation for God's coming reign as attested by the Apostolic Witness. First, Jesus trusted God's reign to *consummate the economy of mutual blessing between God and the house of Israel, and therefore between God and the nations as well.* Second, Jesus trusted God's reign to consummate Israel and the nations in a manner that *reclaimed, redeemed, and restored the lost.* In both cases, Jesus' hope centered on God's fidelity to Israel, yet in such a way that the nations were not excluded from God's consummating and redemptive purposes.[1]

In the first instance, then, Jesus trusted God's reign to consummate the economy of mutual blessing that God had initiated long ago through God's promises to Abraham and Sarah. This theme is evident, for example, in the Lord's Prayer and in the double commandment of love. In the first three petitions of the Lord's Prayer, Jesus instructed his followers to pray for the sanctification of God's name, for the quick coming of God's reign, and for God's will to be done on earth as in heaven. These petitions amplify one another and point to God's coming reign as a place where the covenantal relationship between God and creation will be fulfilled in an eschatological economy of blessing, praise, and righteousness (Matt 6:9f.; Luke 11:2). A vision of reciprocal blessing also informs Jesus' answer to the scribe's question, "Which commandment is the first of all?"

> Jesus answered, "The first is, 'Hear, O Israel: the Lord our God, the Lord is one; you shall love the Lord your God with all your heart, and with all your soul, and with all your mind, and with all your strength.' The second is this, 'You shall love your neighbor as yourself.' There is no other commandment greater than these."(Mark 12:29–31)

The "vertical" economy of love between God and creation entails a "horizontal" economy of love within the created order itself. When the scribe approves Jesus' answer, Jesus in turn replies, "You are not far from the kingdom of God" (v. 34). Jesus' reply indicates that the double love commandment epitomizes not only the Torah but also the claims of God's coming reign.

Jesus expected the consummation of God's coming reign to have special reference to the house of Israel.[2] Indications of this appear throughout the Gospels. Jesus limited his ministry to the land of Israel. Jesus chose "the twelve" as a sign that he was sent to the twelve tribes of Israel (Matt 10:1–5). Jesus spoke of God's reign as a banquet at which the blessed would feast in the company of Abraham, Isaac, and Jacob (Luke 13:28f.). When the Syro-Phoenician woman asked Jesus to drive the demon out of her daughter, Jesus refused, declaring that his ministry was first to the children of Israel (Mark 7:27). Finally, when the disciples asked Jesus when he would "restore the kingdom to Israel," Jesus did not rebuff the disciples' expectation as such, but rather their desire to know times and seasons (Acts 1:6–7).

At the same time, Jesus evidently expected God to consummate God's reign in Israel in manner that *would include the nations within its compass.* When the Syro-Phoenician woman acknowledged Israel's primary claim on Jesus but persisted in her own claim as well, Jesus healed her daughter (Mark 7:29). Of the eschatological banquet with Abraham, Isaac, and Jacob, Jesus said that many would join them "from the east, west, north and south" (Luke 13:29). Finally, even Jesus' selection of "the twelve" suggests that Jesus expected God's reign not merely to gather in the Jewish diaspora but also to revivify the vanished tribes, and *hence to inaugurate a whole new creation.*[3]

Yet this first dimension of Jesus' hope in God's coming reign is inseparable from a second. If Jesus trusted God's coming reign to consummate the house of Israel (and so creation as a whole), Jesus also trusted God's reign to do so in a manner that *reclaimed, redeemed, and restored the lost.* Indeed, Jesus expressly described his ministry as for "the lost sheep of the house of Israel" (Matt 10:6). The lost sheep of Israel were those whose place in the economy of mutual blessing was forfeited, threatened, or denied, whether through their own fault, through the fault of another, or indeed through no clear fault at all. They were the poor, the hungry, the thirsty, and the naked; they were the sick, the crippled, and the possessed; they were the sinner, the tax-collector, the prostitute, the cheat; they were found especially among women, the despised, and the meek. All of these Jesus welcomed in God's name not as barely tolerated outsiders, but as treasured children for whom God had reserved a seat at the very head of the banquet table.

Jesus' mission to "the lost sheep of Israel" confirms rather than cancels his concern for the whole house of Israel.[4] In this respect, there is fundamental congruence between Jesus' ministry and the theological imperative embodied in the biblical Jubilee (Lev 25). Both seek to restore wholeness to the economy of blessing between God and Israel by reclaiming and redeeming those whose place in the economy had become radically threatened. Of course, images of Jubilee are central to Luke's account of the beginning of Jesus' Galilean ministry (Luke 4:16–21; see Isa 58:6, 61:1–2). Jesus inaugurates the prophetic vision of the eschatological Jubilee by proclaiming good news to the poor, release to the captives, recovery of sight to the blind, and freedom for the oppressed. But as Sharon Ringe has shown, the imagery of Jubilee is in fact woven throughout Luke's account of Jesus' ministry, and is present in the other

Gospels as well.[5] In the beatitudes, Jesus limns the borders of God's economy of blessing in a manner that emphatically includes the poor, the grieving, the hungry, and those who are persecuted for righteousness' sake (Matt 5:3–6; Luke 6:20–22). In the Lord's Prayer, Jesus instructs his followers to ask God to release them from their debts, just as they are to forgive those who are indebted to them (Matt 6:9–13; Luke 11:2–4). Finally, in his healings and exorcisms Jesus signals not only the *nearness* but also the *character* of God's coming reign as the restoration of human wholeness.[6]

Both dimensions of Jesus' hope in God's reign, and its consequences for human conduct, are expressed in the following commandments he gave his disciples:

> But I say to you that listen, Love your enemies, do good to those who hate you, *bless those who curse you,* pray for those who abuse you. If anyone strikes you on the cheek, offer the other also; and from anyone who takes away your coat do not withhold even your shirt. Give to everyone who begs from you; and if anyone takes away your goods, do not ask for them again. Do to others as you would have them do to you. If you love those who love you, what credit is that to you? For even sinners love those who love them.
>
> If you do good to those who do good to you, what credit is that to you? For even sinners do the same. If you lend to those from whom you hope to receive, what credit is that to you? Even sinners lend to sinners, to receive as much again. But love your enemies, do good, and lend, expecting nothing in return. Your reward will be great, and you will be children of the Most High; for he is kind to the ungrateful and the wicked. Be merciful, just as your Father is merciful. (Luke 6:27–36)

Jesus' instruction presupposes the fundamental reality of God's economy of mutual blessing but also the fact that this economy is under assault by curse, violence, and enmity. Yet Jesus instructs his followers not to respond to these assaults in kind. Instead they are to live on behalf of God's economy as a whole, even and indeed especially on behalf of the enemy. For in this way, they act as children of the heavenly Father, who also perseveres in blessing those who curse.

"death. . ."

Yet from the outset the messenger and his message encounter incomprehension and resistance among friend and foe alike. Far from inaugurating an economy of mutual blessing between God and the house of Israel, Jesus seems to provoke bewilderment and discord wherever he goes (Mark 5:17; Luke 4:28). Time and again Jesus' closest followers misunderstand and disobey (Mark 6:52; 9:32). Time and again Jesus fails to turn the hearts of his hearers and opponents.

Finally, as though to press the issue, Jesus turns his face toward Jerusalem. There he is initially hailed by the crowds as the promised Messiah. But almost immediately the tide begins to run out on him. In the coming days, the one who consistently embodied God's blessing for others appears ever more isolated and alone. By day Jesus teaches in the precincts of the Temple and debates the authorities. By night he hides in the environs of Jerusalem in the homes of supporters. In a final act of table fellowship, Jesus celebrates the Passover meal with his closest disciples. He blesses God over the bread and cup and announces that God's reign shall have come before he next drinks wine again (Mark 14:25). Still Jesus' isolation increases. One of his table companions prepares to hand him over to the Temple authorities. Jesus retires with his disciples to a garden to pray at night, but his disciples are not able to remain awake. Jesus prays alone (Mark 14:39).

Now things happen quickly. Men with clubs and swords arrest Jesus in the garden. His disciples scatter. He is brought before the Temple authorities, who find him guilty of blasphemy and hand him over in the morning to the Roman governor, Pontius Pilate. Pilate holds an irregular trial and sentences Jesus to death on the strength of false evidence. Jesus is flogged and mocked by gentile soldiers. Nearby, his Jewish followers deny ever having known him. Around nine o'clock in the morning Jesus is taken outside the gates of Jerusalem and crucified between two criminals. About six hours later, Jesus dies, crying, "My God, my God, why have you forsaken me?" (Mark 15:34)

Thus in the person and history of this one herald of God's reign the economy of mutual blessing between God, Israel, and the nations comes to a remarkable confluence and issues in a catastrophic result. The one who trusted God's coming reign to gather in the outcasts is himself rejected by leaders of the house of Israel, handed over to rulers of the gentiles, and crucified. At point after point, members of the human family act in ways that are at once wholly plausible and wholly destructive. "Jews and Romans, Gentiles and Jews, the pious and the impious, the political and the apolitical, rulers and ruled, reflective and frenzied—in a unanimity that extends beyond their differences, they all bring the one chosen by God to the cross."[7]

Yet the wound in the economy of blessing goes deeper still, for at the uttermost point it touches the relationship between Jesus and the one he called *Abba*, the God of Israel. Jesus trusted God's coming reign to bring the ultimate victory of God's blessing over curse, not for himself alone but for all, and especially for the lost. In this faith, Jesus trod a path of obedience until God's promised blessing was wholly hidden under its opposite—under curse, shame, isolation, and abandonment. Thus Jesus became wholly identified with the lost whose case he advocated, even to the point of crying out in abandonment on the cross. The burden of curse, shame, and isolation that he bore was not his own but that of others.

"and resurrection. . ."

Alone among Jesus' devastated followers, the women set out early in the morning to dress Jesus' body for burial. But when they arrived at the tomb everything was other than they had expected. To their astonishment, they discovered that, "Our God turned curse into a blessing" (Neh 13:2; see Gal 3:13–14). The God of Israel had raised Jesus from the dead.

By raising the crucified Jesus from the dead, God vindicates the economy of mutual blessing over against all the destructive powers of sin, curse, separation, and death. God thereby also vindicates Jesus' own faith in the ultimate victory of God's blessing, especially on behalf of the lost and forsaken. The victory of God's blessing over curse is efficacious in the first instance on behalf of Jesus himself: God refused to let the "Holy One experience corruption" (Acts 2:27). But God's victory is efficacious in the second instance on behalf of all those for whom Jesus lived, ministered, and suffered. In light of the resurrection, the crucifixion itself appears in a new and triumphant light. When Jesus entered into uttermost solidarity with the lost, even to the point of dying the shameful death of a sinner and outcast, he did so in continuity with his *Abba*'s own passionate love for the house of Israel and for the whole earthly economy of difference and mutual dependence. Therefore Paul does not hesitate to say that Christ became a "curse" in his death by crucifixion, yet just in this way secured the blessing of Abraham for the Gentiles (Gal 3:13–14).

The resurrection, which God performs on Jesus, is followed by the resurrection appearances, in which Jesus presents himself to others. These meetings are first of all meetings of recognition, forgiveness, and reconciliation. They are then meetings of fellowship and feasting. Finally, they are meetings of sending. Henceforth reconciliation, feasting, and sending mark the phases of renewed fellowship whereby Jesus' resurrection from the dead becomes a power among the living until the day of the Lord's return.

"the victorious guarantee of God's fidelity to the work of consummation. . ."

The gospel, we said earlier, speaks about God's coming reign by speaking about Jesus. Specifically, the gospel proclaims Jesus as the victorious guarantee of God's end-time fidelity to the work of consummation. Each element of the phrase *victorious guarantee* must be given its proper weight. The gospel proclaims Jesus as *victorious* because through the resurrection God vindicates Jesus' trust in the triumph of blessing over curse, life over death, communion over isolation. At the same time, the gospel proclaims Jesus as *guarantee* because while everything about Jesus pertains to God's eschatological reign, Jesus himself is not that reign in its fullness. Jesus is only "the first fruits of those who have died" (1 Cor 15:20). Jesus must be joined by all his brothers and sisters before God's reign is established. Paul describes Christ as God's victorious guarantee in the most compact terms when he writes, "For in him every one of God's promises is a 'Yes'" (2 Cor 1:20). Paul does not say that in Christ all of God's promises are fulfilled but rather that they are confirmed. Paul, moreover, makes clear throughout his writings that God's victory presently appears among Christ's followers not in the form of "fullness," but in participation in Christ's sufferings, a point to which we will return shortly.

In Jesus God demonstrates invincible fidelity to God's overarching work as the Consummator of creation. Here one can only agree with the great christocentric theologians Karl Barth and Karl Rahner, both of whom rightly insist that the gospel is intelligible only as the confirmation and vindication of God's work as Consummator. Barth rightly describes God's covenant with creation as the presupposition of the atonement in Christ, and the atonement as the work by which God upholds and maintains the covenant in the face of sin (*CD* IV/1, 3–78). Barth, however, veers over the edge of Christian gnosticism when he goes on to say that atonement in Jesus brings the history of God's covenant with creation to an end.

In this respect, at least, Rahner is closer to the mark when he speaks of God's work in Christ as establishing the "irrevocability" of history in its orientation toward final consummation.[8] Rahner allows for the incompleteness of covenant history and makes room for the new and unexpected.

"that is, to fullness of mutual blessing as the outcome
of God's economy with Israel, the nations, and all creation."

Yet neither Barth nor Rahner identifies God's work as Consummator in its concrete historical form. God's work as Consummator cannot be collapsed in a Scotist fashion into the relationship that exists between Jesus Christ and the rest of the human family. To proceed thus is to risk perpetually falling afoul of Dietrich Bonhoeffer's admonition, "One cannot and must not speak the last word before the last but one."[9] But neither can God's work as Consummator be identified in a traditional Thomist fashion with one or another abstract account of the Creator's purposes for a generic human race. Rather God's work as Consummator takes concrete shape in the open-ended economy of difference and mutual dependence that continually unfolds between the Lord, Israel, and the nations.

If Jesus is the proleptic enactment of God's eschatological fidelity to the work of consummation, then Jesus is by this very fact the carnal embodiment of God's end-time fidelity toward Israel and toward Israel's future as the place of unsurpassable blessing for Israel, for the nations, and for all creation. By its nature, then, Jesus' resurrection from the dead anticipates a future event whose character as victorious fidelity can no longer be in doubt. That event is God's intervention on behalf of all Israel in keeping with God's promises, such that God's final act of covenant faithfulness toward Israel redounds not only to the blessing of Israel but also to the blessing of the nations and all of creation. Jesus, the firstborn from the dead, is also the first fruits of God's eschatological vindication of Israel's body. In light of Jesus' bodily resurrection, it is certain not only that God will intervene on behalf of the whole body of Israel at the close of covenant history but also that by this very act God will consummate the world.

THE SHAPE OF DISCIPLESHIP

In the life, death, and resurrection of Jesus, God irrevocably upsets the equilibrium of blessing and curse within God's economies of difference and mutual dependence. Jesus thereby frees his disciples to live in such a way that the blessing of others knows no bounds.[10] "We know love by this, that he laid down his life for us—and we ought to lay down our lives for one another" (1 John 3:16).

Few writers have articulated more emphatically than Bonhoeffer the point that Christian discipleship necessarily takes a cruciform shape:

> The passion of Christ is the victory of divine love over the powers of evil, and therefore it is the only supportable basis for Christian obedience. Once again, Jesus calls those who follow him to share his passion. How can we convince the world by our preaching of the passion when we shrink from that passion in our own lives? On the cross Jesus fulfilled the law he himself established and thus graciously keeps his disciples in the fellowship of his suffering. The cross is the only power in the world which proves that suffering love can avenge and vanquish evil. But it was just this participation in the cross which the disciples were granted when Jesus called them to him. *They are called blessed because of their visible participation in his cross.*[11]

Bonhoeffer's insight has nothing to do with a morbid submission to suffering for its own sake. Quite the contrary, we have seen that Bonhoeffer clearly understood the Hebrew Scriptures' central concern for God's blessing, "which includes in itself all earthly good."[12] Moreover, Bonhoeffer insists that the Scriptures' concern for God's blessing is precisely *not* superseded or transcended in the Apostolic Witness. Bonhoeffer immediately goes on to write:

> It would be natural to suppose that, as usual, the New Testament spiritualizes the teaching of the Old Testament here [with regard to blessing], and therefore to regard the Old Testament blessing as superseded in the New. But is it an accident that sickness and death are mentioned in connection with the misuse of the Lord's Supper (The cup of *blessing*, 1 Cor 10:16; 11:30), that Jesus restored people's health, and that while his disciples were with him they "lacked nothing"?[13]

According to Bonhoeffer, even Jesus' cross must not be played off against God's blessing as announced in the Scriptures of Israel:

> Now, is it right to set the Old Testament blessing against the cross? That is what Kierkegaard did. That makes the cross, or at least suffering, an abstract principle; and that is just what gives

> rise to an unhealthy methodism, which deprives suffering of its
> element of contingency as a divine ordinance. . . . *The only
> difference between the Old and New Testament in this respect is that
> in the Old the blessing includes the cross, and in the New the cross
> includes the blessing.*[14]

The cross does not supersede the economy of mutual blessing; it
establishes the outermost point of God's fidelity to it on behalf of
the estranged other. As a result, the cross does not offer redemption
from this world but for it:

> The Christian, unlike the devotees of the redemption myths, has
> no last line of escape available from earthly tasks and difficulties
> into the eternal, but, like Christ himself ('My God, why hast thou
> forsaken me?), he must drink the earthly cup to the dregs, and
> only in his doing so is the crucified and risen Lord with him, and
> he crucified and risen with Christ. This world must not be
> prematurely written off; in this the Old and New Testaments are at
> one. Redemption myths arise from human boundary-experiences,
> but Christ takes hold of a man at the center of his life.[15]

The cross at the center of the public square is what makes the
Gospel an offense to Jew and Greek alike. The cross has nothing
whatever to do with the denial or destruction of Israel's national
privilege. To interpret the gospel in that way is to "nullify the faithfulness of God" (Rom 3:3). The real offense of the gospel is at once
much simpler and much harder: God preserves the economy of
mutual blessing through suffering love, to which Jew and Greek
alike are called to be conformed.

THE CHURCH AMID JEWS AND GENTILES

The resurrection anticipates the eschatological outcome of covenant
history and reveals its character *in nuce* as God's vindication of
Israel's body to the blessing of Israel, the nations, and all creation.
But the resurrection does not have only this ultimate eschatological
point of reference. The resurrection also inaugurates something
new within the open-ended story of God's work as the Consummator of creation. So it was also after the Exodus, when God's deliverance of Israel from Egypt led to God's giving the law at Mt. Sinai
and thus to a further unfolding of God's work as the Consummator
of Israel. In the wake of Jesus' resurrection, the new thing is the

church, the table fellowship of Jews and Gentiles that prays in Jesus' name for the coming of the God of Israel's reign.

To understand this table fellowship more fully, we must consider its relationship to the economy of consummation as this is embodied in the difference and mutual relation of Israel and the nations. To do this, we must explore the relation of the church and the economy of consummation from three perspectives. First, we must examine the economy of consummation within the church. Second, we must examine the church within the economy of consummation. Third, we must examine the church's relation to the eschatological fulfillment of God's economy of consummation. In each case, we will see that the gospel and the table fellowship it founds *confirms* rather than *annuls* the difference and mutual dependence of Israel and the nations.[16]

The Economy of Consummation within the Church

Traditionally, the church has understood itself as a spiritual fellowship in which the carnal distinction between Jew and Gentile no longer applies. The church has declared itself a third and final "race" that transcends and replaces the difference between Israel and the nations. While the historical journey that ultimately issued in this misunderstanding is a complex one, its basic trajectory can be formulated easily enough. What began in Jesus' name as Israel's hospitality toward Gentiles as Gentiles, ended as the Gentiles' inhospitability toward Jews as Jews.[17]

The proper therapy for this misunderstanding is a recovery of the church's basic character as a table fellowship of those who are— and remain—different. The distinction between Jew and Gentile, being intrinsic to God's work as the Consummator of creation, is not erased but realized in a new way in the sphere of the church. The church concerns the Jew as a Jew and the Gentile as a Gentile, not only initially or for the period of a few generations but essentially and at all times. Indeed, the church's fundamental character is revealed in the fact that it is the place where Jews and Gentiles, with equal right, are together with one another.[18] As Friedrich-Wilhelm Marquardt has written:

> The idea that all human distinctions are "transcended" in Christ is falsely understood if one deduces from it the pure meaninglessness of these distinctions. Christ "transcends" not the different circumstances of our various callings but the

apartheids by which we have closed ourselves off from one another. Jesus Christ tore down the "dividing wall" between Israel and the nations, the Chinese and the Berlin walls; he beat down the "enmities" between human groups; he conquered the dualistic global law of human history (Eph 2:14). His work is establishing peace (Eph 2:14–16), but not the nullification of Judaism. And he annuls the Gentiles only insofar as he takes from them their lack of relation to Israel. The nations are contradicted only in the event that they should seek their essence, their identity, in inward absence of relation to Israel, just as must happen to a Judaism which—contrary to its vocation—for its part sets itself exclusively against the nations.[19]

What the church rejects is not the difference of Jew and Gentile, male and female, but rather the idea that these differences essentially entail curse, opposition, and antithesis. Understood in this way, the church is the social embodiment of the doctrine of justification, for justification in its social dimension means the reconciliation of different kinds of people.[20] Reconciliation does not mean the imposition of sameness, but the unity of reciprocal blessing. The church is called to be not simply a household, but a household of households.

Thus the church is not a third column of biblical ontology next to that of the Jews and that of the Greeks, but rather a particular form in which the basic relation between Jew and Gentile is actualized.[21] Jesus' resurrection does not transcend the distinction between Israel and the nations but confirms and realizes it in a new way. To be sure, the church is only a *provisional* form of the relationship of Jew and Gentile, of Israel and the nations. The church is not itself God's reign; it is not the place where God's promises are completely fulfilled to the definitive blessing of Israel and the nations. But the church does realize the fellowship of Jew and Gentile in a promissory way and thereby points forward to the coming of God's reign in hope.

This view of the church underlies the decision of the so-called Council of Jerusalem (Acts 15:1–21; Gal 2:1–10). Those present take it for granted that Jewish followers of Jesus remain obligated to the Torah; at the same time they rule that Gentile followers of Jesus are obligated to observe only the Noachide law. In back of this decision is the belief that what God has done in Jesus engages Jews as Jews and Gentiles as Gentiles. Hence obedience to Jesus is equally possible from either of two vantage points. It is possible from the vantage point of Jews, who continue to observe the Mosaic law in light of Jesus' messianic interpretation of the same. And it is possible from the vantage point of Gentiles, who, without first becoming Jews and hence without incurring obligation to the Torah, nevertheless live in obedience to Jesus as Gentiles. The fundamental vision of the church is one in which difference is *preserved* in a table fellowship of common blessing rather than overcome.

When this understanding of the church is recovered, ecclesiology does not lead inevitably to the eclipse of the body of Israel or to the "demythologization" of Israel's election. Michael Wyschogrod's concern regarding the ecclesial erasure of the distinction between Jew and Gentile is directly addressed.[22] The church can only desire the faithful preservation of the distinctiveness and integrity of Jewish existence wherever this takes place, whether within or without the church. The church, for its part, should repent of having turned its back upon the original determination of the Council of Jerusalem, where the Jewish obligation to maintain Jewish identity was universally presupposed. For the future, it should seek to make clear, in the words of Paul van Buren, that when Jews seek to join the church, this "does not mean that they have no part in the covenant of their people with God. They remain Jews, however irregular their status with their people will be because of past church policy."[23]

The Church within the Economy of Consummation

The church is not the reign of God but a provisional form of the fellowship of Jew and Gentile. Nothing attests to the church's provisional character more eloquently than its almost exclusively gentile character. While the church proclaims a gospel that invites the Jew as Jew and the Gentile as Gentile, Jews for the most part have declined the invitation. This poses an inevitable conundrum for the church. Granted, the conundrum can be dissolved rather easily if one simply denies the starting points out of which it arises. This can be done either by denying God's fidelity toward the Jews, as the church has done for most of its history, or by denying the relevance of the gospel for Jews, as some Christians are tempted to do today. Both positions resolve the conundrum by diminishing the scope of God's promises. They solve the problem by cutting the knot.

It is profoundly instructive that Paul in his Letter to the Romans, the one work in the Apostolic Witness that addresses the issue at hand explicitly and at length, did not cut the knot. Paul regards God's election of and fidelity toward Israel as absolutely fundamental and axiomatic (Rom 3:3; 9:4–5; 11:29; 15:8). Equally axiomatic for Paul is the gospel's all-encompassing significance, "to the Jew first and also to the Greek" (Rom 1:16; see 2:9, 10). Yet, as Paul acknowledges with evident astonishment, Israel has rejected the gospel in overwhelming measure (10:18–21). How is this to be understood? Paul answers by interpreting the gospel as an event that takes place within the context of God's overarching work as the Lord of covenant history (Rom 11).

According to Paul, Israel's no to the gospel is itself an internal and divinely willed part of the way the gospel fits into the world of Israel and the nations. It is God who has brought a hardening "upon part of Israel"—not absolutely and in every respect—but quite specifically with respect to the gospel (Rom 11:25). This hardening is not the same thing as rejection and has nothing at all to do with moral judgment.[24] Nor does this hardening cut Israel off from God's covenantal love and saving power. The point of the hardening is not the punishment of Israel but rather the blessing of the nations. As Leslie Newbigin has put it, "God has hardened the heart of Israel so that the gospel which they reject will—so to say—bounce off to the Gentiles."[25] Israel's no provides time and space for the preaching of the gospel among the nations.

Is it conceivable that the God of Israel would work blessings for the nations by closing Israel's eyes to "so great a salvation?" (Heb 2:3). Could such an action be in keeping with God's character and fidelity? In reply, one might observe that the God of Israel acted in a remarkably similar way once before, in the history of Joseph and his brothers. In that case too, Jacob's sons rejected their especially beloved brother and handed him over to foreigners from the nations, who did with Joseph what they would. For years thereafter, Jacob and his sons could only assume that their brother Joseph was "no more" (Gen 42:13, 36). But Joseph was "yet alive," for God was with Joseph (Gen 45:28). Joseph lived among the Egyptians, while Jacob and his other sons remained ignorant that this was so.

As the well-known story suggests, it is hardly inconceivable for the God of Israel to pursue the ultimate good of Israel in a roundabout way that entails the preliminary blessing of the nations. What is inconceivable is that the living God would at any point annul God's love for Israel or abandon Israel as the ultimate *focal point* of God's blessing. As Paul wrote, "The gifts and the calling of God are irrevocable" (Rom 11:29).

In view of the church's place within God's overarching economy of consummation, the church must guard against two misunderstandings. First, the church should not permit its overwhelmingly gentile character to lead it to forget or minimize its own character as a table fellowship that is open to all persons *as* Jews and *as* Gentiles. It is extremely doubtful whether there has ever been a time when the living membership of the church included no Jews. Yet even if there were such a time, the presence of the church's living Lord, the Jew Jesus Christ, ensures that the church remains essentially a table fellowship of Jews and Gentiles.

Second, the church should not confuse its universal mission with a *uniform* mission. The church does indeed have a commission to proclaim "the good news about the kingdom of God and the name of Jesus Christ" before all the world. But it must do so in a differentiated way. The church is commissioned to make disciples of all the nations (*panta ta ethnē*) (Matt 28:19). It has no comparable commission to seek the "conversion" of the Jewish people. This is especially true of the gentile church. Nothing in the Apostolic Witness remotely suggests the validity of a gentile-Christian mission to non-Christian Jews. Christians should not hide or minimize their faith in conversation with Jews. But the church, above all in its gentile portion, should cease organized mission efforts among the Jewish people. Instead the church of the Gentiles should seek to live before the Jewish people in such a way that Israel can reasonably infer that here the nations of the world truly worship the God of Israel and in this way manifest the truth of its gospel (see Rom 11:13–14).

By accepting these terms of its existence and resisting the temptation to "smooth them out" in favor of a simpler solution, the church demonstrates its readiness to live *in media re*, sustained by faith in the God of covenant history.

The Economy of Consummation and the Limits of the Church

Operating within the framework of the standard canonical narrative, Christian theologians have sometimes held that Israel would convert to the church at the end of the ages and thereby be saved. They have supported this view by appealing to the "mystery" that Paul solemnly declares to his gentile audience near the end of Romans 11:

> So that you may not claim to be wiser than you are, brothers and
> sisters, I want you to understand this mystery: a hardening
> has come upon part of Israel, until the full number of the
> Gentiles has come in.
> And so all Israel will be saved; as it is written,
> "Out of Zion will come the Deliverer;
> he will banish ungodliness from Jacob."
> "And this is my covenant with them,
> when I take away their sins." (Rom 11:25–27)

Yet nowhere in this passage does Paul say that Israel will be saved *through conversion to the church*.[26] Rather, what Paul announces is God's immediate intervention on Israel's behalf at the end of the age: "Out of Zion will come the Deliverer." For Paul, moreover, there is nothing mysterious about this aspect of his announcement. Few themes are more prevalent throughout the Scriptures than God's eschatological intervention on Israel's behalf. Furthermore, Paul's theme throughout Romans 11, and indeed, throughout the whole letter, has been God's fidelity toward Israel.[27] Rather, the mystery that Paul announces touches on a different point entirely, namely, the *manner* in which God will intervene on Israel's behalf. This will happen, Paul affirms, after "the full number of the Gentiles has come in." "*And so*," that is, in this way, "all Israel will be saved."[28]

Although perhaps overly familiar in discussions such as the present one, this Pauline passage has enduring significance because it points clearly to the eschatological limits of the church. The church is not a community that issues directly into God's reign like a river that flows into the sea. A hiatus separates the church and God's eschatological reign that can only be filled by the Lord's free action on behalf of all Israel. This future event, in Berthold Klappert's phrase, is "trans-kerygmatic" and "trans-ecclesiological."[29] It does not depend upon the mediation of the church or its kerygma. "*Out of Zion* will come the Deliverer." The final chapter of covenant history turns on the Lord's relationship to Israel, not the Lord's relationship to the nations, not even the nations who have been gathered into the church. Once again, the Joseph cycle provides the most apt commentary on Paul's expectation. The story reaches its climax in an event that takes place between Joseph and his siblings, while the Egyptians listen from an adjoining room (Gen 45:1–2). The common rejoicing comes thereafter.

This does not mean that the church can or should adopt a posture of christological agnosticism with regard to God's eschatological fidelity toward Israel. Because of the church's faith in Jesus Christ, its hope in God's reign has a quite definite contour. Quoting from Isaiah 59, Paul identifies God's future action on Israel's behalf in messianic terms. Although Paul does not identify the coming messiah by name, Paul's whole pattern of argumentation "from the lesser to the greater" reflects the cruciform imprint of the personal history of Jesus (see Rom 11:12, 15). If God has blessed the nations through Israel's no to the gospel, then how much more can be expected when God acts directly on Israel's behalf at the end of the age!

FINAL CONSUMMATION

The unity of the Christian canon is not best unlocked by insisting that everything in the Bible points toward Jesus Christ. Such a construal of the canon's unity systematically disregards Bonhoeffer's admonition not to speak the last word before the last but one. What results practically is a Christian theology that is triumphalist in its posture toward the Jews and latently gnostic in its grasp of God's purposes for the earth and its history. More helpful for discerning the unity of the canon is the recognition that the Scriptures and the Apostolic Witness are both centrally concerned with the God of Israel and the God of Israel's coming reign of *shalom*. This understanding of the Bible's overarching theme allows Christians to give adequate weight to that divine purpose which is *antecedent* to the gospel about Jesus, namely, the Lord's work as the Consummator of creation. Without doubt everything turns on Christ, but not everything concerns Christ.[30] Redemption is for the sake of consummation, not consummation for the sake of redemption.

According to the Scriptures, the Lord consummates through

the blessing of an other. The open-ended covenantal history that the Lord inaugurates by promising to bless Abraham and "in him" all the nations of the earth is not an epiphenomenon of God's work as Consummator but the work itself. The Lord's history with Israel and the nations is oriented from the outset toward a reign of wholeness, righteousness, justice, and peace; but this outcome is deeply and radically threatened by sin, evil, and oppression. The fall does not lie *in back* of this history but *within* it. Redemption does not mean deliverance *from* this history but liberation *within* and *for* it. According to the Apostolic Witness, the Lord's eschatological fidelity to the work of consummation is proleptically enacted over against all destructive powers in Jesus' life, death, and resurrection. The gospel is therefore "the power of God for salvation to everyone who has faith, to the Jew first and also to the Greek" (Rom 1:16). The gospel summons everyone not to cease being Jews or Gentiles but to glorify the present and future victory of the God of Israel through conformity to Jesus' own solidarity with the other, even to the point of participation in Jesus' sufferings.

The Lord's history with Israel and the nations does not *prepare* for the gospel but *surrounds* the gospel as its constant horizon, context, and goal. This point is confirmed by John's vision of the New Jerusalem (Rev 21). In the new creation, God dwells in a city whose gates are marked by the names of the twelve tribes of Israel (21:12), through which the kings of the earth come bringing "their glory" (21:24). In John's vision, God's work as Consummator comes to fulfillment in an event that has both historical and cosmic dimensions. The cosmic dimension concerns God's creation of a new heaven and a new earth (21:1). The historical dimension concerns God's definitive fulfillment of God's promise to bless Israel and, in Israel, all the "peoples" of the earth (21:3). The guarantor of the two dimensions in their unity is the Lamb, who together with the glory of God is the light of the city of God (21:23). Thus the path to the new creation leads through God's fidelity toward the tribes of Israel, yet in such a way that God's fidelity toward Israel is simultaneously an act of healing judgment and reconciliation between the Lord, the whole human family, and all creation.

For I tell you that Christ has become a servant of the circumcised on behalf of the truth of God in order that he might confirm the promises given to the patriarchs, and in order that the Gentiles might glorify God for his mercy (Rom 15:8–9a).

It is said that even Doeg and Ahithophel shall have a part in the life to come. The angels of the Service say, "If David complains of this, what wilt Thou do?" God replies, "It is my business to make them friends with one another" (Sanhedrin, 105a).[31]

NOTES

Chapter 1

1. Statement of the 1987 General Assembly of the Presbyterian Church (USA); in Alan Brockway *et al.*, *The Theology of the Churches and the Jewish People* (Geneva: WCC Publications, 1988), 111. Key passages from other church statements that explicitly reject the teaching of supersessionism are collected in Clark M. Williamson, *A Guest in the House of Israel: Post-Holocaust Church Theology* (Louisville: Westminster/John Knox Press, 1993), 37. The complete texts of these and many other recent church declarations dealing with the church and the Jewish people are available in Brockway *et al.*, *Theology of the Churches*; Helga Croner, comp., *Stepping Stones to Further Jewish-Christian Relations* (New York: Stimulus Books, 1977); Helga Croner, comp., *More Stepping Stones to Jewish-Christian Relations* (New York: Paulist Press, 1985).

2. Brockway *et al.*, *Theology of the Churches,* 112–13.

3. "The God of Hebrew Scriptures acted in Jesus for all the world" is my working formulation of the central normative claim of Christian faith as attested by the New Testament and subsequent Christian tradition. Like any such formula, mine reflects a constructive judgment about Christian faith as a whole and hence cannot be defended on historical grounds alone. (For the classic statement of this point, see Ernst Troeltsch, "What Does 'Essence of Christianity' Mean?" in *Ernst Troeltsch: Writings on Theology and Religion*, ed. by Robert Morgan and Michael Pye (Atlanta: John Knox Press, 1977), 124–79.) Still, I intend my formula to be as nontendentious as possible without falling into utter vacuity. The statement's threefold structure (subject, action, object) articulates the obvious point that Christian faith concerns a salvific transaction between God and the world whose center is Jesus. The identification of God with reference to the Hebrew Scriptures makes clear that Christians do not confess a hitherto unknown God (the view held by Marcion and repudiated by the church) but rather the same God attested by the Scriptures of the Jewish people.

4. The most complete source for Wyschogrod's theology is his *The Body of Faith: God in the People Israel* (San Francisco: Harper and Row, 1989). In addition, Wyschogrod has written numerous articles on Judaism and Christianity.

5. Wyschogrod, *Body of Faith*, xv, 58–70; "Eine Theologie der jüdischen Einheit" in *Welches Judentum steht welchem Christentum gegenüber*, ed. Hans-Hermann Henrix and Werner Licharz (Frankfurt: Haag and Herchen Verlag, 1985), 45–50, 54.

6. Wyschogrod, *Body of Faith*, 57.

7. Ibid., 56–57.

8. Ibid., 65–70; "Theologie der jüdischen Einheit," 51.

9. Ibid., 66–67.

10. Wyschogrod, *Body of Faith*, xv.

11. Ibid., 256.

12. Ibid., 58.

13. Ibid., 62–63.

14. Ibid., 61.

15. Ibid.

16. Ibid., 63–65.

17. Michael Wyschogrod, "Israel, Church, and Election" in *Brothers in Hope*, ed. John M. Oesterreicher (New York: Herder and Herder, 1970), 80.

18. Wyschogrod, "Theologie der jüdischen Einheit," 54.

19. Wyschogrod, "Israel, the Church, and Election," 79–80.

20. Michael Wyschogrod, "A New Stage in Jewish-Christian Dialogue," *Judaism* 31 (1982), 361f.

21. Michael Wyschogrod, "Christology: The Immovable Object," *Religion and Intellectual Life* 3 (1986), 79.

22. Michael Wyschogrod, "Why Was and Is the Theology of Karl Barth of Interest to a Jewish Theologian?" in *Footnotes to a Theology: The Karl Barth Colloquium of 1972,* ed. Martin Rumscheidt (SR Supplements; Waterloo, Ont.: Canadian Corp. for Studies in Religion, 1974), 102.

23. Wyschogrod, "Christology," 80.

24. Idem., "Karl Barth," 100.

25. Ibid., 99–100.

26. Ibid., 97.

27. Wyschogrod, "Israel, the Church, and Election," 83. See also Michael Wyschogrod, "Letter to a Friend," *Modern Theology* 11/2 (1995), 165–71.

28. Michael Wyschogrod and David Berger, *Jews and Jewish Christianity* (New York: KTAV, 1978), 64f.

29. Wyschogrod, "Israel, Church, and Election," 83.

30. Ibid., 84f.

31. Key essays on the importance of narrative for Christian and Jewish theology are anthologized in *Why Narrative? Readings in Narrative Theology,* ed. Stanley Hauerwas and L. Gregory Jones (Grand Rapids: Eerdmans, 1989). Michael Goldberg advances a similar claim for both Judaism and Christianity in his *Jews and Christians: Getting Our Stories Straight* (Philadelphia: Trinity Press Int'l., 1991), while arguing that the Christian narrative is radically discontinuous with the Jewish narrative in its depiction of God's identity.

32. Because the terms *Old Testament* and *New Testament* are bound up with the logic of the canonical narrative criticized in this book, I refer to the parts of the Christian canon as the Scriptures (or, for clarity's sake, the Hebrew Scriptures) and the Apostolic Witness respectively. *The Scriptures* recommends itself as an alternative to *Old Testament* because it follows the usage of Jesus and the first Christians (see Mark 12:24; Acts 17:2; Rom 1:2). *Apostolic Witness* seems a

suitable alternative to *New Testament* inasmuch as it identifies the characteristic that the church deems the writings to possess that endows them with an authority equal to that of the Scriptures.

33. Charles Wood develops the idea of a canonical construal in *The Formation of Christian Understanding: An Essay in Theological Hermeneutics* (Philadelphia: Westminster Press, 1981), especially ch. 4.

34. Ibid., 109.

35. Ibid.

36. Ibid., 100.

37. Ibid., 99.

38. Dietrich Bonhoeffer, *Letters and Papers from Prison* enlarged edition (New York: Collier Books, 1972), 285–86.

39. Ibid., 282. Emphasis added.

40. This is not to suggest that Bonhoeffer was wholly clear in his own mind about such a connection, or indeed, that he fully recognized supersessionism as a theological problem. Earlier than most, Bonhoeffer perceived the threat that the anti-Semitism of the Third Reich posed both to the Jewish people and to integrity of the church, and he worked to awaken an awareness of this threat in the Confessing Church. Still, Bonhoeffer's theological statements regarding the Jewish people are often quite traditional in conception. See, for example, Dietrich Bonhoeffer, "Die Kirche vor der Judenfrage" in *Gesammelte Schriften,* vol. 2 (Munich: Christian Kaiser, 1959), 44–53.

41. The present work takes its place among a small but growing number of works in English that attempt to draw the consequences of the church's contemporary rejection of supersessionism for dogmatic or systematic theology. Among the most important of these are Paul M. van Buren's multivolume work, *A Theology of the Jewish-Christian Reality* (San Francisco: Harper and Row, 1987–88); and Clark M. Williamson, *A Guest in the House of Israel: Post-Holocaust Church Theology* (Louisville: Westminster/John Knox Press, 1993).

Chapter 2

1. On the history of this development, see Hans F. von Campenhausen, *The Formation of the Christian Bible*, trans. J. A. Baker (Philadelphia: Fortress, 1972); Bruce M. Metzger, *The Canon of the New Testament: Its Origin, Development, and Significance* (Oxford: Clarendon Press, 1987); and Harry Y. Gamble, *The New Testament Canon: Its Making and Meaning* (Philadelphia: Fortress, 1985).

2. Catherine Mowry LaCugna provides a useful overview of the history of the term *economy* in Christian theology in *God for Us: Trinity and Christian Life* (San Francisco: HarperCollins, 1991), ch. 1.

3. Melito of Sardis, *On Pascha*, trans. S. G. Hall (Oxford: Clarendon Press, 1979), 21.

4. Ibid., 55, 57.

5. Karl Barth's theology offers a classic example of the view that holds fast to economic supersessionism while rejecting punitive supersessionism. Barth's position is therefore not inaptly characterized as "radical traditionalism." See

Stephen R. Haynes, *Prospects for Post-Holocaust Theology* (Atlanta: Scholars Press, 1991), ch. 2. Barth's theology is discussed in greater detail in ch. 4.

6. In sum, I distinguish three kinds of supersessionism in the standard canonical narrative: economic, punitive, and structural. The first two designate explicit doctrinal perspectives, i.e., that carnal Israel's history is providentially ordered from the outset to be taken up into the spiritual church (economic supersessionism), and that God has rejected carnal Israel on account of its failure to join the church (punitive supersessionism). Structural supersessionism, in contrast, refers not to an explicit doctrinal perspective but rather to a formal feature of the standard canonical narrative as a whole. Structural supersessionism refers to the narrative logic of the standard model whereby it renders the Hebrew Scriptures largely indecisive for shaping Christian convictions about how God's works as Consummator and as Redeemer engage humankind in universal and enduring ways.

7. Until recently, the First Scottish Confession (1560) was the only creed of the Christian church to refer in detail to God's history with the Jewish people. In that case the treatment entirely follows the spirit of the standard model. See Philip Schaff, *The Creeds of Christendom* (Grand Rapids: Baker Book House, 1985), vol. 3, 437–79, esp. 442–43.

8. On the interpretation of the canon in the second-century context, see Rowan A. Greer, "The Christian Bible and Its Interpretation" in James L. Kugel and Rowan A. Greer, *Early Biblical Interpretation* (Philadelphia: Westminster Press, 1986). General background is available in W. H. C. Frend, *The Rise of Christianity* (Philadelphia: Fortress Press, 1984).

9. Rowan A. Greer develops this thesis in detail in "The Christian Bible." My discussion of Justin and Irenaeus is heavily indebted throughout to Greer's illuminating essay.

10. References to the *Dialogue* and the *Apologies* are taken from the English translation by T. B. Falls, *Saint Justin Martyr* (New York: Christian Heritage, 1948).

11. Justin's "salvation-historical" reading of the Hebrew Scriptures is generally considered his most important advance over the previous generation of Christian writers and the point at which he proves most influential. See von Campenhausen, *Formation*, 98.

12. For Justin's understanding of the church as the "true Israel" against the background of previous Christian exegesis, see Peter Richardson, *Israel in the Apostolic Church* (Cambridge: Cambridge University Press, 1969); and Jeffrey S. Siker, *Disinheriting the Jews: Abraham in Early Christian Controversy* (Louisville: Westminster/John Knox Press, 1991).

13. J. N. D. Kelly, *Early Christian Doctrines*, rev. ed. (San Francisco: HarperSanFrancisco, 1978), 96.

14. See Theodore Stylianopoulos, *Justin Martyr and the Mosaic Law* (Missoula: Scholars Press, 1974), 45–76.

15. Greer, "The Christian Bible," 151.

16. Ibid., 155–76.

17. Kelly, *Early Christian Doctrines*, 22–28.

18. References to *Against Heresies* are taken from the English translation in *The Ante-Nicene Fathers,* ed. A. Roberts and J. Donaldson (Grand Rapids: Eerdmans, 1985), vol. 1, 315–567.

19. Greer, "The Christian Bible," 164.

20. On the whole question, see Eugene TeSelle, *Christ in Context: Divine Purpose and Human Possibility* (Philadelphia: Fortress Press, 1975), esp. chap. 1. The problem should be distinguished from the debate among Reformed theologians in the sixteenth and early seventeenth century regarding "infralapsarianism" and "supralapsarianism." The Reformed debate also presupposed the basic framework of the standard model, but turned on the logical relation of God's specifically *redemptive* decree to save sinners in Christ and God's intention to create Adam and permit him to fall. The infralapsarians held that God's decree to save sinners in Christ logically *follows* God's intention to create Adam and permit him to fall. The supralapsarians held that God's decree to save sinners in Christ while reprobating the rest logically *precedes* even God's decree to create. The question of the place of the incarnation in God's initial consummating plan for Adam does not arise. On the Reformed debate, see Karl Barth, *Church Dogmatics* II/2 (Edinburgh: T & T Clark, 1957), 127–45.

21. Greer, "The Christian Bible," 172–74.

22. See von Campenhausen, *Formation*, 262–68.

23. See Heinrich Heppe, *Reformed Dogmatics: Set Out and Illustrated from the Sources,* trans. G. T. Thomson (Grand Rapids: Baker Book House, 1978), 371–409; and Heinrich Schmid, *Doctrinal Theology of the Evangelical Lutheran Church,* trans. Charles A. Hay and Henry E. Jacobs (Minneapolis: Augsburg, 1899), 508–20.

24. The illuminating exception to the general silence of the church councils regarding the Jewish people appears in the canons enacted by the conciliar fathers, which impose some restrictions on Christian intercourse with Jews and on Jewish economic activity. A summary collection of relevant legislation can be found in James W. Parkes, *The Conflict of the Church and the Synagogue* (New York: Atheneum, 1977), 379–91.

25. Wolfhart Pannenberg, *Jesus: God and Man,* trans. L. L. Wilkins and D. A. Priebe (Philadelphia: Westminster Press, 1968), 34–35.

26. The telling exception is the tradition of *Adversus Judaeos* literature, a polemical genre that served to martial arguments against the Jews. See A. Lukyn Williams, *Adversus Judaeos: A Bird's Eye View of Christian "Apologiae" until the Renaissance* (Cambridge: Cambridge University Press, 1935). Overtly hostile to Israel in any case, the genre was ultimately not incorporated into the standard dogmatic framework.

27. On the distinction between a Scotist and a Thomistic account of God's work as Consummator, see text at note 20 above.

28. Dietrich Bonhoeffer, *Letters and Papers from Prison,* enlarged ed. (New York: Collier Books, 1972), 285–86.

29. Bonhoeffer, *Letters and Papers,* 336.

30. Ibid., 157.

31. Peter Gorday, *Principles of Patristic Exegesis: Romans 9–11 in Origen, John Chrysostom, and Augustine* (New York: Edwin Mellen Press, 1983), 43–102, 226–30.

32. Augustine, *The City of God* 18.46.

Chapter 3

1. The most complete history remains Emanuel Hirsch's five-volume *Geschichte der neueren evangelischen Theologie im Zusammenhang mit den allgemeinen Bewegungen des europäischen Denkens* (Gütersloh: C. Bertelsmann, 1960). For a study that traces the development with special reference to biblical hermeneutics, see Hans W. Frei, *The Eclipse of Biblical Narrative: A Study in Eighteenth and Nineteenth Century Hermeneutics* (New Haven: Yale University Press, 1974).

2. Immanuel Kant, *Religion within the Limits of Reason Alone*, trans. Theodore M. Greene and Hoyt H. Hudson (New York: Harper Torchbooks, 1960). Page references that follow in the text are to this edition.

3. This discussion of Kant's *Religion* and his philosophy of religion in general is informed by Gordon Michalson Jr., *Fallen Freedom: Kant on Radical Evil and Moral Regeneration* (Cambridge: Cambridge University Press, 1990); Bernard M. G. Reardon, *Kant as Philosophical Theologian* (Totowa, N.J.: Barnes and Noble Books, 1988); and Michel Despland, *Kant on History and Religion* (Montreal: McGill-Queen's University Press, 1973).

4. In the *Religion*, Kant states only as much of his moral theory as is necessary for his argument, an example that we follow here. For Kant's moral philosophy, see *Prolegomena to Any Future Metaphysics* (1785) and *The Critique of Practical Reason* (1788).

5. On Kant's understanding of the one true religion and the traditional faiths, see Despland, *Kant*, ch. 10; and Gordon E. Michalson Jr., *The Historical Dimensions of a Rational Faith: The Role of History in Kant's Religious Thought* (Washington, D.C.: University Press of America, 1979).

6. This reversal of concept and narrative is perhaps the classic example of what Ernst Cassirer has called "an exchange of index symbols." "That which formerly had established other concepts, now moves into the position of that which is to be established, and that which hitherto had justified other concepts, now finds itself in the position of a concept which requires justification." Ernst Cassirer, *The Philosophy of the Enlightenment*, trans. Fritz C. A. Koelln and James P. Pettegrove (Princeton: Princeton University Press, 1951), 159.

7. I have revised the English translation by Greene and Hudson by rendering Kant's *Jehowa* as *Jehovah* rather than as *God*. The word *God* needlessly obscures Kant's quite deliberate decision to employ the transliteration of the Tetragrammaton conventional in his day. Although now outdated in scholarly literature, the term *Jehovah* is the contemporary equivalent of Kant's term.

8. Kant refers to Moses Mendelssohn's *Jerusalem, or on Religious Power and Judaism* (1783). Mendelssohn, the most prominent Jewish philosopher of his

day and a celebrated natural law theorist, authored the tract in advocacy of civil and religious liberty for Jews.

9. I have followed the example of most translators and commentators by rendering Schleiermacher's *Gefühl* with "feeling," although it is important to bear in mind that Schleiermacher did not understanding *Gefühl* as mere subjective emotion. As John Macquarrie correctly points out, Schleiermacher understood feeling more nearly as a "'deep-down' experience" that is called forth by our basic apprehension of reality. Macquarrie, *Jesus Christ in Modern Thought* (London: SCM Press, 1990), 195.

10. See, for example, S. W. Sykes, *The Identity of Christianity* (Philadelphia: Fortress, 1984), ch. 4; and Thomas H. Curran, *Doctrine and Speculation in Schleiermacher's* Glaubenslehre (Berlin: Walter de Gruyter, 1994). In the discussion of Schleiermacher, *The Christian Faith*, eds. H. R. Mackintosh and J. S. Stewart (Edinburgh: T & T Clark, 1989), that follows, the work is cited according to paragraph and, when applicable, subsection, e.g., §5.4.

11. Schleiermacher explains and defends the organization of his dogmatics in *On the* Glaubenslehre: *Two Letters to Dr. Lücke*, trans. James O. Duke and Francis Schüssler Fiorenza (Chico, Calif.: Scholars Press, 1981).

12. See ch. 2.

13. On the centrality of the Second Adam motif in Schleiermacher, see Eugene TeSelle, *Christ in Context: Divine Purpose and Human Possibility* (Philadelphia: Fortress Press, 1975), 69–86.

14. One might argue that Schleiermacher's Scotist reading of the Christian story is actually implied by his definition of Christianity. If "everything" in Christianity is determined by its relation to redemption in Jesus, then so too must be God's work as the Consummator of creation. If it were not, a dangerous cleft would open between Christianity as a generic instance of moral monotheism and the distinctively Christian experience of redemption. Schleiermacher's Scotist christology can be understood as a vigorous—if finally unsuccessful—attempt to avoid such a cleft.

15. Mark C. Taylor, *Altarity* (Chicago: University of Chicago Press, 1987), 3.

Chapter 4

1. References are to the English edition of the *Church Dogmatics* (Edinburgh: T & T Clark, 1936–1969). Passages are cited according to volume, part, and page, e.g., *CD* IV/1, 17.

2. Barth develops his doctrine of creation and covenant, like his doctrine of Israel, on a massive scale across a number of volumes. Our concern is not with either doctrine as such but rather with the intersection of the two. Even so, our discussion can only be cursory. The main source for Barth's theology of creation and covenant is *CD* III/1–4, although relevant material can be found throughout Barth's work. A valuable introduction to this aspect of Barth's theology remains Hans Urs von Balthasar, *The Theology of Karl Barth* (New York: Holt, Rinehart and Winston, 1971), 100–50. Important sources for Barth's doctrine of Israel include *CD* II/2, 195–506; III/3, 155–238; and IV/1, 3–78, although once again relevant material can be found throughout his writings.

Useful discussions of Barth's doctrine of Israel include Katherine Sonderegger, *That Jesus Christ Was Born a Jew: Karl Barth's "Doctrine of Israel"* (University Park: Pennsylvania State University Press, 1992); Friedrich-Wilhelm Marquardt, *Die Entdeckung des Judentums für die christliche Theologie: Israel im Denken Karl Barths* (Munich: Christian Kaiser Verlag, 1966); and Berthold Klappert, *Israel und die Kirche: Erwägungen zur Karl Barths Israellehre* (Munich: Christian Kaiser Verlag, 1980).

3. The phrase we have elided reads "and which was fulfilled in Jesus Christ." Barth's understanding of Jesus Christ as the fulfillment of God's covenant with Israel will be treated in the following section. Here we concentrate on Barth's conception of God's covenant with Israel in abstraction from its fulfillment in Jesus Christ.

4. Even the so-called Federal theologians of the seventeenth century, whom Barth acknowledges as his distant forerunners, followed the example of the standard model in this respect. The Federal theologians regarded God's covenant (*foedus*) as key to the interpretation of the Bible but distinguished between God's initial covenant of works and God's subsequent covenant of grace. The first they referred to Adam and Eve, the second to Israel and the church. Barth expressly criticizes these theologians for separating God's initial consummating work from God's subsequent covenant of grace as embodied in God's covenant with Israel and, ultimately, in Jesus Christ (*CD* IV/1, 54–66, esp. 62).

5. Perhaps this broader shift in perspective is the reason Michael Wyschogrod is able to write, "There is nothing more important that I have learned from Barth than the sinfulness of Israel." Michael Wyschogrod, "Why Was and Is the Theology of Karl Barth of Interest to a Jewish Theologian?" in *Footnotes to a Theology: The Karl Barth Colloquium of 1972,* ed. Martin Rumscheidt (SR Supplements; Waterloo, Ont.: Canadian Corp. for Studies in Religion, 1974), 108.

6. For the term *economic supersessionism*, see ch. 2.

7. Important sources for this central Rahnerian concept include "Concerning the Relationship between Nature and Grace" in *Theological Investigations,* vol. 1 (London: Darton, Longman, and Todd, 1961), 297–317; "Nature and Grace" in *Theological Investigations,* vol. 4 (Baltimore: Helicon, 1966), 165–88; and *Foundations of Christian Faith* (New York: Crossroad, 1989), esp. ch. 4. Relevant material is also found throughout Rahner's later essays.

8. Rahner saw the danger of an extrinsic view of grace in the Thomism of the Neoscholastic revival codified in the textbook theology of the nineteenth and early twentieth century. Within the Protestant realm, Karl Barth's view of grace has been frequently charged with "extrincisism," most memorably perhaps by Paul Tillich, who complained that Barth throws the Christian message at his audience "like a stone." Paul Tillich, *Systematic Theology* (Chicago: University of Chicago Press, 1967), 1:7.

9. Rahner, "Concerning the Relationship between Nature and Grace," 298.

10. "The transcendental structures of this single history of each individual and of the human race are historical insofar as, even as permanent and inescapable, they are grounded in God's free and personal self-communica-

tion." Rahner, *Foundations,* 141.

11. Thomas Aquinas, *Summa Theologiae,* I–II, q.110, aa.1–2.

12. On Rahner's relation to Heidegger, see, for example, Anne Carr, *The Theological Method of Karl Rahner* (Missoula: Scholars Press, 1977), 7–58.

13. Martin Heidegger, *Being and Time,* trans. John Macquarrie and Edward Robinson (London: SCM Press, 1962), 33.

14. Karl Rahner, "Über das Verhältnis des Naturgestzes zur übernatürlichen Gnadenordnung," *Orientierung* 20 (1956): 9. Cited in William C. Shepherd, *Man's Condition* (New York: Herder and Herder, 1969), 87.

15. Karl Rahner, "Immanent and Transcendent Consummation of the World," *Theological Investigations,* vol. 10 (New York: Herder and Herder, 1973), 281.

16. Karl Rahner, "Grundsätzliches zur Einheit von Shöpfungs- und Erlösungswirklichkeit," in *Handbuch der Pastoraltheologie,* ed. Franz Xavier Arnold (Freiburg: Herder, 1966), 2/2: 219. My translation.

17. Rahner, "Concerning the Relationship between Nature and Grace," 313.

18. Karl Rahner, "On the Importance of Non-Christian Religions for Salvation," *Theological Investigations,* vol. 18 (New York: Crossroad, 1983), 291.

19. In addition to Schleiermacher, of course, Duns Scotus must be mentioned as a source of Rahner's christology. According to Duns Scotus, the hypostatic union in Christ is the sole basis of all grace bestowed on human creatures at all times, even to Adam before the fall. In a similar way, Rahner affirms that the entire supernatural order, including the grace of Adam, is willed in view of Christ's incarnation. See, for example, Rahner, "The Sin of Adam" in *Theological Investigations,* vol. 11 (New York: Seabury Press), 247–62, esp. 255f.

20. Rahner, *Foundations,* 162.

21. Ibid., 162–63.

22. See Rahner, "The Sin of Adam," 253ff.

23. Rahner, *Handbuch,* 222. My translation.

24. Rahner, *Foundations,* 167.

25. Ibid., 166.

26. Karl Rahner, "History of the World and Salvation History," *Theological Investigations,* vol. 5 (Baltimore: Helicon Press, 1966), 109.

27. Johann-Baptist Metz, "Facing the Jews: Christian Theology after Auschwitz," *The Holocaust as Interpretation,* ed. Elisabeth Schüssler Fiorenza and David Tracy (Edinburgh: T & T Clark, 1984), 27–28.

Chapter 6

1. Following ancient custom, I render the Tetragrammaton as *Lord* in recognition of the holiness of the divine name. In this connection it is worth recalling Dietrich Bonhoeffer's admonition while in prison, "It is only when one knows the unutterability of the name of God that one can utter the name of Jesus Christ." *Letters and Papers from Prison* (New York: Macmillan Books, 1972), 157. The Tetragrammaton does not appear in the Apostolic Writings,

not because some other God is intended but because the practice of not pro-
nouncing the divine name was already well-established in Jesus' time. The one
whom Jesus called *abba* is the Lord, the God of Israel.

2. Dale Patrick, *The Rendering of God in the Old Testament* (Philadelphia:
Fortress Press, 1981), 106n.8.

3. Dietrich Bonhoeffer, *Letters and Papers from Prison* enlarged ed. (New
York: Collier Books, 1972), 336.

4. On the presence of a theology of blessing alongside the more familiar
thelogy of redemption, see Claus Westermann, *Blessing in the Bible and the Life
of the Church,* trans. Kieth Crim (Philadelphia: Fortress Press, 1978); also
Johannes Pederson, *Israel: Its Life and Culture,* 2 vols. (Atlanta: Scholars Press,
1991).

5. Patrick D. Miller, Jr., "The Blessing of God: An Interpretation of Numbers 6:22–27," *Interpretation* 29, 3 (1975): 249.

6. Bonhoeffer, *Letters and Papers,* 374.

7. Leslie Newbigin, *The Gospel in a Pluralist Society* (Grand Rapids: Eerdmans, 1989), 82. Italics added.

8. Bruce Birch, *Let Justice Roll Down: The Old Testament, Ethics, and Christian Life* (Louisville: Westminster/John Knox Press, 1991), 87–91. See also Phyllis A. Bird, "'Male and Female He Created Them': Gen 1:27b in the Context of
the Priestly Account of Creation," *Harvard Theological Review* 74 (1981): 159.

9. Brevard Childs, *Introduction to the Old Testament as Scripture* (Philadelphia: Fortress Press, 1979), 145–46; idem., *Old Testament Theology in Canonical
Context* (London: SCM Press, 1985), 103.

10. Walther Zimmerli, *1. Mose 1–11: Die Urgeschichte* (Zurich: Zwingli Verlag, 1957), 366.

11. Terence E. Fretheim, "The Book of Genesis," in *The New Interpreter's
Bible,* ed. Leander E. Keck *et al.* (Nashville: Abingdon Press, 1994), vol. 1,
410–13. In this connection it is worth observing that the story of Pentecost
(Acts 2:1–13) is *not* a kind of Christian "anti-Babel," as though the Holy Spirit
overcame the diversity of tongues through the introduction of a new divine
Esperanto. Pentecost preserves the diversity of tongues. The new thing is that
"*in our own languages* we hear them speaking about God's deeds of power"
(Acts 2:11).

12. Friedrich-Wilhelm Marquardt, *Das christliche Bekenntnis zu Jesus, dem
Juden: Eine Christologie,* vol. 1 (Munich: Christian Kaiser, 1990), 302f.

13. Walter Brueggemann, *The Land* (Philadelphia: Fortress Press, 1977), 13.

14. Ibid., esp. 4–5, 187–89.

15. See David Novak, *The Image of the Non-Jew in Judaism* (New York:
Edwin Mellen Press, 1983), xiii.

16. The following paragraphs follow closely the stimulating exegesis of Paul
van Buren, *The Jewish-Christian Reality—Part Two: A Christian Theology of the
People Israel* (San Francisco: Harper and Row, 1987), 138–42.

17. Ibid., 141.

18. L. Finkelstein, ed., *Sifre on Deuteronomy* (New York: Jewish Theological

Seminary, 1969), 80. The citation is taken from Niels A. Dahl, "The One God of Jews and Gentiles" in *Studies in Paul* (Minneapolis: Augsburg Publishing House, 1977), 185. For similar passages, see Jacob Neusner, ed. and trans., *Scriptures of the Oral Torah: Sanctification and Salvation in the Sacred Books of Judaism* (San Francisco: Harper and Row, 1987), 191; and C. G. Montefiore and H. Lowe, *A Rabbinic Anthology* (New York: Schocken Books, 1974), 80f., 102.

19. Cited from Montefiore and Lowe, *A Rabbinic Anthology*, 39.

20. Pedersen, *Israel*, 1: 310–35.

21. See Montefiore and Lowe, *A Rabbinic Anthology*, 581f., for texts and commentary.

22. My source for the anecdote is Newbigin, *Gospel*, 80.

23. Compare Fretheim, "Genesis," 345–46.

24. Cited from Jacob Neusner, *Scriptures of the Oral Torah*, 85.

25. Bonhoeffer, *Letters and Papers*, 285f.

Chapter 7

1. So also Walter Brueggemann, *Genesis* (Atlanta: John Knox Press, 1982), 41; Claus Westermann, *Genesis 1–11: A Commentary* (Minneapolis: Augsburg Publ. House, 1984), 276.

2. Compare Terence Fretheim, "Is Genesis 3 a Fall Story?" *Word and World* 14, 2 (1994): 150–51.

3. Phyllis A. Bird, "'Male and Female He Created Them': Gen. 1:27b in the Context of the Priestly Account of Creation," *Harvard Theological Review* 74/2 (1981): 158.

4. Robert Alter, *The Art of Biblical Narrative* (New York: Basic Books, 1981), 180.

5. Terence E. Fretheim, "The Book of Genesis" in *The New Interpreter's Bible*, ed. Leander E. Keck *et al.* (Nashville: Abingdon Press, 1994), vol. 1, 410–14.

6. Cited from C. G. Montefiore and H. Lowe, *A Rabbinic Anthology* (London: Macmillan and Co., 1938), 80.

7. For a discussion of relevant passages, see Walther Eichrodt, *Theology of the Old Testament*, trans. J. A. Baker, vol. 1 (Philadelphia: Westminster Press, 1967), 459–62, 467–71.

8. Dietrich Bonhoeffer, *Letters and Papers from Prison* (New York: Macmillan Books, 1972), 336. Final italics mine.

9. Claus Westermann, *Blessing in the Bible and the Life of the Church*, trans. Kieth Crim (Philadelphia: Fortress Press, 1978), 30.

10. See Martin Noth, *Leviticus,* trans. J. E. Anderson (London: SCM Press, 1977), 183ff.

11. Westermann, *Blessing in the Bible*, 63; Johannes Pedersen, *Israel: Its Life and Culture*, vol. 1 (Atlanta: Scholars Press, 1991), 311–35.

12. Bruce Birch, *Let Justice Roll Down: The Old Testament, Ethics, and Christian Life* (Louisville: Westminster/John Knox Press, 1991), 250f.

13. Karl Rahner, "Nature and Grace" in *Theological Investigations*, vol. 4

(Baltimore: Helicon, 1966), 183.

14. Karl Rahner, *Handbuch der Pastoraltheologie,* vol. 2:2 (Freiburg: Herder and Herder, 1966), 219. My translation.

15. See, for example, Michael Wyschogrod, *The Body of Faith: God in the People Israel* (San Francisco: Harper and Row, 1989), 181–85.

16. Karl Rahner, "Brief Theological Observations on the 'State of Fallen Nature'" in *Theological Investigations,* vol. 19 (New York: Crossroad, 1983), 46.

Chapter 8

1. On Jesus in the context of Jewish restoration theology, see E. P. Sanders, *Jesus and Judaism* (Philadelphia: Fortress Press, 1985).

2. See ibid., 319–40.

3. Ibid., 229f.

4. Peter von der Osten-Sacken, *Christian-Jewish Dialogue: Theological Foundations,* trans. Margaret Kohl (Philadelphia: Fortress Press, 1982), 52.

5. Sharon Ringe, *Jesus, Liberation, and the Biblical Jubilee: Images for Ethics and Christology* (Philadelphia: Fortress Press, 1985); see also John Howard Yoder, *The Politics of Jesus,* 2nd ed. (Grand Rapids: Eerdmans, 1994), ch. 2.

6. Claus Westermann, *Blessing in the Bible and the Life of the Church,* trans. Kieth Crim (Philadelphia: Fortress Press, 1978), 94f.

7. Michael Welker, *God the Spirit,* trans. John F. Hoffmeyer (Minneapolis: Fortress Press, 1994), 209.

8. See Karl Rahner, *Foundations of Christian Faith,* trans. W. V. Dych (New York: Crossroad, 1978), 194.

9. Dietrich Bonhoeffer, *Letters and Papers from Prison* enlarged edition (New York: Collier Books, 1972), 157.

10. Westermann, *Blessing,* 93.

11. Dietrich Bonhoeffer, *The Cost of Discipleship,* trans. R. H. Fuller (New York: Macmillan, 1967), 161. Emphasis added.

12. Ibid., 374.

13. Ibid.

14. Bonhoeffer, *Letters and Papers,* 374. Italics added.

15. Ibid., 337.

16. A thorough examination of the church's relation to the economy of consummation would entail a close examination of Paul's Letter to the Romans, a task that lies beyond the scope of this essay. As Friedrich-Wilhelm Marquardt has observed, "Paul's Letter to the Romans is the New Testament writing in which the basic structure of the Old Testament's understanding of reality not only appears incidentally, but is made the theme itself: *the differentiated relationship which the God of Israel and the Father of Jesus Christ adopts on the one side toward the Jews, on the other side toward non-Jews.* What is the status of this fundamental, salvation-historical difference after the resurrection of Jesus from the dead? That is the leading question of Romans from beginning to end." *Das christliche Bekenntnis zu Jesus, dem Juden: eine Christologie,* vol. 1 (Munich: Christian Kaiser, 1990), 181 (original italics, my translation). Mar-

quardt argues, correctly I believe, that in Romans Paul confirms the fundamental significance of the distinction between Jew and Gentile after Jesus' resurrection. See Marquardt's detailed exegesis, ibid., 181–297. For the brilliant demonstration of a similar thesis, together with a rebuttal of more traditional readings, see Stanley K. Stowers, *A Rereading of Romans: Justice, Jews, and Gentiles* (New Haven: Yale University Press, 1994).

17. See Jeffrey S. Siker, *Disinheriting the Jews: Abraham in Early Christian Controversy* (Louisville: Westminster/John Knox Press, 1991), esp. ch. 8. For a somewhat different view, see James D. G. Dunn, *The Partings of the Ways: Between Christianity and Judaism and Their Significance for the Character of Christianity* (Philadelphia: Trinity Press International, 1991).

18. Marquardt, *Das christliche Bekenntnis*, vol. 1, 233.

19. Friedrich-Wilhelm Marquardt, *Von Elend und Heimsuchung der Theologie* (Munich: Christian Kaiser, 1992), 447. My translation.

20. Yoder, *Politics of Jesus*, 218f.

21. Marquardt, *Das christliche Bekenntnis*, vol. 1, 233.

22. See the discussion of Michael Wyschogrod in ch. 1.

23. Paul M. van Buren, *The Jewish-Christian Reality—Part Two: A Christian Theology of the People Israel* (San Francisco: Harper and Row, 1987), 340. With van Buren I would add, "That [irregular] status [with Judaism] could change, however, if the church were to do all in its power to encourage its Jewish members to remain faithful to Torah. . . . Clearly we move into uncharted waters in this matter, but they are uncharted because the church has not taken up its internal service to Israel as Israel."

24. Jürgen Moltmann, *The Way of Jesus Christ: Christology in Messianic Dimensions* (San Francisco: HarperCollins, 1989), 34.

25. Leslie Newbigin, *The Gospel in a Pluralist Society* (Grand Rapids: Eerdmans, 1989), 83.

26. Bertold Klappert, "Traktat für Israel (Römer 9–11): Die paulinsche Verhältnisbestimmung von Israel und die Kirche als Kriterium neutestamentlicher Sachaussagen über die Juden," in *Jüdische Existenz und die Erneuerung der christlichen Theologie*, ed. Martin Stöhr (Munich: Christian Kaiser Verlag, 1981), 60–61.

27. Klappert, "Traktat," 81.

28. Ibid., 82–86; Sanders, *Jesus and Judaism*, 93.

29. Klappert, "Traktat," 85.

30. Arnold A. van Ruler, *Die christliche Kirche und das Alte Testament* (Munich: Christian Kaiser, 1955), 65.

31. C. G. Montefiore and H. Lowe, *A Rabbinic Anthology* (New York: Schocken Books, 1974), 587

INDEX